An Introduction to Organisational Behaviour for Managers and Engineers

An Introduction to Organisational Behaviour for Managers and Engineers

A Group and Multicultural Approach

First Edition

Duncan Kitchin

ELSEVIER

AMSTERDAM • BOSTON • HEIDELBERG • LONDON • NEW YORK • OXFORD
PARIS • SAN DIEGO • SAN FRANCISCO • SINGAPORE • SYDNEY • TOKYO

Butterworth-Heinemann is an imprint of Elsevier

BH

Butterworth-Heinemann is an imprint of Elsevier
30 Corporate Drive, Suite 400, Burlington, MA 01803, USA
Linacre House, Jordan Hill, Oxford OX2 8DP, UK

First edition 2010

British Library Cataloguing in Publication Data
A catalogue record for this book is available from the British Library.

Library of Congress Cataloging-in-Publication Data
A catalog record for this book is available from the Library of Congress.

ISBN: 978-0-7506-8334-0

For information on all Butterworth–Heinemann publications
visit our Web site at www.books.elsevier.com

Printed and bound in Great Britain

10 11 12   10 9 8 7 6 5 4 3 2 1

Working together to grow
libraries in developing countries

www.elsevier.com | www.bookaid.org | www.sabre.org

ELSEVIER   BOOK AID
International   Sabre Foundation

Contents

Acknowledgements

The route by which I came to write this book was circuitous. Many years ago as an unhappy lecturer in economics, I sought out a yoga teacher, with the hope that I would learn to make my life more content and peaceful. I was fortunate that my teacher was an exceptional teacher of yoga, the late Tina Sessford. I owe her a great debt. Amongst everything else that I learnt from her, I learnt about relaxation. As a teacher by inclination, I went on to teach stress management in public and private organisations, and thus started my interest in organisations.

The next step in the journey was when the University of Sheffield decided that it had too many economists and not enough business studies teachers and offered to give me a year off, on full salary, to do a Master's degree in Organisational Development. I jumped at the chance and a year later returned to teach about organisations and organisational behaviour. So I owe the University of Sheffield a great debt.

After taking early retirement to practice as a psychotherapist, I was invited by the Department of Electronic and Electrical Engineering at the University of Sheffield to teach organisational behaviour to their second year undergraduates. At the same time the Business School of the University of Nottingham invited me to teach an introductory organisational behaviour course to a class that was predominantly engineering students. The challenge and fun of these two sets of students fired my enthusiasm for teaching engineers something that is about human behaviour and is not presented in mathematical and statistical terms. Some of the engineers have loved what I teach and how I teach it, and others have hated it. The ongoing challenge that both groups present has stimulated me to write a book for them, to fill a gap in the market. At the time when I started to turn my lectures into this book, there was not, and at the time of writing there is still no book in the English language that combines Organisational Behaviour and Engineering or Engineers in the title. I have cause to be grateful to those two university departments for inviting me to meet their students. The Department of Electronic and Electrical Engineering (EEE) at Sheffield even offered me an office, a desk and a computer in the early days of writing – how kind and generous. My contacts in EEE have been an ongoing source of support, especially Peter Judd and Richard Tozer, but other colleagues have been warm, welcoming and encouraging to this strange organisations' man.

Over the years I have constantly been challenged to rethink, and introduced to new literature and perspectives, by colleagues, especially George Hespe, Penny Dick, Donald Hislop, Sue Green, Cathy Cassell and Gill Musson. I owe them thanks.

Almost finally, I want to acknowledge the love and support that I have received from my friends and family. Without them life would have seemed bleak. I particularly want to thank my good friend Kevin Dowd, his wife Mahjabeen and their two daughters. They have been wonderful friends over many years. Kevin has been an example of diligence, brilliance and creativity that I have tried to emulate, largely in vain. My sons and their families, and my stepson and stepdaughter and their families, have provided me with enough love, support and distraction to keep me sustained and fresh.

Finally, I dedicate this book to my partner Anneliese, who has borne the costs of its writing with patience and fortitude, and every day reminds me about the joys of living.

Duncan Kitchin
September, 2009
Kingston upon Thames

Preface

This book has grown out of recent enjoyable experiences of teaching engineering students in both the universities of Sheffield and Nottingham. What has emerged from the experience has been the need for a text that is specifically aimed at the needs of engineers and students of engineering. It will also serve a purpose for others wanting a brief introductory text on organisational behaviour.

Because standard organisational behaviour texts are written for business and management students they have proved to be unsuitable for engineers, being both too big for an introductory course (many are between 600 and 1000 pages long), and having a range of topics, and an emphasis, that is unsuited to contemporary engineers and people looking for a brief introduction. Given the unsuitability of these texts, I have found that my lecture handouts have grown year by year. Now I have decided to bite the bullet and go for the ultimate expansion, into a book specifically for engineers and others looking for a brief introduction. A 1000-page book is vastly too long for any introductory course with only 9 or 10 weeks teaching, and these brief introductory courses are growing in number just as the latest editions of established texts are growing ever longer.

Anyone interested in the education of engineers will eventually end up reading the Standards and Routes to Registration (SARTOR) document of the Engineering Council. This document sets out the educational requirements for anyone who wants to be a professional engineer, of whatever recognised variety.

A clear part of the criteria set out in SARTOR is that engineers should have training in Management and Business Topics. This book aims to support courses that go at least some way towards meeting the SARTOR requirements for management and business training. The intention of the book is to meet the practical needs of engineers, both as students and as practising professionals, in addition to their qualification needs.

One of the requirements of SARTOR is that students experience work in project groups. This book starts with a chapter on Groups and Group Processes, meeting the needs of engineers, whether students or professionals, to form groups that will be successful and that will not fail as a result of any of the well-known problems that occur in groups.

Generations of students have told me that they felt empowered because they understood what was happening within organisations and groups. This book aims to empower engineering students and engineers.

SARTOR also writes of the need to be able to work in multidisciplinary and inter-disciplinary teams. What they might well have added, but do not, is that engineers increasingly need to be able to work in multinational and multicultural organisations and teams. To meet this last point, this book looks at the aspects of multiculturalism and the formation of integrated working cultures in multicultural organisations, groups and teams. However, before we can sensibly discuss multiculturalism we need to discuss the nature of organisational culture.

After the discussions of groups and teams, group processes and decision making, organisational culture and international culture, we go on to examine a number of the topics that are necessary for the professional engineer, or anyone working in an organisation.

We look at the Organisational Culture, Motivation, Stress, Organisational Politics, Leadership, Organisational Structures and Communications.

The chapters could have been presented in almost any order, because the nature of organisational behaviour is that all of the standard topics are inter-related. It is not really possible to understand leadership without understanding culture, motivation, international cultural difference, organisational politics, communications and organisational structures. But it is as true to say that it is not really possible to understand organisational culture without understanding leadership, organisational structures and organisational politics. Really, all the topics in this book need to be understood at the same time, but logic tells us that this is not possible, so the chapters have to be in some order, but I do not think that the reader would come to much harm if they read them in the order that took their interest.

In an effort to overcome this problem of needing to understand every topic at the same time, the reader will find that there are many cross references to topics in other chapters, some of which may have been read, some of which may await reading.

Because the world of organisations is becoming so international and diverse, there is a chapter on International Cultural Differences, and in almost every chapter there are references to this chapter so that the reader is constantly challenged to think in international terms. Ideally, each nation should have its own version of each of the topic chapters, but that is clearly not possible, because of problems of the scale of the resulting book, and because much of the development and testing of theories has not been done. There has been some replication of traditional research, and where possible these results are reported. Most of the development of theories and their testing has been done in the USA and Western Europe, and thus we need to be wary about applying them in other countries. By writing the International Cultural Differences chapter, it is possible to invite the readers to apply the content of that chapter to other topics and begin to speculate whether the theories are applicable to their nation.

Almost all traditional organisational behaviour books only look at motivation theories for individuals, so our discussion of the emerging theory of motivating groups serves as a real bonus for engineers who frequently work in groups and who have to set up and manage groups.

The discussion of political processes in organisations pulls together an overarching framework for defining organisations and many of the processes that occur within them. Without such an understanding of political processes in organisations, an engineer would end up feeling, and being, powerless.

The discussion in the Leadership chapter will supplement the earlier discussion of the leadership of formal groups and teams in the Groups and Group Processes chapter.

The chapter on Organisational Structures properly comes near the end of the book, as to understand structures requires an understanding of culture, politics and leadership.

The final chapter is about Communications. It is obvious that organisations are about the relating of people. If people communicate poorly then it is obvious that the organisation will be dysfunctional – it won't work.

Finally, to reiterate, if you understand organisations, then you are powerful and can further your own interest and/or those of the organisation. If you do not understand organisations, you will be powerless and will be tossed around like a leaf on a turbulent river. The aim of this book is to empower the reader with understanding.

List of Figures and Tables

List of Case Studies

Groups and Group Processes

Central to many organisations, and of increasing importance to others, is the existence and operation of groups. Project groups, task groups or teams are a normal feature of the working life of engineers, whether students or fully qualified professional engineers. We shall use the terms "groups" and "teams" and "task" and "project" interchangeably.

In this chapter we are going to look at the definition of a team, how they form, how they work successfully and what causes them to be unsuccessful. As the main purpose of teams is to make decisions, there will be a discussion of decision-making and then an examination of the processes within teams when they are making decisions. What happens within teams is called *group process*, the interactions of individual members of a team that makes a team different than the sum of the individuals that make up the team. Understanding this idea of groups being different than the sum of the individuals is crucial to being a successful member of a team, and is crucial to knowing how to set up and manage teams so that they make a contribution to the organisation that is better than any single individual, or group of individuals who simply have their individual contributions summed. To understand water it is not enough to understand about oxygen and hydrogen, you have to understand how they interact as water. If you are a member of a task or project group or team it is important to understand what is happening in the group so that it does not go "awfully wrong", and so that if it starts to go wrong you can recognise what is happening and correct the process in order to reach a successful outcome.

WHAT IS A GROUP?

There is a big literature defining what constitutes a group. We will look at a few of the obvious and attractive options before settling on a clear and acceptable definition.

Some people have tried defining groups as having a collective fate. Under this definition, the staff of Lehman Brothers would be a group, with their collective fate to be unemployed as the investment bank imploded in 2008. It has been suggested that the European Jews constituted a group, with the collective fate that awaited them in Germany and much of Europe between 1933 and 1945. When you think of your project group, "collective fate" hardly seems to define your sense of why you are a group.

A different way of defining has been to say that a group could be defined in terms of face-to-face interaction. Your project group certainly has face-to-face interaction, unless it is a virtual group that only meets electronically via the Internet. A football crowd also

An Introduction to Organisational Behaviour for Managers and Engineers meets face-to-face, physically in the same place, but your reaction is probably to say that the crowd is very different to your project group, both in terms of the scale of the group (75,000 against 5 or 6) and the degree if intimacy in the meeting. The soccer crowd meets face-to-face, but there is no intimacy, no sense of knowing or getting to know the other members of the group.

So, what does your project group have that leads you to define it as a group? It is a small group of people who meet regularly (either face-to-face or electronically, or a mix of the two), and who know, or get to know, one another. (For a discussion of groups that only meet electronically, see the discussions on virtual organisations in Chapters 8 and 9.) An added criteria might be that as the group evolves there is an emerging set of relationships that develop and people begin to adopt certain roles within the group; perhaps there is a chair, a secretary and a social worker who looks after the pattern of relating in order to prevent or resolve interpersonal conflicts. There may also be an element of a group existing because its members say that the group exists – this is self-categorisation – "a group exists because we all agree that it exists and that we are members of it." The characteristics that we have mentioned help us to define a group, but is rather more of a list than a definition.

A neat definition of a group is given by Brown (2000, p. 3):

> *A group exists when two or more people define themselves as members of it and when its existence is recognized by at least one other.*

Some of what we are going to write about in this chapter is the interaction of one group with another (specifically "in-groups and out-groups"), and the setting up of groups within an organisation, hence the need to include a reference to "…recognized by at least one other."

The definition has a minimum size of two, but there is no reference to a maximum size. Reflection on our experience of groups suggests that as the size of membership grows, a crucial change tends to take place when the membership reaches about eight. Above that number the group tends to break up into subgroups as the difficulty of maintaining a face-to-face discussion with more than eight people grows. Once a group divides, then we have two groups, with the complications that that brings in terms of the relating of the two groups (see the Sherif and Sherif discussion of "in-groups and out groups" later in this chapter).

A British anthropologist, Dunbar, came forward with the maximum size of a group with which any one individual can maintain stable social relationships (Dunbar, 1993). "Dunbar's number", as it became known, is 150. Even at that level, Dunbar estimated that 42% of the group's time would be taken up with social grooming in order to maintain the group. Dunbar's groups are not, however, groups that meet face-to-face and are more akin to the number of "friends" one might have in a Face book list of friends. Later in the chapter we are going to write about Belbin's ideas about what the makeup of a winning decision-making team. Belbin concludes that there are eight or nine separate roles that need to be filled if a decision-making team is to be successful. This, interestingly, fits with the research about the maximum size of group that can sustain face-to-face interaction as a single unified group.

If we use an evolutionist's approach to the size of groups, then we can observe that groups larger than eight or nine rarely seem to exist – they cannot survive in the interpersonal environment – they die or self destruct.

An economist's perspective on groups would suggest that they exist because the benefits of groups outweigh the costs of groups, and that the value of the net output (total benefits less total costs) of groups is normally greater than the sum of the net outputs of the individuals if they were not members of the group. There are net benefits for the organisation from combining individuals into groups.

FORMING GROUPS

Group development

We cannot expect that it is enough to put eight random people into a group and tell them to solve a problem. One of the problems that the author sees regularly with student engineering project groups is that after being put in a room together, they immediately start trying to solve the problem that they have been given.

Tuckman (1965) recognised that successful groups had gone through a number of stages before they could function successfully as a group.

Subsequently, Tuckman and Jensen (1977) added a further stage of AJOURNING (Ending).

The four initial stages are much as the names suggest:

- *Forming*: groups need to form, that is, they need to get to know one another. Before a group of strangers can hope to work together they need to begin to develop relationships with, and a sense of trust in, the other group members. Developing relationship and trust requires them to talk and act together in an emotionally safe way. A sense of belonging to the group needs to develop, with the resulting sense of commitment and obligation; this takes time. If the members of the group are from different cultures, then the cultural assumptions that members bring about relating, sense-making, time-keeping and many other issues will differ very much from one member to another, and the time taken to form will

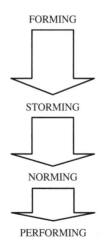

FIGURE 1.1

Tuckman's group development model

be longer than when the members of the group are drawn from a single national culture. Forming is followed by storming.

- *Storming*: this is the process that develops after forming, where group members begin to "fight" with one another over the roles within the group; who is going to chair, who is going to have power and influence. They also need to "fight" over how they will work together; for example, will they work virtually (meeting electronically) or will they be co-located, present in the same room. Storming is followed by norming.

- *Norming*: this is the resolution of the storming and is, in effect, agreements about individual's roles, how they will work together, what are the time-keeping rules, how will the rules be enforced and so on. When the members of the group are drawn from diverse cultures, the process of norming is likely to be slower than for a group with a single national culture. Norming is followed by performing.

- *Performing*: only after the previous three stages have been completed can the group have any real hope of being able to work productively together. During performing there may be a return to storming.

- *Storming*: as the group performs they may discover that some of the norms that they developed together are not functional, and they will have to turn from performing to storm again so that they can renorm. Different national cultures deal with interpersonal disagreements and conflict in very differing ways and thus the storming may be very difficult to resolve for a culturally diverse group. Following this Storming will be:

- *Renorming*: this is agreeing to the new norms that hopefully will be more appropriate and lead to better performing.

- *Performing*: the loop to storming and renorming may have to happen a number of times.

If the group is meeting as a virtual group, with all meeting taking place electronically, then it is clear that at least the forming stage is going to be different and slower than in a co-located group where people meet face-to-face. For a fuller discussion of virtual groups, consult Chapters 8 and 9.

Psychotherapeutic writers have suggested that the sequence is actually:

Forming–norming–performing–storming–renorming–performing

with the possibility of a number of loops through storming to renorming and back to performing. Certainly this sequence is common in psychotherapy groups and is probably a reflection of the essential politeness of the British, who are reluctant to storm until they are sorely tried by the failure of the group to perform with its existing norms. Whatever the sequence, the essential feature of the model is that groups have to spend time developing before they can be functional and productive.

Designing teams: Belbin's winning teams

The situation that Belbin investigated was a business game where teams of executives at a Management School had to make a sequence of decisions about a business, in competition with other teams. His first thought was that if the most brilliant executives were put in the same team, then that would be the winning team. The result was what Belbin called the Apollo Paradox – the team of the most brilliant executives who always did badly. What Belbin eventually discovered was a result of studying the teams that *did* win. He discovered that for a decision-making team to do well, they needed eight different roles to be filled by members of the team. Subsequent research suggested that there were *nine* key roles (Belbin, 1993). If any of these roles was not satisfactorily filled, then the team would be less effective. Belbin developed an instrument (a questionnaire) that showed how much an individual would be drawn to each of the roles. The instrument showed that most individuals would happily fill one, two or sometimes three of the roles and would have little inclination to fulfil the other roles. The roles that an individual fills are a reflection of their personality rather than some level or type of cognitive ability. The questions in the questionnaire were more about what behaviours/roles people found themselves performing in teams. Inclination seems more important than raw ability.

Case Study 1.1: Belbin's roles

Over many years I have invited students and managers to complete Belbin's instrument so that they could see which of the roles they were drawn to. People are usually drawn strongly to one or two roles and occasionally to three roles. They usually have very low scores for all the other roles, indicating that they are not at all attracted to these other roles. When questioned about how they would respond in a group where no-one is fulfilling a particular role which is one of their least favourite, the response is almost without fail that they would not fill the missing role even though they can see that the role is essential to the success of the group. People will say things like "I would never take the role of co-ordinator even though I can see that no-one else in the group has taken that role, and that the group is suffering because there is no co-ordinator."

Question

What would you do if your group had certain roles not being filled and you were aware that the group was likely to fail because of the vacancies?

Belbin's nine roles were:

- *Co-ordinator*: someone who will chair the team and ensure that all of the necessary abilities are present and used and that team goals are clear.

- *Shaper*: this person is something of a driver who motivates team members.

- *Plant*: this is the ideas person, who is creative and innovative.

- *Resource investigator*: this role is literally to investigate the resources available to the group and to ensure that they do not reinvent the wheel.

- *Monitor evaluator*: this is the critical evaluative role that questions ideas and plans.

- *Teamworker*: this role is, in effect, the social worker in the team, who looks after relationships within the group.

- *Implementer*: this person turns ideas into practical implementable plans.

- *Completer*: in the original work this role was called the Completer finisher, and this perhaps captures the role better than the more recent title. This is the person who makes sure that work is done in time, ensures that deadlines are met and ensures that proof-reading is done.

- *Specialist*: this is the ninth role that was added to the original eight. Clearly there is usually a need for someone with expert knowledge about the task that the team has to perform.

The conclusion to be drawn from Belbin's work is very clear; if a team is to be successful it has to be well constructed, with team members who are able to fulfil all nine roles between them. As most people can reasonably competently fulfil two or even three roles, the implication is that a team needs to have at least three or four members if all of the roles are to be filled. We also know that when teams have more than about eight or nine members, it becomes increasingly difficult to maintain face-to-face interaction, and there is a growing probability that the group will split into subgroups. Later in this chapter we will discuss how two or more groups interact with one another (ingroups and out-groups).

Case Study 1.2: Belbin in action

I was working as a consultant in a department of the UK headquarters of a major international computer firm. A problem that I had identified was that the department hired adults and then treated them as children. The leadership style was McGregor's Theory X. (See the Appendix on Theory X and Y.) During the process of trying to change the management style of the department (to Theory Y), the Head of Department decided to set up a series of task groups, each with four or five members. Each group was to try and find products or services that could be developed profitably using the existing resources within the department. These groups were set up without consulting me. When I heard of the groups, I suggested that we ran all of the group members through Belbin's instrument to see how well each group was structured given Belbin's eight (at that time) roles. We then used the extent to which the teams were well structured to predict how well each group would perform. The predictions were almost perfect. The well-structured teams produced creative well-worked reports on time, and the poorly structured groups produced reports (if at all) that were of very little use.

An additional problem that arises within groups with specialist roles is when there are two or more people fulfilling one of the roles, as this may lead to conflict between these individuals – what group needs, or can work with, two co-ordinators fighting for power? The answer is clearly to construct groups with great care, so that the role conflict does not occur.

Another well-known study of team roles was by Margerison and McCann (1990), and interestingly, like many other such studies, it came to very similar conclusions as

Belbin's. Margerison and McCann concluded, like the early Belbin, that there were eight key roles, defined very much like Belbin's, although the basis of their approach was Jung's taxonomy, where people were defined by how they fitted into a two-dimensional matrix, where the dimensions were about how people gathered information (from measuring to collecting information intuitively) and how they processed information (from using intuition through to using theoretical/rational frameworks). [For a brief introduction to Jung's taxonomy see p36 in chapter 2.]

Groups and diversity

There is some evidence that the degree of diversity of a group will influence how it works and how effectively. The growing diversity of groups is inevitable in many organisations as their employees come from increasingly diverse backgrounds. In the UK, for example, the percentage of the workforce formed by women has risen from about 33% in the 1960s up to 50% in the twenty-first century, and with this growth has come an increasing percentage of women in management, banking, the law, accounting, finance and many other areas that used to be dominated by men. There has also been a great increase in the percentage of workforces that come from different nationalities, races, colours, religions, sexual orientations and so on. We have to accept that diverse workforces are a fact of life in many countries.

Research has looked at whether diverse groups, such as project or task groups or decision-making groups, are any different than homogeneous groups. The evidence is mixed (King et al., 2009).

A report flowing out of the London Business School in 2007 reported research which suggested that groups which had equal proportions of men and women were more creative than unbalanced groups in terms of producing the most innovative ideas (Guardian, 2007). Professor Lynda Gratton is quoted as saying "It is not about gender, it is about minorities. Our data shows that whenever anybody is in a minority, they suffer, and as a consequence the team suffers." (Guardian, 2007). An even mix provides a psychologically safe communications climate and ensures self-confidence in members. This finding provides support for the ideas about the in-groups and out-groups of Sherif and Sherif that are discussed later in this chapter. The basic idea is that if you can identify yourself as a member of a category (male, black, gay or whatever defining characteristic) then you can identify others as not in your category, and thus you and the people like you are in the "in-group" and everyone else is in a separate group called the "out-group." Thus diverse groups may split into subgroups which do not co-operate.

Research has suggested that diverse groups will bring together differing ways of sense-making, different knowledge and different theoretical perspectives and thus there are more inputs into creation and problem-solving than in a homogeneous group. Thus the argument is that diverse groups are more creative, and a number of studies back up this hypothesis.

If, however, we look back at Tuckman's idea that groups have to go through a series of developmental stages before they can begin to perform and produce output, then we can hypothesise that diverse groups will take longer to form, storm and norm. Research supports this hypothesis, with the conclusion that whilst diverse groups may be more creative, they take longer before they are creative.

If diversity is inevitable because of the employee mix of organisations, then perhaps the only useful idea to come out of the diversity research is that Tuckman's group development stages take longer in diverse groups. For a recent summary of the diversity research, see King et al. (2009).

Having looked at how groups are defined (Brown, 2000), how they can be successfully structured (Belbin, 1993; Margerison and McCann, 1990) and the impact of diversity on their success (King et al., 2009), we now go on to lay some theoretical foundations about decision-making, before going on to look at what happens within groups as they interact and try and make decisions, Group Processes.

DECISION-MAKING

Like most topics in organisational behaviour, decision-making theory has developed over the years into a complex, and at times, difficult set of theories and frameworks. In this section we intend to look at the basic, useful and key ideas that will benefit people who are, or will ultimately be, involved in the process of decision-making, as individuals and within groups.

The early writings on decision-making were what are called the *modern* approach, that is, where the theory assumed that people were rational economic people who worked in unitary organisations, and where the decision-making process was linear, meaning that there was a simple direct logic – "If I do A then B will happen." Modern approaches meant that the underlying assumption about human behaviour was that people were rational and that in an organisational setting there would be a single unified set of shared beliefs about what policies should be accepted and what should be the goals of the organisation.

The contrast is with *post-modern* approaches; this sounds rather confusing, as post-modern sounds as though it means something about the future. In fact *post-modern* thinking and theorising is what followed *modern* theorising and thinking. Post-modern thinking is based on the idea that organisations are pluralist, that is, there is no unified set of beliefs and goals that are shared by everyone in the organisation, and thus that organisations are characterised by differing goals, conflict, complexity, ambiguity and uncertainty. Post-modernism also no longer believes that individuals are rational decision-makers who are only interested in economic outcomes, that is, only interested in financial outcomes in terms of incomes (wages, salaries and profits).

To understand the ideas around decision-making, it is necessary to begin with a modernist approach so that we can contrast that with a post-modernist approach and have a sense of what is useful in the modernist approach, so that we do not give up ideas that are still useful.

Modernist and post-modernist approaches to decision-making

We can divide decisions into structured and unstructured decisions; these can also be called programmed and unprogrammed decisions.

Structured or programmed decisions are decisions that are easy to make, are made regularly and where there is a rational best solution on which everyone can agree (a modernist perspective). A simple example might be in the case of a building that is getting too cold for the comfort of the work staff during winter. The cold is upsetting the staff. The programmed (structured) decision is to turn up the central heating, to adjust the thermostat. This is not a complex problem about which to make a decision; but even this is more complex than it seems. Not everyone might agree how much too cold it is, and thus some people might complain that they are too hot if the heat is turned up too much. There may also be other solutions – people could be encouraged, or choose, to wear one more layer of clothes when they are at work. Basically, the decisions seem to be about applying rational logic, but it gets more complicated when we allow for people being different (post-modernism).

Unstructured or unprogrammed decisions are about problems that are unique and complex. There is no simple solution or decision that can just be looked up, and simple logic will not provide an immediate answer. For these types of problems the traditional (modern) decision-making model is set out below, as a logical sequence of acts.

- Recognition of a problem

- Search for alternative solutions

- Gather information needed to make a best decision

- Choose criteria for decision-making

- Decide the best solution

- Implement the decision

There are lots of problems with this Modernist approach. It assumes that everyone involved in the decision-making has the same set of values by which they evaluate the decision, that is, the decision criteria are not contentious. Also, it assumes that everyone can agree on what constitutes the problem. In an approach called Soft Systems Analysis (Checkland, 1981) there is the concept of a "mess." A "mess" is where people cannot agree on what constitutes the problem. There are a variety of reasons why this might happen, but they all revolve around differences in perception. In a lovely piece of research (source unknown), a case study about an organisation was presented to a set of executives who came from different functional backgrounds. Each of the executives was told to think of themselves as *general*-manager and to analyse the principal problem that the organisation needed to solve. The result was that the marketing managers saw marketing as the principal problem, the finance people saw finance as the key problem and so on, despite the instruction to adopt the role and thinking of a *general*-manager. Where you stand determines what you see. The cognitive models (theories that different specialists use to make sense of their world) reflect their training and experience – accountants view the world through accountants' eyes, engineers through engineers' eyes and so on.

A more post-modern view of the model would add a seventh stage, which would be Evaluation. This implies an acknowledgement that the information gathered to aid decision-making might not have been correct or adequate (ambiguity), or that the theories implicit in the decision-making may have been wrong, that is, the outcome of the decision may have been unexpected (uncertainty).

The garbage can theory of decision-making

This strangely named post-modernist theory was initially developed by Cohen et al. (1972). The theory says that decision-making in organisations is a messy business with many interacting factors affecting the way that decisions are arrived at – all sorts of things are thrown into the mix that results in a decision, just as many things are thrown into a garbage can.

The theory is essentially about the working out of micro-politics within organisations. If a group of people meet together to make a decision, the decision is a result of the interaction of the members of the group. Each member of the group will have their own interests that they want the decision to further; thus the woman from the research and development department may want the decision to further the interests of her department, or to be a decision that helps her further her career or a decision (or the failure to make a decision) that harms another member of the group over whom she wants revenge. We can see that a group is likely to have members with interests that clash and that their interest is not necessarily what is in the interests of the organisation.

Even if all of the members of the group have the interests of the organisation at heart, they may not agree what is in the interests of the organisation. Some group members may have a short-term orientation and others may have a long-term orientation. (See Chapter 3 on differing time orientations in different international cultures.)

The decision-making can further be confused by the members of the group having different perspectives or perceptions, with accountants thinking and analysing like accountants and marketing people thinking and analysing like marketing professionals. The members of the group may not even be able to agree what the problem is that needs them to decide on a solution (remember the Soft Systems Analysis idea of a "mess" – a problem where people cannot even agree what constitutes the problem – discussed earlier in this chapter).

All these differences need to be resolved in the garbage can before a decision can be made, even if the decision is that they cannot reach a decision. The resolution of the conflict is through the use of power, and this process is a political process, which is discussed at length in Chapter 6.

There are other reasons why a rational economic decision may not come out of the garbage can, but at this point we will only discuss one more post-modernist idea. This is an idea that is discussed in detail in the Hawthorne Experiments (see E. Mayo, in Pugh, 1990), but here we will just anticipate one result of that discussion. This result is the finding that a group will form a set of agreements, norms or cultural elements, one of which may be that the group agrees what behaviour within the group is in the mutual interest of the group members. This agreed behaviour, such as "a fair day's work for a fair day's pay" may not be in the best economic interest of the organisation although it is agreed by the group to be in the group members' best interests.

Bounded rationality

A further problem of decision-making was highlighted when Simon (1960) wrote about bounded rationality. This is the idea that an individual's capacity to handle large amounts of data is limited and that our theories may be inadequate and certainly not rational. Simon argued that if we cannot handle, or have, all the data that we need to make a perfect decision, and if the way that we handle the data is limited by our lack of rationality and appropriate theories, then the best that we can hope for is what he called satisficing decisions – decisions that are good enough. The example that is usually used is that of looking for a needle in a haystack. Finding the perfect needle might take forever, so if we can find one that is good enough for our purpose, even if rusty and bent, then we should settle for that – we should satisfice.

GROUP PROCESSES AND DECISION-MAKING

There have been lots of studies that look at the quality of decisions made by individuals and compare them with the decisions made by groups or teams working collectively. In contemporary organisations, there is a lot more use made of group and team working as opposed to individual working.

Much of the research about the behaviour of groups has centred on what happens within groups when they are making decisions. What happens within groups is called group processes and that is what we examine next.

Group processes

Earlier in this chapter we looked at the way Tuckman (1965) discussed the development of groups through a process that led them to being able to perform effectively. The clear prediction of Tuckman's work was that if you try and get a group to perform too soon after it has been formed, then it may fail to be effective.

In the next pages we are going to examine in some detail what happens within groups – at the processes within groups, that is, at group processes. Some of the topics examined will show the varying ways that groups can work ineffectively, often in terms of the quality of their decision-making. The problems often result from asking a newly formed group to perform before it has gone through all of Tuckman's stages of team development (forming, storming, norming and performing).

A set of related group process problems fall under the heading of *group conformance*. This is a different framework for making sense of some elements of group processes. This is where the individual members of a group tend to conform to some group norm that emerges, and at least partially abandon their own individual judgment. Where possible, we will quote research evidence of how internationally robust these research findings have proved to be. Most of the original group process research has taken place in the USA and in the UK, but the results do seem to replicate internationally. In considering conformance, we will look at the work of Asch (1956), Harvey (1988), Janis (1972), Zimbardo (1972) and Milgram (1963).

Asch: minorities

An early important study of conformance was conducted by Asch. The experiment was conducted in the USA.

Eleven students were briefed that they were to verbally give a unanimous identical wrong answer on certain repetitions of a simple task of judgment. A 12th person was not briefed. The task required the 12 people in the experiment to say which of three straight lines was the same as a standard line. The 12th "innocent" person found themselves repeatedly in a minority of one. Repetitions of the experiment showed that about one-third of the time the 12th person agreed with the wrong decision made by the unanimous majority, and three-quarters of people agreed at least once with the incorrect majority. When people were asked to complete the task as individuals, so that they were not influenced by others, they made correct judgments every time.

The group result rapidly disappeared when the size of the minority began to rise. This (conformance to the majority) is a culturally strong result. Culturally strong means that the result holds in a wide variety of populations in many different countries.

Table 1.1 looks at international replications of Asch's experiment and is based on a table in Smith and Bond (1993).

A meta-analysis by Bond and Smith (1993) suggested that in countries with a collectivist culture, the degree of conformance will be higher than for countries that have an individualistic culture, but Table 1.1 of international results (adapted from Smith and Bond, 1993) offers little in the way of support for their hypothesis (see Chapter 3 for a discussion of collectivist/individualistic cultures). We may also wonder whether the results would be replicated internationally if the participants were not predominately students. Would older and more mature participants produce the same level of conformance?

Asch found that in small group replications of his experiment, as few as three unanimous conspirators were enough to replicate the result of the original experiment (with 11 conspirators), and that further increases in the number of conspirators above three seemed to make little or no difference.

Why do the minority not speak their truth? When the participants in the original experiment were asked why they had agreed with the unanimous majority, most of them said that they knew that the majority were wrong, but that they did not want to be ridiculed or thought "peculiar" by the majority. Only a small minority thought that the majority were correct. In a subsequent repetition when the "innocent" was allowed to write down

Table 1.1 International Replications of Asch's Experiment on Conformance

	Subjects	**% Errors**
Original Asch study	Students	37%
8 Later USA studies (averaged)	Students	25%
4 British studies (averaged)	Students	17%
Holland	Students	24%
Brazil	Students	34%
Hong Kong	Students	32%
Japan	Students	25%
Japan	Sports club members	51%
Japan	Students not known to each other	27%
Fiji	Indian teachers	58%

their answer after hearing the views of the wrong majority, the conformance rate fell to about one-third of the previous conformance rate. We may speculate that conformance may be particularly high in Eastern cultures, where saving "face" is important.

The degree of conformance also falls when the group is not the newly formed group of the experiment, but is a collection of people who know one another.

To avoid this problem of conformance, it seems that we should avoid using newly formed groups and also that writing down our decisions without hearing the judgments or decisions of others may be useful.

We may also adopt a different view, which is to rejoice that about two-thirds of people did not conform to the unanimous majority. We should also note that the effect very rapidly reduced as the minority rose above one. Perhaps we have no need to worry about conformance.

Other experiments have been conducted about conformance, two of which, Milgram (1963) and Zimbardo (1972), are particularly famous and worrying.

Milgram's shocking experiment

Milgram arranged for there to be a set of people who were "learners" and a set who were "teachers", with a researcher running the experiment. The "teachers" were told that they were to administer electric shocks to the "learners" if the "learner" made a mistake. It was explained to the "teachers" that this was a serious piece of research about learning. Large numbers of "teachers" demonstrated that they were prepared to give electric shocks of up to 400 and more volts, even though they could hear the "learners" begging for the shocks to end and could see the "learners" reacting physically to the shock. In a subsequent experiment, two associates of the experimenter would urge that higher shocks should be given, but the experimenter would say that the "teachers" could suggest the level of the shock and that the lowest suggested shock would be the one used. In this subsequent experiment the "teachers" accepted the two associates' suggestions and did not take the option of reducing the shocks. In reality there were no electric shocks as the "learners" were actors playing at being shocked.

This is clearly a shocking experiment in every sense of the word, as it implies that people will do dreadful things so long as an authority figure says that it is acceptable.

The experiment has been replicated, and a representative sample of the results is shown in Table 1.2 (adapted from Smith and Bond (1993)).

We note that in the replications, the results were similar whether the participants were students or the general population; also, the more collectivist societies were not more conformist.

The work by Milgram would certainly seem to suggest that the members of a group might agree to enact unethical or illegal decisions if an authority figure assured them that it was alright. Social psychology seems to suggest that people may conform to some group norm in decision-making because they respect authority or because they want to maintain their membership in the group.

Milgram may offer an explanation of why employees will enact illegal or immoral instructions from an authoritarian boss. This may explain the way that Robert Maxwell could raid the pension funds of the companies of which he was the Chief Executive Officer the way that Conrad Black could divert funds into his private pocket; and the way that senior executives at Enron could enrich themselves whilst bankrupting their

Table 1.2 Replications of Milgram's Experiment

Country	Subjects	% Obedient
USA (Milgram)	Male/female general population	65%/65%
USA	Students	85%
Italy	Students	85%
Germany	Male general population	85%
Australia	Male students	40%
Australia	Female students	16%
UK	Male students	50%
Jordan	Students	62%
Spain	Students	>90%
Austria	General population	80%
Holland	General population	92%

company. An Internet search will provide many websites that will outline the illegal and dubious practices that these individuals and organisations got their employees to undertake.

Zimbardo's pathology of imprisonment

Zimbardo (1972) ran an alarming experiment about the way that people's behaviour can be changed not only by their membership of a group but also as a result of having a role. He recruited about 24 "normal" young men from middle-class backgrounds and then randomly split them into a group of prisoners and a group of prison guards and put them into a mock-up of a prison for 2 weeks. The guards could make up their own rules. The experiment was abandoned after only 6 days to save Zimbardo (!) from more distress as a result of what was unfolding before his eyes. Some of the guards had become tyrannical and brutal and the remaining guards unquestioningly implemented the brutal regime designed by the brutal guards. Zimbardo reported that "It was no longer apparent to most of the subjects... where reality ended and their roles began." Again, just as in Milgram, we see people prepared to behave in an immoral or unethical manner, or failing to argue against the immoral or unethical behaviour. The dynamics of why people in groups can behave in these ways is very complex and unresolved, but we need to be aware that groups are capable of making bad decisions as a result of group processes. Groups may fail to make rational or moral decisions because of the processes within the group.

Abilene Paradox

The Abilene Paradox was discovered by Harvey (1988). This is a fascinating example of how individual members of a decision-making group can all conform to, and accept, a decision with which *none* of them agree. This possibility was first observed by Harvey, not in a newly formed group but in a cohesive family group, which was obviously long established, so this is not a problem arising because a group has not gone through all of Tuckman's group formation stages.

The members of the decision-making group were a father-in-law, a mother-in-law, their daughter and her husband. The group was together, having a perfectly agreeable afternoon. The father-in-law, wanting to do something for his son-in-law, suggested that they drive 53 miles on a hot and dusty day to Abilene, in Texas, in the USA, in order to have a meal together. The son-in-law, in order to please his father-in-law (who "obviously" wanted to go to Abilene), agreed that this was a good idea, although he privately did not want to make the journey. Subsequently, when told what the two men were proposing, the two women agreed that a trip to Abilene for a meal would be a nice outing. The whole family, having agreed to go to Abilene, made an unpleasant journey and had a poor meal, before returning home through the heat and dust. On their return they each owned up to the fact that they had not wanted to go to Abilene for a meal, and had only agreed to the decision because the others had been enthusiastic. They had all agreed to a decision with which none of them agreed!

This is a failure as a result of not speaking your truth. The interesting question is why they had not spoken their truth. Perhaps they did not want to be a kill-joy, or they did not want to spoil the others' pleasure either individually or collectively, or they felt that by agreeing they would maintain their membership of the group.

How are you going to get around this danger of going to Abilene? The obvious answer is to speak your truth – but that may be easier said than done if you strongly wish to maintain your membership of the group, and fear that if you speak out then you will be marginalised or cast out of the group.

Case Study 1.3: How many of you have been to Abilene?

My experience is that if you tell this story to any group of managers and then ask "How many of you have been to Abilene?" almost everyone in the group will have a rueful grin on their face as they remember their professional visits to Abilene.

Question

Have you ever been to "Abilene" – how did it happen?

Shift to extreme

This is another situation where individuals have a tendency to conform to some emerging group norm, but in this case the group norm that emerges is not the average of the individual decisions. Again it is a problem that occurs in decision-making groups, when they are newly formed. It has also been observed to occur when the decision-making group is long established but meets only rarely, which seems to make it act much like a newly formed group where the members are unfamiliar with one another.

The initial research was by Stoner (1961) where he looked at decision-making when there was an element of risk, and compared the decisions made by individuals and by a group. One of the dilemmas used was as follows: "An electrical engineer may stick with his present job at a modest but adequate salary, or may take a new job offering considerably more money but no long-term security." The participants were asked to judge the lowest acceptable level of risk at which the engineer should accept the risky alternative. They then discussed the level of risk in a group and had to arrive at a unanimous group decision. The unexpected result was that over a number of decision-dilemmas, the group agreed on riskier decisions than the average of the individual decisions. Subsequent research using similar situations showed that the move was not always to riskier group decisions, but was to more extreme group decisions; a move to more or less extreme risks. It seems that if we look at the average of the individual decisions then if the average was towards high risk, the group decision would move towards an even riskier decision; and if the average individual decision was towards a low level of risk, then the group decision would move towards an even lower level of risk. This later result is called the polarization or shift to extreme phenomenon. A full discussion of this research can be found in Brown (2000).

Decision-making by groups where there is risk attached to the outcome is such a common situation in organisational decision-making that we should perhaps be wary of using newly formed or infrequently meeting groups to make such decisions.

Sherif and Sherif: in-group/out-group

Sherif and Sherif (1953) reported on the results of their studies of how two groups interact. Their results were very strong and have important implications for organisations, although it is only a part of their findings that are relevant to decision-making. They broke up friendships and formed two groups. The groups then were involved in activities, including some where the groups competed with one another. The members of the groups were then asked to assess their group and the other group. The recurring result was that the members of a group (the in-group) would view their group in a very positive way and would evaluate the other group (the out-group) in a very negative way, even though some of their earlier friends were in the out-group.

Subsequent studies have shown that the distorted assessments of the in-groups and out-groups occur whatever the basis for group membership. The distortion can occur between groups defined by:

- Blue eyes and brown eyes

- Men and women

- Heterosexuals and homosexuals

- Real Madrid and Barcelona (soccer clubs)

- The Marketing Department and the IT Department

- Engineers and accountants

- Jew and Muslim

- Jew and Gentile

- Catholic and Protestant

- Japanese and Chinese

The list is endless and seems capable of accounting for very many conflicts between defined groups. All that seems necessary is that you can define yourself as a member of one group and that another set of people, or an individual, belong to an identifiably different group.

Freudians suggest that we disown that which is negative in ourselves and project it onto others – the others, the out-groups, have all of our disowned negative aspects projected onto them – they become scapegoats.

Case Study 1.4: Stop being in role!

Running a managing-change module with a group of senior executives, I set up a role-playing exercise about an organisation that wanted to implement a consultant's report about computerisation. I split the executives into groups each representing a different group of employees; these were the senior management, the middle management, the shop-floor staff and the secretarial and administrative staff. Within two hours, the degree of conflict between the groups was amazing and almost frightening. The conflict and anger between the groups continued even after the "game" was terminated. It took a determined effort to get people to stop being angry and oppressed shop-floor workers (or whatever group they had been) and remember that they were actually all senior executives who liked one another.

I have run this and similar exercises on a number of occasions and every time members of the in-group will "rubbish" the out-group(s) within only a few minutes.

Questions

1. What does this observation say about interdepartmental co-operation within an organisation?
2. What might you expect to happen if a committee breaks up into sub-committees?

The standard way to overcome the problems arising from in-groups/out-groups is to organise a super-ordinate goal, that is, a goal that can only be achieved by the co-operation of the two or more groups.

The impact of in-group/out-group theory on decision-making is that a group that is searching for information in order to make a decision, or that needs to have its proposed decision evaluated, will be reluctant to turn to an out-group for assistance; the group is likely to isolate itself (see Group Think on p18 of this chapter).

We have now assembled enough theory to make some sense of a theory about faulty decision-making called Group Think.

Group Think

Group Think was defined by Janis (1972) as "a deterioration of mental efficiency, reality testing and moral judgment that results from in-group pressures" and was put forward as a way that very cohesive groups fail to make good decisions. A typical definition of cohesiveness is "… (the) strength of group members' desires to remain in the group and their commitment to the group", Gibson et al. (2000). Implicit in this definition is that the group is not a newly formed group of strangers.

Group Think was "discovered" by Janis in 1972. He sought to explain the group processes that had led a number of cohesive high profile groups to make poor decisions. Amongst the decisions were the USA's decision to support an invasion of Cuba at the Bay of Pigs in 1961, the decision to escalate US military involvement in Vietnam in 1965 and the Watergate scandal of 1973 (when the US President Nixon, and a group of close colleagues, decided to try and cover up a decision to "bug" the opposition party's offices in the Watergate Building) (Janis 1972, 1982). Janis put forward a number of features as being characteristic of groups that made poor decisions:

- A high level of group cohesiveness was central to poor group decision-making.

- The groups were characterised by being isolated from, and isolating themselves from, information and ideas from outside the group.

- The groups rarely searched systematically through alternative policy options as a way of appraising the merits of the policy that they had settled upon.

- The groups were often under time pressure to reach speedy decisions.

- Finally, the groups were nearly always dominated by a very directive leader who had a strong personal sense of the best decision, which they tried to impose on the group.

These five factors lead to strong pressures on group members to conform to the group decision and argument, and will lead to three key symptoms that will be demonstrated by groups suffering from Group Think:

- A very cohesive group exerts pressure on dissenting group members to conform to a group view. We have seen conformance to a group norm when we looked at the work of Asch (1956), Milgram (1963) and Zimbardo (1969) earlier in this chapter, but these were in newly formed groups and not cohesive ones. The Abilene Paradox did, however, arise in a cohesive group.

- An illusion of unanimity and correctness ("Our decision is the best logically and morally"), which inhibits the search for alternative decisions and the questioning of the decision that the group has made. Milgram's shocking experiments would seem to offer some explanation of how a group can act immorally; and Sherif and Sherif's in-group/out-group research offers some explanation of why groups may not search outside the group for alternative solutions.

- Other groups and individuals (out-groups) are negatively stereotyped. We have come across this earlier in this chapter when we looked at the ideas of Sherif and Sherif (1953) about in-groups and out-groups.

Subsequent research has suggested that whilst Janis was correct in his conclusion that group processes can lead to poor decision-making, his emphasis on the centrality of group cohesion was misplaced.

Research by Hart (1990) and Kramer (1998) also suggested that Janis's conclusion that group processes were entirely to blame for the Bay of Pigs, Vietnam and Watergate was too simplistic. Their research suggested that all three situations could be as well explained by looking at the political context and the wider socio-political context.

The importance of group cohesion as the basis of Group Think was overthrown by Tetlock et al. (1992) and Peterson (1997). Tetlock re-analysed six of Janis's (1982) examples of Group Think, plus two cases of good decision-making processes, and concluded that the six cases of Group Think all displayed less group cohesion than the examples of good, or vigilant, decision-making processes. The conclusion drawn was that factors related to procedural or structural defects (such as inappropriate leadership style) explained poor decision processes and not cohesiveness.

Peterson looked at the way the management teams of seven prominent companies made decisions during successful and unsuccessful periods of trading. The conclusion was that successful economic performance was associated with the more cohesive management teams and strong leadership, the reverse of Janis's conclusions.

We can make sense of this in terms of Tuckman (1965) (who we discussed earlier in this chapter), who suggested that for teams to be effective they have to go through a process of group development (forming, storming, norming and performing). Until a group has gone through these stages it cannot really hope to perform well, and this series of stages sounds very much like the stages that a group would go through in order to become cohesive. From this we have the hypothesis that for a group to perform successfully, it needs to be cohesive in some sense – the opposite of Janis.

When we think of strong and directive leadership, it makes us reflect on the meaning of the terms. A directive leadership could be autocratic, in the way that Janis suggested would be part of the process of Group Think, or it could be strong and directive by apportioning roles and ensuring that the group process was appropriate in how the group gathered information, shared it, analysed it and made decisions (the way that Belbin's Co-ordinator would control a decision-making group – see earlier in this chapter).

A final research finding about cohesiveness that further confuses the matter comes from the work of Moorehead and Montanari (1986), who found that the cohesiveness of student project groups was unrelated to their performance.

What is clear, when browsing through many alternative organisation behaviour texts, is that Janis's view that cohesiveness is the basis of Group Think has been accepted by many writers who have failed to notice the social psychology literature that clearly demonstrates that cohesiveness is not a necessary or sufficient condition for poor group decisions. Readers wanting a beautifully written summary of the social psychology literature about groups should turn to Brown (2000).

Janis was correct to point to the possibility that group processes might lead to poor decisions, but it seems clear from research that this is likely to be the result of poorly structured groups (Belbin, 1981), autocratically directive group leaders and the mini-mising of out-groups (Sherif and Sherif, 1953). Most of the other dysfunctional processes in groups (e.g. conformance) only seem to happen in newly formed groups or groups that meet only rarely.

Autocratic directive leadership where the leader pushes the group towards a preferred conclusion or decision can be a source of poor process, but can be overcome by ensuring that everyone in the group gets to speak and contribute, that individuals specialise in parts of the data collection and analysis, and that there is the appointment of a "devil's advocate", whose role is to try and find fault with the group's ideas and proposals so that the group does not fix on a single proposal too quickly.

Social loafing and labouring

We have looked at a number of problems that arise when individuals come to work together in a group, and now we look at some further problems which compare the productivity and efficiency of individuals when they work as members of a group.

Latane et al. (1979) observed what he called *social loafing*, which was the way that the sum of individual efforts in a group was less than the sum of the efforts of individuals working as individuals. This social loafing seems to occur very widely in groups. Karau and Williams (1993) reviewed 78 studies which compared individual effort when working in groups and as individuals, and found that nearly 80% of the studies showed evidence of social loafing. The earliest study of this problem was by Ringlemann (1913), where he measured how hard an individual could pull on a horizontal rope and then looked at how hard groups of people would pull on the rope. On average the first individual would exert a pull of about 85 kg, but seven pulling only managed 450 kg (that is, an average of only 64.5 kg) and the larger the group, the lower the average individual pull. This loafing seems to apply to a wide range of group activities when compared with solitary individual efforts, applying, for example, to problem-solving and brainstorming.

Clearly it is important to work out why the loafing occurs and to find ways to reduce it, or even how to get a synergy effect, where output of the group is greater than the sum of the individuals – this latter situation being called *social labouring*.

Steiner (1972) suggested that social loafing was most importantly effected by problems of co-ordination of individual effort within the groups and by group processes. In addition, he suggested that individual motivation might be effected by being a member of a group. Tuckman (1965) suggests that groups need to learn to work together and that newly formed groups are unlikely to be able to co-ordinate their efforts. Earlier in this chapter, we looked at a range of interpersonal processes that occur within a group, both newly formed and established, which reduce the potential effectiveness of the group. Research by Latane et al. (1979) suggested that members of a group were less motivated to do their best, especially if the other members of the group could not know how hard the individual was trying to contribute to the group task. In one experiment, Latane et al. (1979) had people shouting. He found that people shouted less loudly in a group than as individuals even though the task was to maximize the level of sound. Even when every member of the group was blindfolded and had white noise played through earphones, the level of sound produced by each individual was lower than their individual isolated best, but was higher than when they were in the group without earphones and blinds. He concluded that the motivation to contribute to a task is reduced in a group.

When we look at brainstorming it has been found that the best results come from individual brainstorming where the ideas are then pooled in the group, who then combine and evaluate the ideas that were produced individually. The volume of ideas and the quality of the ideas is higher when working as individuals. Taylor et al. (1958) found that when the individuals' ideas were collected together into a group, and the identical ideas eliminated, the collected individual ideas numbered on average 68 as compared with only 37 ideas produced by the interacting group with the same number of members. Individual brainstorming is improved by giving individuals an ambitious target for the quantity of ideas generated, or even just telling them that their performance will be compared with a standard of performance to be stated later (Paulus and Dzindolet, 1993; Szymanski and Harkins, 1987).

International cultural differences in relation to the collectivist/individualistic nature of national cultures (Hofstede, 2001), can be expected to have an impact on the presence or absence of social loafing, and it seems that there is generally less social loafing in eastern cultures that are characterised by a more collectivist culture (Brown, 2000).

WHY CAN WE EXPECT GROUPS TO MAKE BETTER DECISIONS THAN INDIVIDUALS?

This does not seem to be a difficult question to answer. We know that a group will have more information when the information of its individual members is pooled. We can also expect that if a problem is intellectually very difficult to solve, then a group is on average more likely to have a member who can solve the problem than if we ask individuals to solve the problem. Shaw (1932) showed that more intellectual problems will be solved by a group than if an individual is set to solve the problem, but that each solution achieved will take longer. The greater time can be put down to two causes; there is likely to be social loafing in a group, whether established or newly formed, and the complexity of the communications between the members of the group, as they interact in seeking to find a solution, will take a lot of time.

Not only is there more information in a group, but there are also more theories that can be pooled to solve the problem. We will also see, in Chapter 6, that the political process aids the discovery of weak and faulty arguments.

Case Study 1.5: Surviving the desert as a group

In teaching students about the relative merits of individual and group decision-making, I have often set them a problem that they answer as individuals and then address the same problem as a group. The problems used are often survival problems where the students are asked to imagine that they are the only survivors of a plane crash in some inhospitable location, like the Arctic tundra or a hot and sandy desert. They then have to decide which of a list of artefacts, that they have, are the most and least important to their survival. Producing the "best" answer requires a lot of knowledge and the ability to use that knowledge.

Continued

Using these types of exercises with management students, the result was that about 95% of the groups obtained a better score than the average individual who made up the group. This result is the usual result that is quoted for these types of decision exercises. However, with electrical and electronic engineering students, more than half the groups did worse than the average individual team member. I have never satisfied myself why the engineers get such different results year after year. My only thought is that a high proportion of the engineers are from the far East where there are few deserts or frozen areas – do they just have less knowledge to pool?

A conclusion from the ideas about the pooling of ideas, theories and arguments is that we may usually expect that groups will solve more problems, or produce better solutions, but at greater cost (more people and more time taken). If costs are higher and more time taken, then we should only use groups when the decision does not have to be taken very quickly and where the benefit to the organisation of good decisions outweigh the extra costs. If the building is burning down, it is not a good idea to convene a meeting to discuss the evacuation of the building, and deciding what sandwiches to order for a departmental sandwich lunch is hardly an appropriate use of scarce resources (time).

CONCLUSIONS

There are really too many conclusions to summarise, and thus I recommend that you look into each section of the chapter for the conclusions and the advice on how to effectively use groups, or when to avoid using groups.

REFERENCES

Asch, S.E., 1956. Studies of independence and conformity: a minority of one against a unanimous majority. Psychological Monograph 70 (9).

Belbin, R.M., 1981. Management Teams: Why They Succeed or Fail. Heinemann Professional Publishing.

Belbin, R.M., 1993. Team Roles at Work. Elsevier Butterworth Heinemann.

Brown, R., 2000. Group Processes: Dynamics Within and Between Groups, second ed. Blackwell.

Checkland, P., 1981. Systems Thinking, Systems Practice. John Wiley, Chichester.

Cohen, M.D., March, J.G., Olsen, J.P., 1972. A garbage can model of organizational choice. Administrative Science Quarterly 17 (1), 1–25.

Dunbar, R.I.M., 1993. Co-evolution of neocortical size, group size and language in humans. Behavioural Sciences 16 (4), 681–735.

Gibson, J.L., Ivancevich, J.M., Donnelly, J.H., 2000. Organizations: Behaviour, Structure, Processes. McGraw-Hill, Irwin.

Guardian, 2007. <www.guardian.co.uk/uk/2007/nov/01/gender.world>.

Hart, P., 1990. Group Think in Government: A Study of Small Groups and Policy Failure. Swets and Zeitlinger, Amsterdam.

Harvey, J.B., 1988. The Abilene paradox: the management of agreement. Organisation Dynamics (Summer 1988), 17–43 [The full text is available on Google Scholar under "Abilene"].

Hofstede, G. H., 2001. Culture's Consequnces; Comparing Values, Behaviours, Institutions, and Organizations Across Nations, 2nd edition, Sage.

Janis, I., 1982. Victims of Group Think, 2nd edition, Houghton-Mifflin.

Janis, I., 1972. Victims of Group Think. Houghton-Mifflin.

Karau, S.J., Williams, K.D., 1993. Social loafing: a meta-analytic review and theoretical integration. Journal of Personality and Social Psychology 65, 681–706.

King, E.B., Hebl, M.R., Beal, D., 2009. Conflict and co-operation in diverse workgroups. Journal of Social Issues 65 (2), 261–285.

Kramer, R.M., 1998. Revisiting the Bay of Pigs and Vietnam decisions 25 years later: how well has the group think hypothesis stood the test of time. Organisational Behaviour and Human Decision Processes 73, 236–271.

Latane, B., Williams, K., Harkins, S., 1979. Many hands make light the work: the causes and consequences of social loafing. Journal of Personality and Social Psychology 37, 822–832.

Margerison, C., McCann, D., 1990. Team Management. W.H. Allen.

Milgram, S., 1963. Group pressure and action against a person. Journal of Abnormal Social Psychology 67, 371–378.

Morgan, G., 1997. Images of Organization, second ed. Sage.

Moorehead, G., Montanari, J.R., 1986. An empirical investigation of the group think phenomenon. Human Relations 39, 399–410.

Paulus, P.B., Dzindolet, M.J., 1993. Social influence processes in group brainstorming. Journal of Personality and Social Psychology 64, 575–586.

Peterson, R.S., 1997. A directive leadership style in group decision making can be both a virtue and vice: evidence from elite and experimental groups. Journal of Personality and Social Psychology 72, 1107–1121.

Pugh, D.S. (Ed.), 1990. Organisational Theory: Selected Readings, third ed. Penguin Books, Harmsworth.

Ringlemann, M., 1913. Recherches Sur Les Moteurs Animes: Travail De L'homme. Annales de l'institut National Agronomique, second series 12, 1–40.

Shaw, M.E., 1932. A comparison of individuals and small groups in the rational solution of complex problems. American Journal of Psychology 44, 491–504.

Sherif, M., Sherif, C.W., 1953. Groups in Harmony and Tension: An Integration of Studies on Intergroup Relations. Octagon Books.

Simon, H.A., 1960. Administrative Behaviour. Macmillan.

Smith, P.B., Bond, M.H., 1993. Social Psychology Across Cultures: Analysis and Perspectives. Harvester Wheatsheaf.

Steiner, I.D., 1972. Group Process and Productivity. Academic Press.

Stoner, J.A.F., 1961. A Comparison of Individual and Group Decisions Including Risk. Unpublished thesis. MIT, School of Management.

Szymanski, K., Harkins, S.G., 1987. Social loafing and self-evaluation with a social standard. Journal of Personality and Social Psychology 53, 891–897.

Taylor, D.W., Berry, P.C., Block, C.H., 1958. Does group participation when using brainstorming facilitate or inhibit creative thinking? Administrative Science Quarterly 3, 23–47.

Tetlock, P.E., Peterson, R.S., McGuire, C., Chang, S., Feld, P., 1992. Assessing political group dynamics: a test of the group think model. Journal of Personality and Social Psychology 63, 403-425.

Tuckman, B.W., 1965. Development sequences in small groups. Psychological Bulletin 63, 384-399.

Tuckman, B.W., Jensen, M.A.C., 1977. Stages of small group development revisited. Group and Organizational Studies 2 (4), 419-427.

Zimbardo, P., 1969. The human choice: individuation, reason and order versus deindividuation, impulse and chaos. In: Arnold, W.J., Levine, D. (Eds.), Nebraska Symposium on Motivation, vol. 17. University of Nebraska Press.

Zimbardo, P.G., 1972. The pathology of imprisonment. Society 9 (6) [Available on Google Scholar under "Zimbardo"].

Organisational Culture

Organisational culture only became a topic of interest in the 1970s when academics began to seek to understand why Japanese companies were so successful, on the world stage, in a growing number of industries. Japanese motorcycles, cars, shipbuilding and electronics, amongst other products and industries, were rapidly moving to dominate the world market. Implicit in this was that the domestic industries in the rest of the world were coming under severe competition and were losing market share, with firms going bankrupt and having to shed staff. People began asking whether there was something special about Japanese firms that marked them out as different from firms in other countries; some magic ingredient that made them more successful. The conclusion drawn was that it was the culture within Japanese firms that was making the difference.

In the 1980s, three path-breaking books emerged from the growing journal article literature, Deal and Kennedy (1982), Peters and Waterman (1982) and Schein (1985). These books reflected and created a great rise in interest in what organisational culture was, how culture developed, whether a strong culture was important and whether it could be managed. We will now go on to look at these four questions.

WHAT IS ORGANISATIONAL CULTURE?

There are as many definitions as there are writers on organisational culture. Below we set out some definitions that will let you begin to develop a sense of what organisational culture might be.

- The glue that holds an organisation together.

- The way we do things around here (Marvin Bower, former Managing Director of Mckinsey and Company).

- The set of attitudes, values, goals and practices that characterise an institution or organisation (Merriam-Webster's online Dictionary).

- The beliefs, values, myths, legends and stories that are held in common.

- Collective sense-making.

- A pattern of shared basic assumptions that the group learned as it solved its problems of external adaptation and internal integration, that has worked well enough to be considered valid and, therefore, to be taught to new members as the correct way to perceive, think and feel in relation to those problems (Schein, 1992, page 12).

All of the definitions imply that culture is a set of shared rules, beliefs, behaviour, values and systems that are held in common by the people who make up the organisation.

Now we will give a couple of examples of culture that will hopefully add to your understanding of the basic ideas of culture set out in the definitions above.

What do we mean by "collective sense-making"? We mean that we need to share the same way of making sense of what we have seen, heard or read. There is a nice story about the painter Picasso, which may be apocryphal, but is so delightful that we hope that it is true. Picasso was asked by a very rich businessman to paint a portrait of the man's wife. Picasso refused on the grounds that he did not paint commissioned portraits, but the man persisted and eventually a fee was agreed that was so huge that Picasso agreed to paint the portrait. The woman came and sat for Picasso, and the husband was very eager to see the result. The finished portrait was in Picasso's style at the time, where the woman's features had been rearranged. The husband protested that the portrait was nothing like his wife. Picasso allegedly said, "So what *does* she look like?" The man opened his wallet and took out a small photograph of his wife and gave it to Picasso. "Oh" said Picasso, "She's very small and flat!" This is an example of people using two completely different frames of reference to make sense of their experience.

Another nice example, where culture was not shared, is based on a story (source not known) of a young man and a young woman from two different cultures entering an art gallery. The man looks across at the woman and thinks, "what an attractive woman, I would like to make her acquaintance." The woman looks across at the man and thinks how much she would like to make his acquaintance. They go their separate ways round the gallery until they end up in front of the same painting. The man starts a conversation by saying how beautiful the painting is, knowing that gradually he will draw the woman into conversation, until in the end he will be able to suggest that they go together to have a coffee (this process being the way that men in his country start the process of getting acquainted). The woman's shocking response to his comment about the painting is to say, "I like you too, where shall we go?" Her cultural rules are completely different than his.

CRITICAL VERSUS MANAGERIAL PERSPECTIVES OF ORGANISATIONAL CULTURE

There are two ways that we can look at what the definitions collectively are saying. One is called the *managerialist* perspective and the other is the *Critical* perspective.

The *managerialist* perspective sees the rules, beliefs, behaviours, values and systems as relatively fixed, that can be set, formed and changed by management.

The *critical* perspective suggests that the shared rules, beliefs, behaviours, values and systems grow out of the interactions between the members of the organisation with one another, and are thus a function of the individuals that make up the organisation and the environment (both internal and external to the organisation) within which they interact.

The managerialist perspective

This perspective was the first to be developed, and had the attractive implication that if management could work out what a successful culture looked like, then they would be able to design and impose such a culture, and the organisation could move rapidly to being more successful, however success was defined. This approach appealed to managers as it implied a clear role for managers and leaders – guidance as to what managers and leaders should do. In most societies, such certainty is welcomed, and uncertainty is to be avoided, although, as we will see in the International Cultural Differences chapter, attitudes towards uncertainty vary from one country to another.

In the automotive industry early efforts to impose at least some elements of the organisational culture to be found in Japanese car plants failed to bear fruit. For example, efforts to introduce quality circles and team working did not work, or at least they could not be quickly imposed.

The literature of quality circles in the UK is a catalogue of failed initiatives. A quality circle can be defined as

> *… a small group of 6 to 12 employees doing similar work who voluntarily meet together on a regular basis to identify improvements in their respective work areas using proven techniques for analyzing and solving work-related problems coming in the way of achieving and sustaining excellence leading to mutual upliftment of employees as well as the organisation. It is "a way of capturing the creative and innovative power that lies within the workforce". (http://www.mahapwd.com)*

When we examine this definition, we can perhaps begin to see why quality circles failed in the UK and many other "western" economies, and learn something about the nature of organisational culture. The first sentence of the definition talks of a group coming together. In the 1960s and 1970s, the UK was a very individualistic society, unused to working in a collective team or group way. During these times, many Britons would have found collective working strange and disconcerting. By contrast, Japanese society was, and is, very collectivist (see the chapter on International Cultural Differences) and thus quality circles were an entirely natural and comfortable form of organisation that grew out of, and was compatible with, national culture. When we look at the last sentence of the definition of quality circles we see reference to "…capturing the creative and innovative power that lies within the workforce." In the 1960s and 1970s in the UK, the belief of many managers was a Theory X view (see the Appendix on Theory X and Y) with managers believing that their workers were lazy, uninterested in work and could not, or would not, be creative. If this was the management's belief, then it is easy to see that management would not believe that quality circles could work, and thus the tender plant of quality circles was planted in unsuitable soil – quality circles did not fit the existing national or organisational culture and were thus doomed to failure, as was the usual experience of quality circles in the UK.

Case Study 2.1: Culture as beliefs

I was working as a change consultant in a department of an international organisation. All the managers, at the level I was working at, were British. For a variety of reasons, one of these managers was very much a Theory X manager who believed that his subordinates were lazy and unprepared to be creative. One of the change initiatives that I was trying to introduce was that staff should be treated in a Theory Y manner, because at the time the department was hiring adults and then treating them like children who could not be trusted, resulting in a high staff turnover of 100% per year. This theory X manager introduced the changes requested of him, where staff were invited to be creative and responsible, and were told that they would not be as heavily supervised and audited as they had been up to that point. The subordinates were deeply suspicious of the change, as they believed that their manager did not trust them. For them to change their behaviour, as a result of changing their beliefs about their manager, they needed to see that the new policy was adopted long term. Sure enough the manager was soon peering over their shoulders and remonstrating with them for not changing their behaviour. There was a collective sigh from the staff, "We knew he wouldn't change", and the manager said, "You see, I knew they wouldn't change!"

Beliefs, a part of organisational culture, are hard to change just by management imposing a new policy.

Question

1. How could this policy have been introduced so that it had a better chance of succeeding?
2. How do you get your staff to believe you?

Footnote

The manager in question was sacked because he could not/would not change the way he managed. Another manager in the department resigned because he did not want to work for an organisation that was so stupid as to trust its workforce. The other managers introduced the policy, with some relief, as they were Theory Y managers who had been working in a Theory X department. The department eventually reaped the rewards of a motivated and creative staff once the staff came to believe that the change was a permanent change in management style, and staff turnover improved 100%.

Not only was the early experience of the managerialist perspective on organisational culture that elements of a "foreign" organisational culture could not be transplanted easily into a different culture, but also that if you could succeed in changing the cultural beliefs, values and behaviours, this change took a very long time to occur, as it met very considerable resistance to change. In a seminal account of the changing of the organisational culture of ICI (then the largest chemicals company in the UK), Pettigrew (1985) showed that radical change of an organisation's culture usually took between 5 and 10 years to achieve.

Formal and informal, espoused and enacted cultures

The managerial and critical perspectives provide some insight into an observed situation in organisations. If you ask managers about the culture of their organisation, they will often explain to you what the culture is, and it always seems to indicate that the culture is one that enables the organisation to be successful, even though the organisation may be less than successful. What they have told you about is the formal or espoused culture – what it is supposed to be. If, however, you ask the workforce about the rules, values and practices that are actually defining the organisation, or if you stay long enough to become aware of the beliefs, values and so on that actually define the organisation and the way that it works, then you become aware of the informal or enacted culture – how things actually are, as opposed to how the senior management would like them to be. The enacted or informal culture is the culture that has developed through time as a result of the interaction of the actors in the drama. The espoused or formal culture is the one that the most senior people in the organisation would like to be the case, the one that flows from the managerialist perspective.

MODELS OF ORGANISATIONAL CULTURE

Schein

Schein (1985) developed a metaphor of organisational culture as an iceberg. The essence of an iceberg, in this case, is that the majority of the iceberg is below the surface of the water and we cannot see what it is that supports the part of the iceberg that is above the water surface and visible.

   Schein suggested that there were three layers of organisational culture, two of which were below the water line, Basic Assumptions and Values, and one of which was visible and above the water line, Artefacts.

Artefacts

Artefacts are the things that we can observe in an organisation. We can observe the technology, the buildings, furniture, what is on people's desks, the decoration of rooms, the artwork and posters on walls, people's behaviour, what they say and how they say it, how meetings are conducted, how decisions are made and how the organisation is formally structured. Artefacts are the objects and behaviours that an observer will see and hear, that are elements of the culture, but which cannot be understood until the organisational culture is understood.

Case Study 2.2: The IT firm's artefacts

I was visiting for the first time an organisation where I was going to be doing some consulting. I drove up to the HQ, where a notice directed me to an underground car park. At the entrance to the car park was a barrier with an intercom. I explained who I was and who I had come to visit. The barrier rose and let me into the car park. Inside, some of the parking bays were labelled with names, some with titles (Managing Director, and so on), some with no labels and a few were

Continued

labelled "Visitors". I parked my car and made my way to the main door of the HQ; the door was locked but there was an intercom; I again explained who I was and who I was visiting. The door clicked open, to let me into reception. The reception was bleak but luxuriously furnished. I registered and was given a badge to wear that said who I was and who I was visiting. I was told that Mr Graves was on the second floor. I went to leave the reception, only to find that the door out of reception was locked. I had to wait until someone came to escort me to Mr Graves on the second floor.

During my first day, I interviewed a series of staff members, in a private room set aside for the purpose. Everyone answered my questions in a whisper. Sometimes they would draw on a flip chart to illustrate a point that they were making. Every person I interviewed checked with me that what he/she said would be treated in confidence, turned the flip chart from the door, and took his/her drawing away with him/her.

Everything that I had experienced and seen since my arrival were artefacts of organisational culture, but I did not know, at that time, how to make sense of them: why was the organisation so security conscious, why were the car-parking bays labelled as they were, why was everyone so secretive? I was to subsequently learn why these artefacts were as they were.

Question

People are by nature eager to make sense of what they experience. What are your guesses/hypotheses about the beliefs and values of the organisation that lie under the observed artefacts in the IT organisation?

Case Study 2.3: The heavy engineering firm; SIMPLY NOT THE BEST

I was visiting my executive MBA student in the heavy engineering firm where he was a production manager. I knew that the firm had been struggling for a number of years and had on three occasions in the last decade had to cut its staff due largely to falling levels of orders for the steel rolling mills that they manufactured. I was shown round the machine shop, a vast building full of massive metal working machines, including a milling machine that was the size of a small detached house. Many of the machines and much of the walls were covered with pin-up pictures of naked or scantily clad women. My student said that he repeatedly had the pin-ups taken down, but they reappeared overnight. My gaze was drawn to the huge milling machine; stuck to the side of the machine was a headline torn from a newspaper; "SIMPLY NOT THE BEST" it read.

Question

What have you learnt about this engineering firm and its culture from the artefacts that I have described and the one item of organisational history?

Values

Schein argues that the artefacts that we can observe are manifestations of the values that constitute part of the organisational culture. Implicit in the iceberg metaphor is that the values are below the surface of the water, and thus not obvious to the observer who sees and hears only the artefacts.

But what are "values"? Hyde and Williams (2000) define personal values as:

'Underlying and relatively stable dispositions which people [in the organisation] use to guide their actions and decisions and to help them make judgments about what is right and wrong'.

(The [ ] words are an addition to the original quote)

Writing about a Government organisation, Hyde and Williams (2000) give as examples of organisational values a belief in:

- The importance of staff diversity

- Professionalism

- Continuous improvement

- Staff well-being

- Service to clients

The implication of this is that what you see and hear in organisations, the artefacts, ranging from the physical structure of the building and the behaviours that you observe are all to be understood in terms of the values that the staff members hold in common. Organisational members will usually be able to list the values of their organisation, if asked.

The managerialist approach to culture implies that management may design and impose the organisational values. The critical perspective suggests that values cannot be imposed if they differ from the personal values of the individuals. If the imposed values are at variance with the personal ones, then it is likely that either the imposed ones will be ignored, or the people who cannot accept them will leave the organisation (Hyde and Williams, 2000).

Basic assumptions

Just as the artefacts are manifestations of the values, so the values are manifestations of the basic assumptions. Basic assumptions are sometimes referred to as TFGs (Taken for Granteds) – beliefs that everyone in an organisation shares that do not have to be made explicit, as they are "taken for granted". Values flow from these basic assumptions. Schein (1985) suggested that the basic assumptions are things like the nature of truth, of human activity, of relationships and the nature of human nature. If we reflect on this list, we realize that the basic assumptions will be profoundly influenced by the national culture in which we have grown up. For example, the basic assumptions about women, their role in society, and what they can and cannot do, should and should not do and what is appropriate behaviour will all be aspects of national culture, and will vary quite a bit from one country to another. In the International Cultural Differences chapter, the example statements that would be typical of feminist/individualist/uncertainty avoidant, etc. societies, as discussed by Hofstede (2001), are examples of basic assumptions (see pages 50-53). In the same chapter, the statements about management that Laurent (1983) asked different nationalities of managers to agree or disagree about are also examples of basic assumptions (see pages 55-57).

In a marginally different definition of organisational culture than his 1992 definition, in 1985, Schein referred to basic assumptions as being "...invented, discovered or developed..." (Schein, 1985).

What we have just argued is that what is invented, discovered or developed is very much influenced not only by what happens as the organisation develops, but also by the national culture that people bring into the organisation. Recently, discussing this material with an Australian colleague, June Scott, she made the point that some countries are now so diverse in terms of the ethnicity of their citizens that we are unlikely to be able to characterise an Australian national culture anymore since there is a shared British or American culture. To look for a single shared national culture, that might be reflected in the basic assumptions of an organisation, we may have to look at those countries that do not have ethnically diverse populations, perhaps like China; but even in China there is considerable diversity. In many countries the basic assumptions that emerge within an organisation, as it develops, are very likely to reflect more about the shared experiences within the organisation than the diverse national cultures that employees bring into the organisation, just as Schein described.

Johnson's cultural network

In describing organisational culture, Johnson (1988) described a network of interlocking elements of an organisation that, together with a central paradigm that informs the elements, constituted the culture of an organisation. What is a paradigm?

A philosophical and theoretical framework of a scientific school or discipline within which theories, laws and generalizations and the experiments performed in support of them are formulated; broadly they are a philosophical or theoretical framework of any kind (Merriam_Webster's online Dictionary).

The elements reflecting Johnson's (1992) central paradigm were:

- Organisational structures

- Control systems

- Power structures

- Symbols

- Stories and myths

- Rituals and routines

In effect, the central paradigm is the equivalent of what Schein (1985) calls the organisation's culture. That is, the set of shared basic assumptions that are developed through time within the organisation.

The elements are then the manifestations of that central paradigm:

- *Structure and the control systems* will reflect the basic assumptions shared by the staff of the organisation. If the staff are essentially Theory X and believe in Scientific

Management, then the lack of trust in people, the perceived need to be in control and monitoring and auditing processes within the organisation will mean that we are likely to observe a bureaucratic organisation that will be hierarchical, rule bound and highly regulated (for a discussion of Theory X see the Appendix on Theory X and Y. For a discussion of Scientific Management and Organisational Structures, see the Organisational Structures chapter).

- *Power structures* define who has power, how decisions are made and how conflicts are resolved (for a full discussion of Power Structures, see the Organisational Politics chapter).

- *Stories and myths* may well be stories and anecdotes that tell you something about the history of the organisation that led to the basic assumptions that are collectively accepted in the organisation. Thus you may hear stories about what the organisation did in economic hard times that support the current beliefs about the sacrifices that staff are expected to make when economic problems arise again. Perhaps the organisation chooses to cut salaries rather than to reduce the level of staffing and research and development (R&D), because there is a shared belief that a loyal staff is a key to success in that industry, and a shared belief that it is a strong R&D basis that ensures the future products and services that will sustain the organisation in the future.

- *Rituals and symbols*: in universities, part of the culture of the organisation is the ritual of graduation ceremonies where people wear medieval clothing (symbols) to indicate the historical and ongoing pursuit of learning and scholarship. If people wear medieval gowns and mortarboards at graduation ceremonies, then it must be because it continues to serves some function and is part of the culture.

Bate's approach to culture

Bate (1994) captures much that is of the essence of the ideas put forward by Schein and Johnson. Bate's idea about organisational culture can be captured in a single sentence:

> *Organisations do not have cultures, they are cultures.*

Implicit in this statement is that every aspect of an organisation is an aspect of its culture; every aspect is a manifestation of its culture. Thus we can think that the organisation structure, strategy, decision-making processes, payments systems, information systems, management style and any other aspect of the organisation that we can think of is a manifestation of the organisational culture, is a part of the culture or is the culture. To take just one example, we can see that the strategy of an organisation and how that strategy is developed are a reflection, a manifestation, of the way that people think and feel in that organisation, and the way that they think and feel is a manifestation of the beliefs and values that they hold in common. In Schein's iceberg model the artefacts were supported by the values of the organisation, and the values were supported by the basic assumptions of the organisation. This is essentially what Bate was saying explicitly – every aspect of an organisation is a manifestation of the organisation's culture, except that Bate says that they are not manifestations of the culture, but are the culture, parts of the essential whole that is the organisation's culture. In the

Organisational Structures chapter, there is a discussion of how every aspect of an organisation is a manifestation of the personality of the founder or the long-term chief executive officer (CEO), and of how the culture of the organisation is a manifestation of the founder's or CEO's personality.

CLASSIFYING CULTURES: THE TAXONOMY OF ORGANISATIONAL CULTURE

A number of writers have felt the need to classify cultures, or have argued that we can classify cultures into a relatively small number of types, to have a taxonomy, see for example Handy (1985) and Quinn and McGrath (1985). We write later in this chapter that every organisational culture is formed from the interaction of a unique set of factors, so that we can expect that no two organisations will have identical cultures. Does this mean that it is a pointless exercise to look for a way of classifying cultures into a few categories?

When you read the Organisational Structures chapter, you will see that the literature suggests that a limited set of types of organisational structure will evolve as a result of the relatively few forces that determine the structure of organisations. The people who argue for a taxonomy also argue that the culture of an organisation is predominately a function of the organisational structure. Handy (1985), for example, argues that bureaucratic/mechanistic organisations will have what he calls a Role Culture, which will be based around rules, authority, formality and scientific management. In what follows, we set out Handy's taxonomy of organisational cultures, and those of a number of other writers.

Handy's taxonomy

■ *Power culture*: this culture can be pictured as a web, with the power in the organisation concentrated at the centre and with the powerful people in the organisation being target driven and less interested in how the targets are met. It can be quite an aggressive internal environment with politics playing an important role as power is used to make and resolve decisions. This culture enables organisations to respond quickly to a changing external environment and depends on trust, empathy and personal communications for its effectiveness.

■ *Role culture:* this is the formal, bureaucratic, rule-bound organisation that we referred to earlier.

■ *Task culture*: this culture is sometimes called a matrix culture, where task groups are formed, that are made up of staff from all of the specialisms that need to have an input into decision making and enactment. Power is spread widely through the organisation and flows from expertise rather than position power or charisma (see the Organisational Politics chapter for a full discussion). Engineering project groups would be a good example of task cultures.

■ *Person culture*: this is the culture where individuals come together to share resources. The individuals work very much as free-standing experts, but share central facilities. Law firms often have this form of culture where administration and secretarial services are provided centrally.

Quinn and McGrath's taxonomy

Quinn and McGrath (1985) suggest that cultures can be categorised into four classifications as a result of where the organisation falls on two criteria. They look at the extent to which the organisation has an internal or an external focus when relating to the environment - does the organisation work hard at market research, checking on new production techniques and the actions of their customers and rivals, or are they more focussed on what is happening within the organisation, how decisions are made, how the organisation is structured and the internal systems. The second dimension is the extent to which the organisation is focussed on being flexible and adaptable, or focussed on developing certainty and predictability within the organisation. From these two dimensions, four cultural classifications arose:

■ Flexibility and external focus - a Developmental culture

■ Flexibility and internal focus - a Consensual culture

■ Predictability and internal focus - a Hierarchical culture

■ Predictability and external focus - a Rational culture

A gendered taxonomy

In the literature on gender in organisations, writers (see for example, Collinson and Hearn, 1994) talk of masculine and feminine organisational cultures, and even subdivide the masculine cultures into a variety of different masculine cultures, set out below.

■ *Tradition authoritarianism*, which is maintained via bullying and the use of fear.

■ *Gentlemen's club*, where women are patronised and the assumption is that only men can lead.

■ *Entrepreneurialism*, where the organisation is task orientated and long working hours are the norm.

■ *Informalism*, where the culture is boyish, "larky", with elements of sporting and sexual rituals (sexual humour, visits to "male" organisations like strip clubs and lap dancing establishments).

■ *Careerism*, where expertise and bureaucratic career progression are valued highly.

■ *Gender-blind*, where everyone is treated as though they are male, and gender differences are not acknowledged.

- *Feminist pretenders*, where the organisation supports equality and the absence of discrimination against women, but it is the responsibility of the women to be proactive about equality.

- *Smart macho*, where the culture is all about aggressive career development, long hours and being work-centred. In this situation women are seen as weak and uncommitted if they have families that lead to them taking career breaks and time off to manage their family's events.

Jungian taxonomy

Jung's taxonomy of human personalities (Morgan, 1997) looks at personality in terms of how people gather information about the world (measuring versus intuition or feeling) and how they process information (rationally/theoretically versus intuitive), and results in four possible combinations:

- Measuring (gathering) and rational/theoretical (processing)

- Measuring (gathering) and intuitive (processing)

- Intuitive gathering and rational/theoretical processing

- Intuitive gathering and intuitive processing

We have been suggesting that the taxonomists may be people who measure information and then process it rationally/theoretically – they only feel comfortable with numbers and certainties and thinking, and are uncomfortable with uncertainty and ambiguity. We might at this point recall the joke about there only being two types of people; those who think there are only two types of people and those who do not think there are only two types of people.

If we just take the classifications of Handy (1985) and Collinson and Hearn (1994), then an organisation might be classified as having a power culture (when we examine organisational structure) and a gentlemen's club culture (when we examine the organisational culture from a gender perspective). We see that the culture of the organisation has two inter-reacting/overlapping cultural labels.

However, if we use Handy (1985), Collinson and Hearn (1994) and Quinn and McGrath (1985), then we may classify an organisation with three cultural labels.

We can easily see that the labelling and classifying of the culture are getting more and more complex, suggesting that the search for a simple taxonomy may be a waste of time, that says more about the psychological needs of the taxonomists, that flow from their personalities, than it says about the organisations.

You need to draw your own conclusion as to whether the search for a taxonomy of organisational cultures is a useful exercise.

HOW IS ORGANISATIONAL CULTURE FORMED?

The managerialist perspective assumes that culture can be designed, implemented and changed by the management of the organisation. This approach assumes that cultures can be designed in a rational way, or in a way that suits or reflects the personality of the founders. When we look at the Leadership chapter, we will examine the extent to which leaders make organisations in their own image and the extent to which the culture reflects the leadership.

If we look at the alternative critical perspective, presented in the definition of culture given by Schein (1992), on page 25, 26 of this chapter, then we see a clear implication that the culture comes about as the result of the interaction of the people in the organisation over a period of time as the organisation forms and develops in the environment in which it finds itself.

Let us reflect on some of the factors that may interact together to form the organisational culture:

- *The professional training and qualifications that the staff bring to the organisation*: if we think of engineers, they have learnt a way of thinking and problem solving that is central to engineering education and the nature of the job of being an engineer. In addition, we may expect that there may be a particular type of personality that is drawn to engineering as a career, or at least a limited range of personalities, that are drawn to engineering and that are necessary to succeed as an engineer. As an example, it has been my experience that if you run engineering students through Belbin's Team Roles instrument, then only a very small proportion will have the personality that fits them to want the role of Chair or Co-ordinator. Conversely, we may expect that accountants and finance staff will come with their particular and different ways of thinking, analysing and problem solving, again related to their training and their personality. In effect we are suggesting that each professional group within an organisation has its own distinct professional culture formed out of its training and personality types. The organisation's culture will emerge partly as a result of the interaction of these differing professional cultures.

- *The differing national cultures that the staff bring to the organisation*: in the International Cultural Differences chapter we will see that the beliefs, values and behaviours of people differ not only between individuals but also between countries. Some countries have a different attitude to uncertainty; some will be more masculine or feminine than others. We will also see that beliefs about what are appropriate behaviours and expectations of managers will differ between countries. If cultures differ between countries, and there is evidence to suggest this (Hofstede, 2001; Laurent, 1983; Dunkel and Meierew, 2004), then we can expect that within an organisation with an internationally diverse workforce, the culture that emerges will be the result of the interaction of the differing national cultures within the organisation.

- *Gender*: if men and women differ in the way that they think and feel, in their beliefs and values or in their behaviours, and there is evidence to support this (Linstead, Fulop and Lilley, 2004), then the gender mix of the organisation will have an impact on the emerging organisational culture. When we discuss leadership in the Leadership chapter we will see that there is evidence that suggests that women lead, on average, in a different way than men, and thus the gender makeup of the management will be manifested in the organisational culture that emerges as a result of the interaction of staff within the organisation.

Case Study 2.4: A Japanese IT firm in the UK, and its women

Japanese national culture is very masculine. In this Japanese-owned IT firm's UK HQ, it was noticeable that there were no female managers. This arose for two interlocking reasons that formed part of the culture of the organisation. The most senior managers, who were all Japanese men, believed that women were not equipped to be managers, that they did not, as women, have the qualities that a manager needed (although different countries have differing views as to what qualities a manager needs, Laurent, 1983). The British women working for the organisation believed that they would never be promoted into management in a Japanese organisation, and they pointed to the absence of women managers to support their belief. As a result of their belief, the women only stayed with the organisation for a short period of time, until they had accumulated enough experience to be appointed as managers in UK-managed organisations, and then they resigned. The result was that the Japanese senior management said, "You see, women can't be trusted to stay long term in an organisation, and thus we are right not to appoint women managers." The other part of the process was that because the women left after a short time, the UK managers could never point to the qualities and experience of the women in order to challenge the Japanese cultural beliefs about women. This element of culture was imported from Japan but was never challenged or changed because of the way that the women and the Japanese managers interacted.

Question

How might you try and change this element of culture, in this organisation, with its diverse workforce?

- *Founder/leader*: a key factor in the formation of the organisational culture is likely to be the personality, beliefs and values of the founder of the organisation, or the characteristics of the long-term CEO. Because these people have the power to try and impose certain structures, systems and rules on the organisation, these are powerful elements in the interaction out of which the organisational culture emerges. This idea of leader's influence on culture will be discussed more fully in the Leadership chapter.

- *Size, age and structure*: the size of an organisation may well have an impact on its culture. Small, newly formed organisations are likely to have a loose structure that has not been formalised, and the whole of the staff may be involved in making policy and formulating solutions to problems. But, as organisations grow larger, jobs become more specialised, and the structure often becomes more formalised and people's daily experience of working will evolve and change. All of these changes are part of culture changing, as the culture has to fit the organisation as it evolves, or the organisation and culture become dysfunctional and the organisation fails.

■ *External environment*: in Schein's (1992) definition (page 25–26 of this chapter), we see that culture develops as the organisation learns to overcome problems of adoption to the external environment. Thus, for example, changes in the law may require that things are done differently, as may changes to technology and market structures and conditions.

We can see that there are many factors that interact to form the organisation's culture, and, as the external and internal environments are constantly changing, we can expect that the result of all these factors interacting is that the culture will be constantly changing and evolving.

Subcultures

We have been writing as though there will be a single shared culture within an organisation that is the result of the ongoing interaction between the individuals and stakeholders inside and outside the organisation, much as Tuckman (1965) suggested that group norms will develop in a small group or team as the members interact and go through the process of group development – forming, storming, norming and performing. However, in the previous section of this chapter, about the evolving of an organisational culture, we referred to the importance of the professional training and education of the employees. If an organisation is structured into functional departments, with separate departments of finance, marketing, engineering and so on, we may then expect that within a single department there will be intense interaction between people with the same education and training, and thus in the engineering department, full of chartered engineers, for example, there will be a strong engineering culture that is different than the strong accounting culture that develops in the accounting department that is full of professional accountants. The result is that there will be a series of subcultures that have to interact at the boundaries between departments, rather than a single organisation-wide culture. Even in a university each student population within different departments will tend to develop differing cultures. Somehow, even the clothing style of students of law and of archaeology tend to be quite different, as do their attitudes towards study and many other aspects of departmental student culture. Many years ago, when the author worked as an economist at Unilever's HQ, the staff of the IT department could be instantly distinguished from the economists by their casual style of dress and their more relaxed attitude to work and time keeping – the culture of the two departments was quite different in some respects even though we all worked for the same organisation.

The implication of subcultures is that liaison people, who work at the frontiers between two or more subcultures, have to learn the subcultures and how to interact with the other subcultures if they are to be effective.

CAN ORGANISATION CULTURES BE MANAGED?

Throughout this chapter, we have mainly written as though culture cannot be managed, but perhaps it is time to address this issue directly.

The managerial perspective on organisational culture believes that culture can be designed and implemented and thus can easily be changed. Earlier in the chapter we referred to Pettigrew's seminal work on the UK chemical giant ICI, where the finding was that it took between 5 and 10 years to radically change the culture of the organisation (Pettigrew, 1985).

Schein (1992) suggests that there are 11 different ways to change organisation culture, and that the effective technique depends on the stage that the organisation has reached in its life cycle from Founding and Early Life, Organisational Midlife and Maturity and Decline. Below we set out these 11 techniques:

Founding and early life

- *Incremental change through evolution*: here the culture gradually evolves as the organisation exists for a growing period of time and works out how to survive and prosper.

- *Self-guided evolution through organisational therapy*: this is cultural change that comes about as a result of members of the organisation deliberately putting time on one side to look at how the organisation is progressing and whether the processes are appropriate for the agreed aims of the organisation.

- *Managed evolution through hybrids*: here the culture is changed as a result of the internal promotion of managers who have new ideas about how the organisation needs to be in the changing environment. The new ideas are acceptable because the promoted managers are "one of us" and are not outsiders. Their revolutionary, or different, ideas may come from consultants, outside contacts or other sources of different perspectives. Mikhail Gorbachev was a hybrid in the Soviet Union, who rose up through the political ranks whilst secretly harbouring different views about how the country should be run. When he became Head of State, he started the process of rapid change of the USSR culture. We appreciate that the USSR could hardly be described as a culture at an early stage of its cultural life, but Gorbachev is a good example of a hybrid!

Organisational midlife

At this stage in the life of the organisation, the founder(s) and/or their family may no longer numerically dominate the management and decisions have to be made about how the organisation will develop in the future; which products, markets and technologies.

- *Change through systematic promotion from selected subcultures*: this is a process of cultural change that comes from recognising the important subcultures as they develop in the organisation as it moves from birth, infancy and a unified culture. Having recognised the subcultures that are important for the developing organisation, the leaders of those subcultures are promoted into positions where they have the power to shift the organisational culture towards greater functionality in the changing internal and external environment. This approach to cultural change is a more deliberate version of change through hybrids.

- *Change through organisational development*: organisational development is the planned change process, managed from the top, that considers both the technical and the human sides of the organisation, using internal and external consultants for diagnosis, planning and implementation.

- *Change through technological seduction*: the introduction of new technology means that new systems have to be developed, new skills acquired and the distribution of power is altered by the new technology. Thus the deliberate introduction of new technology introduces forces that lead to changed culture.

Maturity and decline

- *Managed change through infusion of outsiders*: this is exactly what it sounds like. The mechanism may be to bring in a new CEO from outside the organisation, or to bring in one or more new outside directors onto the board. There is then an element of shock, new thinking, and the new executives have no investment in the old culture, and don't stand to lose face, as the previous executives might if they changed the culture for which they had been responsible, and the staff expect changes to be introduced.

- *Change through scandal and explosion of myths*: when something goes disastrously wrong for an organisation, either internally, or when those outside the organisation are made aware, then the shock waves and the subsequent post-mortem may well unfreeze (Lewin, 1951) the organisation's culture and make changes more possible and acceptable, or even essential. A classic example would be the disaster for NASA when the Challenger space shuttle exploded as a result of inappropriate decision-making processes and inappropriate public relations priorities. Sometimes the scandal can be manufactured within the organisation by a whistleblower.

- *Change through coercive persuasion*: this approach is about putting consistent and continuous pressure on people to change their beliefs, values and behaviours whilst providing support and security and making it impossible to leave the organisation. This approach can work with those people who want or need to go on working, but will not be effective with people who are prepared to retire or stop working rather than change.

Case Study 2.5: An engineering firm: retire rather than change

I was doing some stress management work with an engineering firm that manufactured twist drills and bits. They had decided to introduce computer-controlled machines. All the machinists were offered training and job security. A number of the highly skilled and experienced machinists refused to have anything to do with the new machinery. They said that they were too old to learn about computers and computer-controlled machines. In a city blighted at the time with unemployment, they chose to resign or take early retirement. The machinists who took the retraining, with all that implied in terms of changed culture, accepted the offered security and rejected the near certainty of unemployment.

Case Study 2.6: A chemicals firm: "I will not attend a course."

I was asked to consult over a strange cultural situation that had arisen in a small chemicals firm with about 80 employees, which made chemicals for the photographic industry. The CEO had been on a course that suggested that if employees were learning something new, then they would go on learning and thinking at work, and productivity and quality would rise and waste would diminish. What they learnt did not matter. The firm instituted a policy that every employee had to be doing a course. It could be anything, languages, woodwork, photography, computing, anything; it didn't have to be related to chemical production. Most of the staff signed up for courses, with their fees paid by the company. Productivity, quality and waste all changed in the desired manner – thinking workers could not switch off their thinking and problem solving when they came to work.

The culture of the organisation had clearly changed, but there were a small minority of workers who refused to sign up for any course on any topic, even though company policy implied that they would be sacked if they continued to resist.

Question

What beliefs, values, behaviours (personal culture) meant that these workers refused to change even with the threat of being sacked?
Unfortunately I didn't get the consultancy contract, so I never learnt what was going on in their minds, or whether the CEO did sack them.

- *Change through turnarounds*: this approach is likely to use a mixture of the previously listed cultural change mechanisms, but is based on the understanding of the senior management that the organisation has to change drastically if it is to survive or continue to thrive. This senior management perspective has to be understood and accepted by the whole organisation, even if coercion has to be used.

- *Change through reorganisation and rebirth*: this is basically the death of one organisation and the culture that defines it, and its rebirth in a very different form that develops a new and different culture. This situation is likely to occur when a firm is bought by another, or is merged with a dominant partner, with the resulting removal of many of the existing staff, complete with their cultural assumptions and behaviours.

One of the difficulties that these 11 techniques encounter is that the culture is formed not just by the rules and actions of the management, but as a result of the interaction of all the people within the organisation within their constantly changing external environment. The management cannot control the thinking and the beliefs of the organisation's people, which are likely to be constantly changing, and it clearly has no chance of controlling the external environment. An organisation cannot control the national legal framework within which the organisation operates. Even less can the firm control the international legal framework. The rapid and unpredictable rate of technical change that influences what goods and services can be produced, and in what manner, is also beyond the control of most organisations, and yet will clearly have an impact on the organisation's culture.

Change in organisations is very much about the political processes of resolving conflicting interests. The use of politics in organisations in order to bring about change, and thus cultural change is discussed in some detail in the Organisational Politics chapter.

Field theory

One way of making some sense of the complex interactions of the many forces that results in a culture, and the changing and evolution of organisational culture(s), is called Field Theory. Field theory, which in the social and organisational context was developed by Lewin (1951), suggests that an organisation is much like a rapidly flowing stream where the state of the water (organisation) at any point in time is the result of the interaction of the changing river banks, and the changing river bed, as the water scours the earth and rocks in the banks and bed, and the gradient of the river, and the rain that fell in earlier times and that has only just reached this location in the river, the extent to which it filled the river and whether someone has just felled a tree which has fallen in the river, and so on.

Each variable interacts with every other element in the field at any moment in time and is influenced by the interaction of all of the elements in the field in all earlier time. Thus field theory implies that the series of elements that are interacting is likely to be very numerous, and that we may not have any adequate theories that predict how the elements will interact.

We can say that almost the only result that comes out of field theory, as applied to organisations, is that if the management changes some element in the field, with a view to changing the culture, then the culture will change, but the sequence of interactions is so complex that we cannot predict what the outcome will be at any point.

We also need to remember that field theory implies that the process of interaction is continuous and thus the culture (the field) will be constantly changing. Heraclitus, an ancient Greek philosopher remarked "No man ever steps in the same river twice, for it's not the same river and he's not the same man." Each person in an organisation is a field in their own right, and is subject to constant change and evolution as they are influenced by their reading, their thinking, the changing views of their partners, the international news and so on. Each of these "Person Fields" is in a constant process of change and thus all of the "Person Fields" in an organisation are changing elements in the greater field that we call the organisation and the fields that make up the greater field that we call the organisation's external environment.

Writers of change management write about the so-called butterfly effect in Chaos Theory, where it is speculated that the single act of a butterfly flapping its wing may cumulatively, through a series of positive and negative feedback loops, have a profound effect at a later time, as the result of the direct and indirect effects are accumulating, such as causing a tropical storm or some other major environmental change. A simple, but profoundly important example of the butterfly effect is to imagine how world history might have changed if, after the First World War, a gassed German private soldier called Adolf Hitler had caught a cold when his immune system was run down, and, as a result, developed pneumonia and died. The working out of the subsequent history of the world might have included the absence of a Second World War.

It is clear that there is an important overlap between chaos theory and field theory, and that together the implication is that organisational culture may be too complex to predict or manage. All that is predicted is that if one element of organisational culture is deliberately changed, then the whole culture and all its elements will change, but in a way that is difficult or impossible to predict. We may even get a change that is the opposite of what we want.

A clear and fascinating account of chaos theory and the butterfly effect and the process of change in organisations can be found in Morgan (1997).

Case Study 2.7: The engineering firm's negotiating position

This Sheffield firm clearly would have liked a workforce that believed what the management said, and yet every year, when it came to the annual round of wage negotiations, the management made an offer to the workforce and said, "We have done all the sums and this is the final and best wage offer that we can make, and if we were to offer more, then there would have to be cut backs in the level of employment as the firm would be less competitive and would lose orders." Every year there would then be a meeting with the trade unions who would reject the pay offer and threaten industrial actions unless the offer was improved. Every year the offer would be improved several times before a settlement was reached, without redundancies.

Question

1. What do you think was the unions' belief about the management?
2. What do you imagine were the beliefs of the management?
3. How do you think that the management could get the unions to change their beliefs?

Case Study 2.8: An engineering firm and its workers' disbelief

The management went to the unions and explained that owing to a change in international competiveness the firm was no longer competitive ("Just look at the decreasing profits on the Balance Sheet") and that there would have to be reorganisation and new technology if the firm was to survive, and there would be inevitable redundancies, but this was a once-and-for-all change; and, if the unions cooperated, then the firm and their employees could go on to a bright future. The unions accepted the new situation and brought in the new practices, technology and redundancies. Two years later the firm came back with the same story, and then again in another 3 years, each time because the world market for their products had again changed and their competitors had been constantly been introducing improvement in their manufacturing processes.

Question

1. What do you think the unions believed about the management after the third round of cuts?
2. How possible is it for the management to manage the beliefs of their workforce?

WHY DOES ORGANISATIONAL CULTURE MATTER?

We started this chapter by commenting that the growth in interest about organisational culture resulted from the observation that some countries were beginning to dominate certain industries and that research seemed to indicate that it was differences in organisational culture were making the difference. The conclusion drawn by the early writers on organisational culture, for example Deal and Kennedy (1982) and Peters and Waterman (1982), was that organisational success was a result of a strong and appropriate organisational culture.

These findings were quickly thrown into doubt when a series of the excellent and successful organisations, with clear and strong cultures, that had been studied by Peters and Waterman, began to perform badly, lose market share and report falling profits.

Schein (1992) summed up many subsequent writings when he suggested that what was needed was not only a strong culture that was functional, but that the culture had to be appropriate and capable of evolution so that it remained appropriate to the changing external environment within which the organisation had to function.

Kotter and Heskett (1992) looked for clear evidence that profitability and success were related to strong cultures. They developed a measure of the strength of an organisation's culture (the degree to which a single clearly defined organisational culture could be observed throughout an organisation) and then looked at how closely this was correlated with net income (a measure of profit), the rate of return on capital, and the rate of growth of the stock (share) price (roughly equal to the rate of growth of the stock market share price). There were 202 US corporations in their sample. The measure of cultural strength was made in 1987 by asking the six most senior executives in each of the 202 corporations to value the strength of the other corporations' culture in the sample over the previous decade. The three performance variables were averaged over the period 1977–1988. The results showed that there was no statistically significant correlation between the strength of organisational culture and net income growth, between cultural strength and rate of return on capital or between cultural strength and the rate of growth of the stock price. Evidence thus seems to suggest that if there is a link between organisational culture and organisational success, then it is not a simple and unambiguous relationship.

CONCLUSIONS

Simple reflection seems to suggest that knowledge of an organisational culture must be important in the functioning of an organisation; we only have to think what it would be like to work in an organisation where we did not understand the culture, where we did not understand what behaviours were acceptable or permissible. How would it be to work in an organisation where we knew what the formal rules were about how to be promoted, but we did not understand what we actually needed to do in order to be promoted, that is, if we did not know what the informal, enacted culture of the organisation was? Working in an organisation without knowing the culture would be like trying to play a game with many other people when you did not know the name of the game or the rules.

We might also conclude that an organisation without a culture cannot be an organisation. A group of people working together cannot succeed as an organisation until a shared culture begins to develop.

Finally, we might reflect that when we are seeking to join an organisation as an employee, it is really rather important that we understand the culture of that organisation, or at least the part of the organisation that we are going to join, as there is no greater misery than working in an organisation where your personality does not fit with the prevailing culture. What a shame that it takes so long to discover and understand the culture(s) of an organisation.

REFERENCES

Bate, S.P., 1994. Strategies for Cultural Change. Butterworth-Heinemann.

Collinson, D.L., Hearn, J., 1994. Naming men as men: implications for work, organization and management, Gender, Work and Organization, 1 (1), 2-22.

Deal, T., Kennedy, A., 1982. Corporate Cultures: The Rites and Rituals of Corporate Life. Addison-Wesley.

Dunkel, A., Meierew, S., 2004. Cultural standards and their impact on teamwork – an empirical analysis of Austrian, German, Hungarian and Spanish culture differences. Journal of Eastern European Management Studies 9 (2).

Handy, C.B., 1985. Understanding Organisations. Penguin.

Hofstede, G.H., 2001. Culture's Consequences; Comparing Values, Behaviours, Institutions, and Organizations Across Nations, 2nd edition, Sage.

Hyde, P., Williams, B., 2000. The importance of organisational values. Part 3: choosing and implementing organisational values. Focus on Change Management 68, 10-14.

Johnson, G., 1988. Rethinking Incrementalism, Strategic Management Journal vol. 9 pp. 75-91.

Kotter, J.P., Heskett, J.L., 1992. Corporate Culture and Performance. Free Press, Macmillan.

Laurent, A., Cultural Diversity of Western Conceptions of Management, International Studies of Management and Organization, vol. 13, no. 1-2, Spring/Summer, 1983, pp. 75-96.

Lewin, K., 1951. Field Theory in Social Science. Harper Row.

Linstead, S., Fulop, L., Lilley, S., 2004. Management and Organisation. Palgrave, Macmillan.

http://www.merriam-webster.com

www.mahapwd.com/isoandqualitycircle/qc.htm

Morgan, G., 1997. Images of Organization. Sage.

Pettigrew, A., 1985. The Awakening Giant: Continuity and Change in ICI. Basil Blackwell.

Peters, T.J., Waterman, R.H., 1982. In Search of Excellence: Lessons from America's Best Run Companies. Harper & Row.

Quinn, R.E., McGrath, M.R., 1985. The transformation of organizational cultures: a competing values perspective. In: Frost, P.J., Moore, L.F., Louis, M.R., Lundberg, C.C., Martin, J. (Eds.), Organizational Culture. Sage.

Schein, E.H., 1985. Organisational Culture and Leadership. Jossey-Bass.

Schein, E.H., 1992. Organisational Culture and Leadership, second ed. Jossey-Bass.

Tuckman, B.W., 1965. Development sequences in small groups. Psychological Bulletin 63, 384–399.

International Cultural Differences

So far we have looked at how small groups form and develop and how organisational culture forms and develops. Now it is appropriate to look at international cultural differences so that we can have some sense of how these differences impact on small group norms and organisational cultures and subcultures.

When we looked at the formation and development of small groups, we noted that this can be seen as going through a process of forming, storming and norming so that they can subsequently perform in a satisfactory manner. In engineering departments there is a pattern of internationalism that is reflected in the large international mixture of students; and increasingly engineering firms and consultancies are staffed by a growing mixture of nationalities, and work in a growing range of countries.

We noted that the norms that develop within the small group are as a result of the interaction of the group members through time. Clearly, the more different the members of the small group, the longer it will take for them to form and norm as a cohesive group with agreed ways of working together. If different nationalities have different beliefs, values, attitudes and ways of sensemaking, then clearly we can expect that the process of norming will take longer in a multinational small group than in a non-diverse group.

We have strong anecdotal and research evidence that the beliefs, values, attitudes and ways of sensemaking differ very strongly from one nation to another. This is not to say that everyone in a country shares the same beliefs, values, attitudes and ways of sensemaking, but we can say that there are patterns that characterise a country. For example, we could almost certainly agree that the attitude towards time and time-keeping is different in Germany and India. If you were invited to dinner by a German for 20.00 then they would expect you to arrive at 20.00, but an Indian guest is likely to think that any time between 20.00 and 22.00 was what the invitation meant. The Indian guest arrives relatively early at 21.00 to find that their dinner is in the bin, put there by their German host who had assumed that their Indian guest was not able to come. This is of course a trivial example, but realistic. How to behave, and what is acceptable behaviour, is something that is only learnt by growing up in a country or by living there for many years.

Cultural differences between countries are not just domestic but are also about behaviour, rules, values and sensemaking within organisations in different countries. Two key researchers have looked at the cultural differences between nations that matter within organisations, Hofstede (1980, 2001) and Laurent (1983).

HOFSTEDE

Hofstede's work has been very seminal in the sense that it has shaped the way that most researchers have approached intercultural research or the way that international cultural differences have been used in organisational research.

In investigating international cultural differences, Hofstede was faced with the problem that the culture within an organisation was a result of both the organisational culture that had developed through the interaction of the employees over a period of time (Schein, 1992) and international cultural differences. In order to unentangle these two factors, Hofstede came up with a novel solution: he looked at the culture within a single organisation which had branches in a variety of countries. In this way, he hoped that the differences he observed in culture would reflect national differences not organisational cultures. Hofstede sent out questionnaires about beliefs, values and behaviours (all of the generally agreed elements of organisational culture) to employees in the branches of IBM (the computer firm) in 40 different countries. The response was enormous, and he received 116,000 completed questionnaires.

In analysing the questionnaires, Hofstede (1980) came to the conclusion that there were four distinct dimensions of cultural difference that distinguished one country's culture from that of another. In the second edition of his book, Hofstede (2001) added a fifth dimension of cultural difference. In order to make an important point about the nature of national culture research, we will look at the four dimensions of 1980 before we look at the fifth dimension of 2001.

Hofstede's (1980) four dimensions of international cultural difference were Masculinity/Femininity, Uncertainty Avoidance, Individualism/Collectivism and Power Distance.

Masculinity/femininity

Masculine nations are those that give importance to assertiveness, dominance and independence, and feminine nations are ones that give importance to interdependence, compassion and emotional values. In his 2001 book, Hofstede reported Japan as the most masculine country and Sweden as the most feminine country. In masculine countries, men and women are likely to strongly agree with statements like:

- Sex roles in society should be clearly differentiated; men lead and women follow.

- Ambition and assertiveness provide the motivation behind behaviours.

Whereas in feminine countries, they are likely to strongly agree with statements like:

- Sex roles should be flexible; sexual equality is desirable.

- The quality of life is more important than personal performance and visible accomplishments.

We suggest that these "typical" statements are the national cultural equivalents of the Basic Assumptions that Schein (1992) wrote about when discussing organisational culture, which we discussed earlier, in the Organisational Culture chapter. These are beliefs about life and society that are so basic to people that they are taken for granted and are likely to be out of awareness.

The second of Hofstede's dimensions of international cultural difference is Uncertainty Avoidance.

Uncertainty avoidance

This dimension is about the extent to which nations are comfortable with an uncertain future, or are, alternatively, comfortable with the future being uncertain. Those countries characterised by discomfort with uncertainty will make efforts to reduce uncertainty, trying to implement some form of insurance against future uncertainty, or develop structures of rules within which the individual can feel certain, or work within industries that develop and change only slowly with little uncertainty about future production, products and markets.

In countries with low uncertainty, avoidance people are likely to say things like:

■ Life is inherently uncertain and is most easily dealt with if one takes one day at a time.

■ There should be as few rules as possible, and the rules that cannot be kept should be changed or eliminated.

In countries with a high level of uncertainty avoidance, people are likely to say things like:

■ The uncertainty in life is threatening and must be fought continuously.

■ Having a stable life is extremely important.

In Hofstede (2001), the nation most alarmed by uncertainty was Greece, and the nation most at ease with uncertainty was Singapore. When we look at Singapore, we see that two of its major industries, electronics and finance, are ones associated with rapid change and uncertainty. If we accept Hofstede's findings, then we would not expect to find such uncertain industries playing an important part in the Greek economy, and they do not.

Individualism/collectivism

Individualistic nations emphasise the pursuit of individual goals, needs and successes. Collectivism emphasises group needs, satisfactions and performances.

In individualistic countries, you are likely to find people agreeing with the statements:

■ "I" is more important than "we".

■ Success is a personal achievement. People are more productive when working alone rather than in groups.

At this point, you might like to think of the material in the Groups and Group Processes chapter that strongly suggests that groups, on average, make better decisions than the average individual, despite various problems of group processes, such as Group Think.

In comparison, in a collectivist culture we are likely to hear that people agree with the following statements:

- "We" are more important than "I".

- Every member of society should (or does) belong to a group that will secure the members' well-being in exchange for loyalty and occasional self-sacrifice.

The second of these statements speaks of "society", but in very individualistic societies people may not even think in terms of there being a society that exists; they may think only in terms of the aggregate of individuals. Famously in the 1970s and 1980s in the UK, the then Prime Minister Margaret Thatcher, seemed to hold the view that society didn't exist, or, at the most, that it was an unimportant concept.

The highest individualism score was for the USA and the lowest was for Guatemala (Hofstede, 2001).

If we look at the list of individualism/collectivism scores, then we note that the four countries with the highest individualism scores were USA, Canada, Australia and the UK. We might be tempted to some easy explanation, which sees highly individualistic countries as those formed by immigrants, who we might expect would be individualistic, as they are the type of people who believe that they can improve their life by taking the initiative and emigrating. Beware, the British (with the third highest Individualism score) were a major source of the people who formed the USA, Canada and Australia, and thus we might expect that the people remaining in the UK would be the collectivists; the individualistic having emigrated! Casual theorising is difficult.

The last of Hofstede's (1980) original dimensions of cultural difference was Power Distance.

Power distance

This dimension of cultural difference is the degree to which members of a society accept differences in power and status amongst themselves.

There has been an ongoing debate about the extent to which Hofstede's dimensions are unique and distinct, or the extent to which they have overlapping sub-elements within the dimensions. Here we can see the problem very clearly, as power distance implies that decisions will be made by the "few" and not by the "many", which in turn implies autocracy/individualism compared with democracy/collectivism. Here, we could argue that power distance and individualism/collectivism overlap.

The types of statements that people in a country with a high level of power distance would agree with are:

- Power holders are entitled to special rights and privileges.

- Superiors and subordinates are different kinds of people.

In a country with a low level of power distance they are likely to make statements like:

- Superiors should be readily accessible to subordinates.

- Power depends on purpose and consequences – it is neither good nor bad.

Hofstede (2001) found that the country with the highest level of power distance was Malaysia and the one with the lowest was Austria.

Long-term orientation (LTO)

This fifth dimension was included following a paper by Hofstede and Bond (1988), where they looked at Asian cultural values. What they realised was that in Hofestede's (1980) original survey of cultural values, the questions that he had included in his questionnaire originated from a European mind, which thought in a way that was determined by his European cultural heritage and ways of thinking and making sense of the world. If Asian and Far Eastern cultures were different, then the questions asked, and the implicit culture, would be different. As a consequence, Hofstede's findings published in 1980 reflected those aspects of culture that were shared by Europe, North America, Asia and the Far East. Aspects of culture that were unique, to varying degrees, to Asia and the Far East, would not show up in questionnaires designed by a European cultural mind.

The fifth dimension reflected differences between countries that were influenced to greater and lesser extents by Confucian thinking. At one extreme were countries that believed in the importance of the values of persistence, ordering relationships by status and the observation of that order, thrift, and having a sense of shame. These were countries with a high long-term orientation (LTO) score. At the other extreme were countries with a low LTO score that were characterised by the values of personal steadiness and stability, protection of "face", respect for tradition and the reciprocation of greetings, favours and gifts.

The descriptions of low and high LTO are not without some ambiguity, as we note that "face" is a very important element of Chinese society, as is reciprocity through what is called guanxi (Warren et al., 2004) (social capital built up through the social exchange of favours or gifts), and yet China has a very high LTO score. By "face" we mean that people care very much about "saving face", about their value or, standing in the eyes of others, their prestige. Currently in China, people would rather have no car than own an unimpressive car – the Chinese do not have entry level cars.

The following are the types of statements with which people with LTO will agree:

■ Nice people are thrifty, and sparing with resources.

■ People should adapt traditions to new circumstances.

Statements with which people with a short-term orientation will agree are:

■ Nice people know how to spend.

■ People should respect traditions.

One of the reasons that this fifth dimension of cultural difference has become of great interest, especially in the West, is that it seems to be related to the rate of economic growth. Just at a casual level, there seems to be a clear relationship between the rate of economic growth and the LTO score. This will be obvious if we list some of the LTO scores from Hofstede (2001):

> *China 118, Hong Kong 96, Taiwan 87, Japan 80 South Korea 75, Brazil 65, India 61, Thailand 56, Singapore 48, Netherlands 44, Bangladesh 40, Sweden 33, Poland 32, Germany (F.R.) 31, Australia 31, New Zealand 30, USA 29, Great Britain 25, Zimbabwe 25, Canada 23, Philippines 19, Nigeria 16 and Pakistan 0.*

The clue to the rapid economic growth effect would seem to be two elements of the high LTO orientation, namely persistence and thrift. Persistence seems to imply that you have a long time horizon and that you are prepared to go on working even if success does not come quickly. Thrift implies that a high percentage of income is saved, and this is certainly true for China with its double-digit percentage Gross National Product (GNP) growth rates in recent decades and its amazingly high savings as a proportion of income. In 2005, more than 50% of Gross Domestic Product (GDP) was saved in China; in comparison the savings ratio in the UK for the same year was 2% (Meyer, H., *www.global-policy.com*). In the slow growing European and North American countries, the savings ratio is very low compared to China. The high level of savings in China is at least partially a reflection not only of LTO based in Confucian Dynamism, but also of Chinese culture in the sense of culture being manifested in artefacts and policies (see Chapter 2). In China the virtual absence of social security provision means that the citizens have to have savings in anticipation of illness, unemployment and the need to care for elderly relatives (the latter made more urgent by the general State policy of each couple being allowed to have only one child).

LAURENT

The work of Laurent (1983) looked at a different aspect of differing international cultures; he looked at the attitudes and beliefs of managers, to examine whether they differed between countries. When he did his research, in 1983, he found that managerial beliefs and attitudes even within Europe differed very much from one country to another. His research has not been replicated, but it sounds a warning not to assume too easily that the beliefs and attitudes of managers will be the same within Europe. The implication is that we can expect to find significant differences between any two countries, even when they are geographically close to one another, when we examine managerial beliefs and attitudes. For differences in the cultures of Eastern European countries, see Dunkel and Meierew (2004).

Laurent examined 817 middle and senior managers who were about to start courses at INSEAD, the international business school near Paris. He argued that it was important to work with them before they had started any courses at INSEAD, as he did not want their responses to be influenced by the education they had received at INSEAD. The students came from a wide variety of European countries and the USA.

Laurent asked the students to agree or disagree with 60 statements about the role and nature of management and managers. These statements were grouped into four broad categories:

- Organisations as political systems

- Organisations as authority systems

- Organisations as role formalization system

- Organisations as hierarchical systems

In the succeeding section, we set out the results that he obtained for a sample of just seven of the statements. The results are the percentage of managers from that country who agreed/disagreed with the statements.

Just as the "typical" statements about Hofstede's dimensions of cultural difference can be seen as equivalent to Schein's Basic Assumptions, so too we can see Laurent's statements as equivalent to Schein's Basic Assumptions.

The first of Laurent's statements that we are going to examine is as follows:

- In order to have efficient work relationships, it is often necessary to bypass the hierarchical line (hierarchical systems). (See Chapter 8.)

This means that it is acceptable to go to your boss's boss if you cannot get, or anticipate that you cannot get, what you want from your boss.

Disagree

Sweden 22%, UK 31%, USA 32%, Netherlands 39%, France 42%, Germany 46% and Italy 75%.

We can imagine a joint venture between a Swedish firm and an Italian firm. The Italian managers would probably be outraged and amazed that so many of their Swedish managerial colleagues would bypass their managers; and the Swedish managers would be similarly amazed that their Italian colleagues would not bypass their managers to get what they wanted.

Case Study 3.1: The danger of bypassing your manager

Consulting in a Japanese organisation's UK headquarters, I asked a wide cross-section of sales executives whether they would bypass their managers if they could not get what they wanted from their manager; everyone except one said "yes, of course!" I asked the one who had said "No" why he would not bypass. The answer was "I was sacked from my last job for bypassing my manager, and I am not prepared to take the risk of it happening again, until I know my current manager's beliefs and attitudes better than I currently do now." Clearly employees need to know not only what is culturally acceptable in their country and organisation, but also about the beliefs and behaviours of their managers. We need to beware of making easy international cultural statements even when on average they are true. The case also emphasises that it takes time to learn the culture of an organisation that you have just joined.

- Most organisations would be better off if conflict could be eliminated forever.

Agree

Sweden 4%, USA 6%, Netherlands 17%, UK 13%, Denmark 19%, Switzerland 18%, Germany 16%, Belgium, 27%, France 24% and Italy 41%.

If we contrast the two extreme countries in the list we see that in Sweden, the view of 96% of managers was that conflict is functional and serves as a useful purpose, whereas in Italy only 59% of managers share that view. We may expect that decision-making processes are often different in Sweden and Italy - the process of strategy and policy-making is different.

The idea that conflict is functional is to be found in much US management literature, and this suggests that management research and writing may well reflect the US national culture rather than some universal truth; by extension, management research, writing and training will reflect the culture of the country where it takes place.

- It is important for a manager to have at hand precise answers to most of the questions that their subordinates may raise about their work (hierarchical systems).

Agree
Sweden 10%, USA 18%, Netherlands 17%, Great Britain 27%, Denmark 23%, Switzerland 38%, Germany 46%, Belgium 44%, France 53% and Italy 66%.

This statement is about the extent to which a manager is required to have detailed knowledge about the jobs of the people who report to them. Detailed knowledge implies that the manager has done all the jobs and that promotion is internal with managers steadily rising up through their department and organisation. There are clearly implications here about management training and promotion rules. A Swedish organisation is unlikely to recruit, train and promote managers in the same way as an Italian organisation. An Italian manager is going to find the experience of working for a Swedish organisation very strange – what is expected of them is very different from that in Italy.

- The manager of tomorrow will be, in the main, a negotiator (authority systems).

Agree
USA 50%, Switzerland 41%, Germany 52%, Denmark 63%, Sweden 66%, Great Britain, 61%, Netherlands 71%, Belgium, 84%, Italy 66% and France 86%.

Whilst the differences between countries are less pronounced than for some of the other statements, there is still a marked difference.

- Most managers seem to be more motivated by obtaining power than by achieving objectives (political systems).

Agree
Denmark 25%, Great Britain 32%, Netherlands 26%, Germany 29%, Sweden 42%, USA 36%, Switzerland 51%, France 56% and Italy 63%.

Clearly this statement is about the extent to which political behaviour is important within management. When you read about political systems in Chapter 6, you will see that power is the resource that enables conflicts to be resolved; the possession of power ensures that as a manager you win the decision battles – you get what you want. The results would seem to indicate that Italian organisations are a lot more political than those in, say, Denmark. To be a manager in Italy, you need to be much more politically minded than if you work in Denmark.

- When the respective roles of the members of a department become complex, detailed job descriptions are a useful way of clarifying (role formalization systems).

Agree

Sweden 56%, USA 76%, Netherlands 71%, Denmark 87%, Great Britain 86%, France 87%, Belgium 89%, Italy 90%, Germany 89% and Switzerland 91%.

The responses to this statement suggest that there is a significant difference in attitudes and beliefs between the group of countries Sweden, USA and Netherlands, and all the other countries. In Denmark, Great Britain, France, Belgium, Italy, Germany and Switzerland, formality and a clear structure are clearly very important to managers, much more than the other group of three countries.

- An organisational structure in which certain subordinates having two direct bosses should be avoided at all costs (hierarchical systems).

Agree

Sweden 64%, USA 54%, Netherlands 60%, Great Britain 74%, Denmark 69%, Switzerland 76%, Germany 79%, Belgium 84%, France 83% and Italy 81%.

This particular element of managers' beliefs is important because of the growth of matrix organisations, organisations where there are many working parties or task groups who have memberships drawn from many different functional departments. When developing a new product, a working party may be made up of staff from the Research and Development Department, the Marketing Department, the Production Department and so on. In this situation, a member of a task group or working party will have the head of the working party as a boss as well as the head of their functional department.

THE PRACTICAL IMPLICATIONS OF HOFSTEDE'S AND LAURENT'S RESEARCH

When reflecting on the practical use of the work of Hofstede and Laurent, it is important to remember that Laurent's managerial attitudes and beliefs and Hofstede's dimensions are not only to be found in managers and leaders, but also may reflect the beliefs, attitudes and behaviours of the workforce below the level of managers and leaders. Thus, for example, in a country with a high power distance level, if a foreign manager from a low power distance culture tried to introduce workforce empowerment, we are likely to observe that the workforce would resist empowerment. The manager might want to introduce empowerment because they have seen it to be effective in their home economy, where the level of power distance is low, but they will now fail as they are going against the culture of their host country.

Laurent

Laurent (1983) concludes that "…the national origin of European managers significantly affects their views of what proper management should be." (p. 77). If we accept this conclusion then it has a number of implications for the recruitment, training and promotion of managers in international companies.

In Chapter 2 we showed how the structure and other systems in an organisation are manifestations of the culture of the organisation, where the culture is at least in part formed by the beliefs and attitudes of the people who make up the organisation.

An Italian company will have an Italian set of definitions of what a manager does, how they manage, what skills and qualities they require and is thus unlikely to recruit a manager from Sweden or Denmark, where the definitions of what a manager does, how they manage and what qualities and skills a manager requires, are very different.

A manager who wishes to broaden their experience by going to work in another country is likely to find that their managerial beliefs and behaviours conflict with those in their host country. They will quickly have to learn the managerial culture of their host country or they will fail. The following mini-case study appears elsewhere in this book, in the Appendix on Theory X and Y, but it seems appropriate to reproduce it at this point as an illustration of how differing national beliefs about management result in differing behaviours.

Case Study 3.2: The chief executives

I was teaching a course for the senior executives of a major European car manufacturer and we were looking at organisational culture and beliefs. On the course were two Chief Executives, one from the company's Belgium business and the other from the company's French business. I asked each of them if they required their assembly line staff to clock on and off at the start and end of each shift, that is, to electronically register the time when they entered and left the assembly plant. One Chief Executive said, "Of course they have to clock on and off; I can't trust them to start and end on time unless I make them "clock"." The other said "No, I don't make them clock; why would I do that?"

Each man could not understand the belief and behaviour of the other, but it is hard to believe that French and Belgium car assembly workers are really so different just across a common national boundary.

Question

How difficult might it be if the French Chief Executive was sent to head up the Belgium organisation?

A multinational organisation has branches or operations in a variety of countries. They could get into this situation by setting up branches or by taking over organisations in the country where they wish to have a presence. If new branches are set up, then the structure of the foreign branch will probably be determined by the beliefs and attitudes of the management in the home country, but then they may find that it is difficult to recruit local staff who can work in that structure. The overseas staff will have their own national and different set of beliefs about what the job of a manager entails, what experience and training they should have, how staff are to be rewarded and controlled, how organisations should be structured and so on. There will be a clash of cultural beliefs and practices between the HQ and their branch in the overseas country.

All the research on changing organisational culture, and the experience of psychotherapists, suggests that changing people's beliefs, attitudes and behaviours is a very slow process, if it is possible at all. The alternative to recruiting local staff is to send out expatriate staff, but that will still lead to clashes with any local staff who work in the organisation. Expatriate staff will be culturally "blind" when placed in a "foreign" country, and thus are likely to find it difficult to interact with local labour, suppliers and customers.

Case Study 3.3: The US management consultancy in the UK: a clash of cultures

Some years ago, I worked for a short time as an associate with a well-known US consultancy that was newly breaking into the UK market. They were in essence selling leadership courses to senior executives in the UK and Europe. The courses included written materials in English, but it was US English. In vain, I argued with the lead consultants from the USA that the material would have to be rewritten in UK English, as it was often confusing or ambiguous to Britains. The Americans were convinced that the material was clear and unambiguous.

I was reminded of Winston Churchill's observation that the UK and the USA were two nations divided by a single language, and of the UK comedian Jasper Carrot writing material with a pencil, when in the USA; having made several writing errors he went to the hotel reception and asked for a rubber; to his astonishment he was asked how many he wanted, and replied "only one, I don't make many mistakes." If you don't understand the ambiguity in this story then you are suffering from a cultural problem arising from the difference between a rubber and an eraser in US and UK English.

Hofstede

We can also reflect on the implications of Hofstede's conclusions that there are key differences between countries in respect of five cultural dimensions: masculine/feminine, individualism/collectivism, uncertainty avoidance, power distance and LTO. Hofstede (2001) speculates in depth about the impact of his five dimensions of cultural difference on the culture of organisations. He suggests that six aspects of organisational culture will be impacted by his five individual cultural differences:

- Planning, control and accounting

- Corporate governance

- Motivation and compensation

- Leadership and empowerment

- Management development and organisational development

- Performance appraisal and management by objectives

Planning, control and accounting: Hofstede (2001) looks at a number of studies concerning the relationship between his five dimensions and planning, control and accounting. The conclusions are not very clear-cut and often hypothesised relationships are contradicted. At a general level, we may expect that power distance, uncertainty avoidance, masculinity/femininity and LTO will have an impact on planning, control and accounting.

High uncertainty avoidance would lead us to expect that there would be careful and detailed short-term planning and strategy making in order to minimise uncertainty. Watson (2006) defines strategic management as "The element of management work that concerns itself with taking the organisation as a whole towards the long-term" (p. 353). What is not clear is whether the planning and strategy would be by experts whose job is to plan and form strategy, or that strategy-making emerges as the result of many small short-term decisions made by many people through all layers of the organisation. Where there is high power distance, we can expect that the planning and strategy will be made by people at the top of the organisation. Obviously the time horizon of the planning and strategy will be affected by whether there is a long- or short-term time horizon in the country. We may thus expect that planning and strategy development will vary between cultures, so that people from one country may be surprised by how organisations in another country plan and develop strategy.

Research quoted by Hofstede (2001) suggests that the form and function of accounting also differs between countries, and we know, for example, that in the UK there are more accountants per head of the population than in any comparable developed nation. This clearly says something about the British culture and marks it as different from other countries. Hofstede (2001) comments that in countries with a high level of power distance, accounting systems are often used to justify the decisions of top power holders. He goes on to argue that in countries with a high level of uncertainty avoidance, accounting systems will contain more detailed rules about handling different situations.

Feminist organisational writers have argued that the typical masculine manager is, through personality, more likely to seek strong control of an organisation and thus be more interested in measuring what is happening in the organisation through strict and detailed accounting systems. This feminist theorising is nicely set out by Linstead et al. (2004).

We see that firms and individuals moving between countries will find differences in the way that individuals and organisations plan, develop strategy and account for what is happening. The way that other nations think and act, and their organisation systems, will seem strange and even wrong.

Corporate governance: corporate governance is the set of processes, customs, policies, laws and institutions affecting the way a corporation is directed, administered or controlled. (www.wikipedia.org). Hofstede (2001) discusses how some of his cultural dimensions influence goverance. Individualism/collectivism seems to explain the pattern of ownership of organisation, for example, in the UK (the third most individualistic country in Hofstede's research, out of 53 countries), 61% of the 100 largest companies had dispersed ownership, where no single share holder owned more that 20% of the shares, whereas in Italy (the 23rd most individualistic) and Austria (the 24th/ 25th most individualistic) no large companies had dispersed ownership.

Power distance was found to be positively correlated with dominant ownership, and co-op structured organisations were essentially found only in feminist countries and not in culturally masculine cultures.

Motivation and compensation: in countries with a high level of individualism, we sometimes also see high levels of masculinity, like the USA, where we see that the popular motivation theories are about individual motivation. Theories of group motivation have developed much later and are not to be found in the average US Organisational Behaviour text book. Why would an individualistic society be interested in group motivation? Power distance is also likely to affect motivation. In the chapter on Motivation, we see that targets that are set participatively are likely to be more motivating than targets that are set by managers, but the extent that this is true is likely to depend on the level of power distance in the culture. Where power distance is high, we are unlikely to see participative target setting as acceptable to either the managers or the followers. Collectivism is also likely to affect whether an organisation contains groups or individuals who need motivation.

How people are rewarded is also clearly about individualism and collectivism. In an individualistic culture, the compensation (the total income, in whatever form) that one receives for work effort is going to be related to individual effort and acheivement. In a collectivist culture, both motivation and compensation will be about group effort and achievement.

Leadership and empowerment: Laurent showed clearly that the beliefs and behaviours of leaders vary significantly from one country and culture to another. Some of these differences make sense in terms of Hofstede's five dimensions. High power distance will cleary result in leaders and followers being further apart, and may lead to leaders distrusting their workers (Theory X – see the Appendix on Theory X and Y) – remember the Mini-case about the French and Belgium Chief Executives on page 58 of this chapter. If we look forward to the various management/leadership styles discussed in Chapter 7 - Leadership, then it is quite easy to see which of Hofstede's dimensions would fit with the various leadeship styles – autocratic, transformative, transactional, participative, delegating, laissez-faire, masculine, feminine, relational and task orientated. It is easy to see that important explanatory dimensions are power distance, masculinity/femininity, individualistic/collectivistic and uncertainty avoidance. We can also expect that empowerment – the spreading of responsibilty and power throughout the organisation – is unlikely to happen in cultures with high levels of power distance and uncertainty avoidance.

Management development and organisation: in order to develop managers through training and appropriate experience, it is necessary to agree what managers and leaders do, and what skills they need to have in order to be effective. In a feminine culture, the role and style of leadership and management is likely to be very different than in a masculine culture – the managers that you recruit, the experience that you give them and the training that you provide, are going to be very different. The conclusions are likely to be very similar if the dimensions of difference that we look at is power distance, or individualism/collectivism, uncertainty avoidance LTO.

Organisational development is about the development and changing of organisations (including managers) so that they are more effective in the environment in which they find themselves. Changes in structure, stategy and decision making, reward and promotion schemes, staff development skills and so on will all clearly be affected by Hofstede's dimensions.

Performance appraisal and management by objectives (MBO): performance appraisal is about appraising how an individual is succeeding or failing in their job, considering what they are doing well (what skills are well developed) and looking at those skills that need to be improved or acquired. MBO is a development of performace appraisal that looks at performance against clearly set (and probably numerical or quantifiable) targets. These topics are the bedrock of individual development and come from the USA, although there have been efforts to apply them in a growing range of countries, where often they fail to make a useful contribution to the success of organisations. The USA is very individualistic and fairly masculine, and thus it should come as no surprise when appraisal and MBO have failed to be translated to countries with a very different culture than in the USA. Individualistic appraisal and MBO are clearly going to need considerable ajustment, at best, if they are to be transferred to organisations in collectivist countries.

GENERAL CONCLUSIONS

What are the lessons to carry away from this chapter?

If you are working with people from another country, they are unlikely to share all, or any, of your beliefs, values and behaviours with regard to organisations. Their beliefs, values and behaviours are not always wrong and yours are not always right, they are just different. You are going to have to find a way to work together, and that may well take lot of time and may require that you always check out your beliefs, values and behaviours.

If you go to work in another country, you will have to work hard at learning to understand the host culture. You can take nothing for granted and will need to constantly check your knowledge about your host culture.

If you are a member of a multinational task group, working party or committee, you need to remember the work of Tuckman (1965) discussed in Chapter 1, where he stressed that groups take time to norm before they can perform. In a multicultural group the storming and norming will take even longer than in a single culture group.

If there is a simple conclusion, it is that you should take nothing for granted when you need to work with the culture of another country – observe, question and never assume that your culture is the best or the most appropriate, it is just different from the culture of other countries.

REFERENCES

Dunkel, A., Meierew, S., 2004. Cultural standards and their impact on teamwork - an empirical analysis of Austrian, German, Hungarian and Spanish culture differences. Journal of Eastern European Management Studies 9 (2).

Hofstede, G.H., 1980. Culture's consequences: international differences in work-related values. Sage.

Hofstede, G.H., 2001. Culture's Consequences; Comparing Values, Behaviours, Institutions and Organizations Across Nations, second ed. Sage.

Hofstede, G., Bond, M.H., 1988. The Confucius connection: from cultural roots to economic growth. Organizational Dynamics 16 (4), 5-21.

Laurent, A., Spring/Summer 1983. Cultural diversity of western conceptions of management. International Studies of Management and Organization XIII (no.1,2), 75-96.

Linstead, S., Fulop, L., Lilley, S., 2004. Management and Organisation; A Critical Text. Palgrave, Macmillan.

Meyer, H., www.global-policy.com.

Schein, E.H., 1992. Organizational Culture and Leadership, second ed. Jossey-Bass.

Tuckman, B.W., 1965. Developmental sequence in small groups. Psychological Bulletin 63, 384-399.

Warren, D.E., Dunfee, T.W., Li, N., 2004. Social exchange in China: the double-edged sword of guanxi. Journal of Business Ethics 55, 355-372.

Watson, T., 2006. Organising and Managing Work. Prentice Hall.

www.wikipedia.org.

Motivation

4

There are many definitions of motivation in the literature, for example:

The cognitive, decision-making process, through which goal-directed behaviour is initiated, energized, directed and maintained.

(Buchanan and Huczynski, 2004, p. 241)

As early as 1981, Kleinginna and Kleinginna found 140 different definitions of motivation in the academic literature, each of the definitions more or less amounting to the same thing.

In everyday terms, motivation is about getting people to work to the maximum of their ability, and this is what this chapter is about.

It has been argued by Seivers (1986) that there was never a need to motivate individuals, or for theories about motivation, until the development of factories that made work become narrowly defined, boring and repetitive. The physical basis of this was a series of inventions in the UK's Industrial Revolution during the eighteenth and nineteenth centuries. The intellectual basis was to be found in the writings of Adam Smith in his seminal work, The Wealth of Nations, published in 1776. In his book, Smith wrote of a pin mill, a factory where pins were made. He demonstrated that if the process of making pins was broken down into a series of individual operations, the total output of pins could be greatly increased if each worker concentrated on just one of the operations (the division of labour), so that they became very skilled and dexterous, and wasted no time moving from one operation to another, which would involve the putting down of one set of tools and the picking up of another set. Under this regime, work became boring and unfulfilling, with workers doing a narrowly defined job, and/or working as machine minders. The range of jobs that they did, and skills that they needed, had been drastically reduced.

This industrialisation of work became even more pronounced with the development of Scientific Management (see Chapter 8) in the USA and Europe, in the first quarter of the twentieth century, as a result of the writing of Frederick Taylor (Taylorism), and the development of the assembly line by Henry Ford in his motor car assembly business (Fordism). For a fascinating account of Scientific Management see Taylor's own submission to the House of Representatives in the USA in 1912, in Pugh (1990). Under these regimes that made work unfulfilling, and that rewarded people only with money and not with any sense of achievement or fulfilment, peoples' level of motivation fell away, and productivity (output per worker) declined.

Scientific Management and Fordism were essentially about the production of manufactured goods, but in the late nineteenth century and the early twentieth century there was an analogous development in the efficient production of services. Here the principal innovation was the bureaucratic organisation, where the organisation and management of the organisation were broken down into small carefully designed jobs where variety of work and individual discretion over how the job was to be done was minimised, in the name of efficiency and control. For a fuller discussion of Bureaucracy, see Chapter 8. Another key theorist writing in the early twentieth century was the Frenchman Fayol (Pugh, 1990), who recommended guidelines for the management of organisations, which fitted neatly with bureaucracy.

A response to these problems resulting from work organisation arose broadly in three ways. The first response was the development of a Human Relations approach, based on the unexpected results of the Hawthorne studies (Mayo, 1949). These studies showed that the reward from working, that might motivate people, was partly about the interaction of workers with one another in a social context. The second response was to the ideas of Maslow (1943) that people need to find life, including work, fulfilling, and this resulted in a whole series of individual motivation theories, some of which will be discussed later in this chapter. The third response was to further explore Maslow's ideas about peoples' need for self-actualisation and the subsequent motivation theories that flowed from this idea of self-actualisation. These theories looked at how jobs and the work experience could be enriched and made more fulfilling, so that the nature of work could revert back to what it was before industrialisation (see for example the work of Hackman and Oldham, 1980, on job enrichment).

The topic of motivation is inevitably interwoven with the topics of leadership, organisational culture, international cultural differences and organisational structure. Motivating employees within a bureaucracy is likely to be very different from motivating them within an organic matrix style organisation, as the structures and cultures differ, but also the type of people who choose to work in such organisations will have very differing personalities (see Chapter 8). Despite this need to study a number of aspects of Organisational Behaviour at the same time, we have to discuss them separately, but this and other chapters will make cross-references to other chapters and relevant topics.

We need to be careful when we look at theories, as they almost all have been developed (and tested, if tested at all) in the USA or European countries. We should question whether people differ enough between countries for the theory to be less than generally applicable.

The standard textbook discussion of motivation looks only at the motivation of individuals, which is rather strange given the prevalence of group and team working in modern organisations, and particular national cultures (remember the individual versus collectivist nature of different national cultures, as discussed by Hofstede (2001), in Chapter 3).

In the next sections of this chapter we will look at theories of individual motivation. A recurring theme will be self-actualisation, which implies that jobs are more motivating if they have been enriched by increasing the range of skills to be exercised and the degree of responsibility and empowerment that the workers are encouraged to accept (see Hackman and Oldham, 1980). Finally, we will go on to look at the motivation of groups.

MOTIVATING INDIVIDUALS

Theories about motivating individuals have long been subdivided into two subsets. There are theories about *what* motivates individuals, and these are called Content theories. There are also theories about *how* individuals are motivated, and these are called Process theories. The distinction will become clearer in the subsequent discussion.

CONTENT THEORIES OF MOTIVATION

Maslow's theory

Maslow (1943) was essentially a social psychologist, some of whose work was applied to individual motivation.

He proposed that all people had needs that could be arranged in a hierarchy. The needs were about these individuals as people, and about these people as individuals. We could talk of these needs as *life needs*, because in Maslow's writing there was nothing to suggest that these needs could only be met through work, but we need to remember that these are the people who go to work with the same set of *life needs* as they have outside work, and that work may enable them to meet their needs. He argued that people are motivated by the opportunity to fulfil these needs, and that in the work situation they might meet these needs if they worked in particular ways – they might be motivated to work. The hierarchy of needs is an ordering, with the basic needs at the bottom. His argument was that the most basic need had to be met before the next higher need was of any concern and could act as a motivator. Below is the hierarchy of needs:

Self-actualisation;

Ego needs;

Social needs;

Security needs; and

Physiological needs.

If people do not have their basic physiological needs met for food, warmth and shelter then they are highly motivated to work if working will enable them to meet these basic physiological needs. People will work if, by doing so, they can meet their unfulfilled need for food, warmth and shelter. The money paid for the work will enable the purchase of food, warmth and shelter, or it may be provided in kind, instead of money, by the employer.

If you are hungry then you will work for food, but after you have eaten enough then hunger will not motivate you, until you are again hungry. Having satisfied this need, then you will be motivated by the possibility of meeting your next most important need, for security – a secure source of income, medical care and perhaps provision for old age and retirement from work. Then you will be motivated by the need to fulfil your need for a social dimension to your life ("No man is an island, entire of itself; every man is a piece of the continent, a part of the main…. Any man's death diminishes me, because I am involved in mankind;" Donne (1624)). We almost all have a need to belong, to be part of a social grouping from which we can get a sense of belonging. It is no chance that one of the most terrible forms of punishment and torture is solitary confinement. Enforced isolation usually results in mental health illness. The sequence goes on with ego needs – the need to feel good about yourself, often resulting from some form of feedback from other people about you as a private individual or as an employee. Finally there is self-actualisation – the need to fulfil your potential, to use all of your talents to the fullest. Self-actualisation is very much what we talked about when we talked of jobs ceasing to provide a sense of achievement and interest when Scientific Management, the factory system and bureaucracies became dominating factors.

Note that Maslow argued that as each need is met, it no longer acts as a motivator.

All of this probably sounds very sensible, full of common sense and hard to dispute, but let us reflect. Many people have argued that this is not a complete list of needs, that they may not be in this order, and that they may even depend on the individual's stage of life. The most extreme argument is that needs are emergent (Watson, 2006) and will constantly change as the stage and context (both private and in employment) of a person's life changes.

As it stands, the theory says that everyone has the same needs, in the same order and that the items in the list, and their order, are fixed. We don't have to reflect for very long to see that this is too rigid, and doesn't reflect the realities of life. Yes, everyone needs to meet their physiological needs as a first thing, and then their security needs (however, in the UK we are seeing an emerging pattern of people choosing not to make adequate arrangements for their old age through saving for pensions), but then after these first two needs, the ordering is less obvious, and people may move to and fro between needs, including back to needs that had been previously met. Let us imagine a young single woman who earns enough to meet her physiological and security needs, and meets her social and ego needs outside her workplace (in her private non-work life), and is trying to see just how successful she can be at work in terms of promotion and career building (self-actualisation). Our young woman now starts a family with her partner, and, on returning to work after maternity leave, now has different priorities. What may now matter most to her is to maximize her income, even if this means putting less priority on making a long-term career – she has moved back from self-actualisation to security. However, as the child or children get older she may again move to being motivated by self-actualisation through career development. This is just one example where a person moves through the hierarchy and back again. This example is set in a particular cultural context of women going back to full-time work after the birth of a child. In other cultures, mothers may well not return to work ever, or not for many years. There is thus a cultural context to the hierarchy of needs.

What has Maslow's theory to tell us that is useful if we are trying, as a manager, to motivate our workforce? It is a useful theory, although hardly surprising, that people can be motivated at work by giving them the opportunity to meet their needs through their work. The main difficulty is that each individual's needs may be difficult to ascertain, may change and people may move to and fro through their needs. The implication seems to be that to fully motivate your staff, you need to know each of them individually.

Other Content theories tend to be variations on Maslow's ideas about needs, their fulfilment and the importance of finding work that is fulfilling and a source of self-actualisation

Aldefer's ERG theory

Aldefer (1972), like Maslow, suggested that people are motivated by the opportunity to fulfil their needs at work. The important difference from Maslow was that he believed that people could regress back to previously fulfilled needs if their efforts to meet higher level needs were frustrated. He categorised the needs into three:

Existence – this is in essence Maslow's Physiological and Security needs;

Relationship – this is in essence Maslow's Social needs; and

Growth – this is in essence Maslow's Ego and Self-actualisation needs.

The benefits for managers from Alderfer's theory are essentially the same as those from Maslow's theory that were noted in the previous section. As with Maslow, an essential factor in motivation is the ability to achieve self-actualisation through working. The clear implication is that employers can motivate staff by offering fulfilling work.

Herzberg's theory

Herzberg (1966) based his theory on 12 different investigations of a diverse range of employees, that included lower-level supervisors, professional women, agricultural administrators, men about to retire from management positions, hospital maintenance personnel, nurses, food handlers, military officers, teachers, housekeepers, accountants, foremen and engineers, where he asked about motivation, satisfaction and dissatisfaction in the work context. He found that there were some factors that were motivators, and that there were other distinct factors which caused dissatisfaction if they were not present (he called these latter factors Hygiene factors). He concluded that the absence of dissatisfaction was not the same as satisfaction. This conclusion probably was a result of the way the research participants were questioned. We may well feel that the absence of dissatisfaction must be satisfaction, although that was not what Herzberg argued. The important idea that follows from Herzberg's theory, perhaps for the first time, was that satisfaction and motivation are not the same thing, that a satisfied workforce is not necessarily motivated.

Motivators:
- Responsibility;
- Advancement;
- Growth;
- Achievement; and
- Recognition.

It is noticeable that these motivating factors are essentially the same as Maslow's ego and self-actualisation needs, and grow out of the human resource approach that was triggered by the Hawthorne experiments of the 1920s that led on to an interest in job redesign, enrichment and empowerment (Hackman and Oldham, 1980).

Hygiene factors:

■ Interpersonal relations with peers, subordinates and senior staff;

■ Job security;

■ Working conditions;

■ Salary.

The implication of the absence of the hygiene factors is not that staff will be less motivated, but that they may resolve their dissatisfaction – because of the non-fulfilment of their implicit contract (see the discussion of implicit contracts at page 75 of this chapter) - by a variety of behaviours which might include the withdrawal of goodwill, dishonest behaviour, absenteeism or leaving the job through resignation.

How useful is Herzberg? Managers have accepted Herzberg's theory rather readily, as it seems to offer conclusions that are clear-cut and easy to enact. There is, unfortunately, little research testing the theory, and thus little research support, and the theory has not been shown to be culturally robust, given that it has not been replicated over a range of countries. It also suffers the same problems as Maslow's theory by not treating the motivator factors as being emergent and individual.

McClelland's theory

McClelland (1961) argued that the needs that motivate us may well be made significant as a result of the socialisation process that we experience as we grow up. He argued that the three main learned needs were the needs for power, achievement and affiliation. Note how these needs reoccur when we discuss leadership theory in Chapter 7.

An interesting departure from other theories is that McClelland suggests how we can determine which factors are the key motivators for an individual. This can be done using a questionnaire (see, for example Thrash and Elliot, 2002), or through the use of Thematic Apperception Tests (TATs). Figure 4.1 is an example of a picture used in TATs. The idea is that a series of pictures are shown, and the individual has to write a story of what they "see" in each of the pictures in the form of a brief one-paragraph story. What the individual "sees" is a projection of part of their personality, and thus it tells us something of the way that they have learnt to make sense of their world. We project our own internal world onto the picture in order to make sense of it, and thus we reveal something of our own needs. If you doubt that different people will see different things in a picture, than just ask your friends to tell you the story that they "see" in the picture; you may be surprised by the number of different types of stories, but they are all likely to say something about achievement, power or affiliation.

It is still a matter of some controversy whether TATs are reliable – give the same result each time, and/or are valid – that they actually predict people's motivating needs.

McClelland's work seems to contribute only a little to motivation theory, except the useful idea that individual's needs may be individual to them, and a reflection of their life experiences, rather than Maslow's notion of needs as the same for everyone, and genetically determined. However, his theory does suggest that if we can discover

FIGURE 4.1

TAT PICTURE
Source: <web.utk.edu/~wmorgan/tat/tattxt.htm>.

a person's motivating needs through the TAT test or questionnaires, then we can offer to meet those needs in exchange for motivation.

Content theories treat people as though they are black boxes, where we know *what* motivates them, but we do not know what cognitive processes are going on inside their heads. We now move on to process theories. These make an effort to explain the cognition (thinking) that goes on in the motivation to behave in one way rather than another.

PROCESS THEORIES OF MOTIVATION

As with the previous section on Content theories, this section will not be a comprehensive coverage of theories, but will highlight some of the main theories.

Operant conditioning theory

This theory has a broad common-sense appeal. It is based on the work of Skinner (1947). Skinner showed that with pigeons, if you rewarded behaviour that you desired, then the desired behaviour would be repeated. Extending this observation, he showed how animals can be "taught" quite elaborate behaviours. Subsequent works by Skinner and other researchers have suggested that if there is punishment for a behaviour that is not wanted, then that behaviour will be eliminated.

It seems to be an easy and "sensible" step to extend these findings from birds and animals to human beings. In everyday terms, people will do things if they expect to be rewarded, and will not do those things that bring no reward or bring punishment. All we have to do is to find out what constitutes a reward or a punishment and then we can "train" people. An unexpected finding of this research was that intermittent rewards worked better than rewarding every performance of the desired behaviour.

Research and reflection suggest that using this approach may not be as easy as it is with animals. Humans are lot more complex and sophisticated than Skinner's animals; they are capable of recognising that they are being conditioned and adjust their response – or so one might hope – see, for example, the following case study.

Case Study 4.1: Payment schemes and motivation

A computer firm's sales staff were paid £15,000 basic salary, and in addition were paid extra salary for each unit of sales that they made. Each of them were given a target level of sales, and if they reached that then their total salary would be £30,000; half basic and half sales commission.

Each time they reached their sales target, the management would raise the target that had to be achieved in order to receive £15,000 of commission, (the rate of commission was decreased) – the staff had to run quicker and quicker to stand still! The author had expected the staff to protest and refuse to perform, or to leave, but they did not, as they knew that the alternative employers paid in a comparable way.

Additionally there was, for the author, a further unexpected part of the staff motivation. The author, in an effort to motivate people to invest more time in the short run in order to build up relationships with customers, so that long-term sales would be increased, investigated the staff's response to moving from a 50%/50% basic/commission split, to 60%/40% split, right up to a 100%/0% split. Most people wanted some movement in this direction, but by 80%/20% they had all said "no further". All of them said "What would be the fun of knowing what your monthly income would be?" The author (an uncertainty-avoidant academic) had assumed that certainty, and the implicit management trust that the staff would work hard on a basic-only salary, would be motivating, but for these staff, a measure of uncertainty was motivating.

Question

What lessons are there to be learnt about motivation from this case?

Expectancy theory

This theory was the result of the work of Vroom (1964).

The first part of the theory asks the question, "How probable is it that what I am doing will lead to a first level desirable outcome, like more rapid promotion, or improved appraisals as a result of working harder?"

The next part of the theory is the probability that the first level outcome will lead to a second level outcome like a pay rise, self-actualisation or some other reward.

The last part of the theory is the individual's valuation of the second level outcome.

The outcome is: if it is seen as very probable that the initial behaviour will lead to a first level outcome which very probably will lead to a second level outcome that is valued by the individual, then the individual will be highly motivated to work hard at the initial behaviour.

If the effort is unlikely to lead to the first level outcome (for example, promotion, or a good appraisal, etc.), or the first level outcome is unlikely to lead to the second level outcome (a pay rise, or self-actualisation, etc.), or the second level outcome is not valued, then the individual will not be motivated.

The motivation is about subjective probabilities and the valuation placed, by the individual, on potential rewards.

The strong points of the theory are that it represents a coherent theory of the cognition within the black box; that it admits to each person having their own unique needs that are satisfied by their behaviour; and that each individuals' valuation of the rewards of effort is not prescribed – needs, and valuations of those needs, are unique to each individual.

The limitations are that the theory assumes a rational, economic man decision maker. We are also left with no guidance as to how the individuals estimate probabilities, how they value ultimate rewards, or what the rewards are.

An economists' perspective on expectations theory

In assessing the value of expectancy theory, we also need to think about how we calculate the present value of future benefits.

If we are going to work harder in the present in order to gain a future benefit, then we need to compare the current cost (working hard in the present) with the future benefit to see if there is a net gain. What is the value now (in the present) of a benefit that I only receive in the future? If I offer you $10 (substitute your home national currency) in a year's time or $7 now, which would you accept? If you cannot choose (are indifferent) between $10 and $7, then the present value of $10 in a year's time is $7, and that is what you compare with the "cost", the sacrifice that you have to make now, in order to get the $10 in a year's time.

Your intuition will tell you that I have not allowed in this calculation for the probabilities. If there is only a 70% chance of the $10 in a year's time, then $7 is the expected value in a year's time, that is, $7 is the sum whose present value I have to calculate.

This approach assumes that we each have an intuitive sense of probabilities and that we have at least a subjective estimate of costs, benefits and time preference. Even if we cannot make numerical estimates of probabilities, costs and benefits, it is likely that we will have a sense of probabilities improving or worsening, or costs and values rising or falling, and thus that we can adjust our behaviour, especially if only one of the factors has changed.

Notice that this theory of present value, as set out above, implicitly assumes that to work harder is a cost and that to be more motivated at work is a sacrifice. Contemporary writing on the topic of working suggests that simply working may be a reward, a benefit, rather than a cost. Research suggests that people would continue to work even if they no longer needed to because they had become independently rich. This finding is internationally robust, in that the finding holds across a range of industrial countries, with no exceptions. In a survey quoted in Noon and Blyton (1997), approximately half of Britons, USA citizens, Belgians, and Dutch would continue to work if they became independently rich, although they would work under different conditions (a different job or shorter hours). The same report found that two-thirds of Japanese would continue to work at the same job even after becoming independently rich. Clearly then, people choose to work for reasons in addition to their need for a cash payment for working; work can be rewarding in itself.

Equity theory

This process theory of motivation was first clearly set out by Adams (1963). In many ways it is hardly a motivation theory, in that it does not give clear indications of what has to be done in order to get people to be more motivated. However, it is important to consider Equity theory as it forms the foundation of the modern approaches to motivation, which are encapsulated in the literature about Implicit Contracts.

The theory looks at the total costs to an individual of working in an organisation and compares this with the total benefits of working. Clearly, we expect that the ratio will exceed 1 in a subjective evaluation, as the value of the benefits of working must exceed the cost of working if the individual is to choose to work.

Suggested costs and benefits of employment (Watson, 2006) are set out in Table 4.1.

The theory requires that individual A compares his/her ratio with that of a reference person (RP) or comparator.

$$\frac{\text{Total benefits (A)}}{\text{Total costs (A)}} \quad \text{vs.} \quad \frac{\text{Total benefits (RP)}}{\text{Total costs (RP)}}$$

If the ratio of benefits to costs is lower than that for the comparator, then the individual feels under-rewarded for the costs they bear. The reason that the theory is not

Table 4.1 Costs and benefits of working

Employee costs (inputs)	Employee benefits (rewards)
■ Physical effort	■ Money
■ Mental effort	■ Job satisfaction
■ Initiative	■ Personal growth
■ Risk of fatigue, injury, stress	■ Social reward
■ Compliance – acceptance of a degree of management control	■ Security
	■ Power
	■ Status
	■ Career development

really a motivation theory now becomes apparent. The theory predicts that if the comparator's ratio is fixed, and beyond the control of individual A, then there are three logical options to change the ratio to match that of the comparator so the work situation is equitable or fair:

■ They can reduce their costs by reducing their inputs into the job.

■ They can increase the rewards for doing their work.

■ Some combinations of changing costs and benefits so that the overall effect is to reduce the ratio of costs to rewards.

Logically, the theory predicts that something will change, but what? If it was a theory of motivation then it would predict that A would have reduced his/her work effort, that is, their level of motivation – but it does not.

What Equity theory also does is to invite us to think of the importance of interpersonal equity in the workplace. It also starts us thinking about the whole idea of implicit contracts in the workplace; that is, we can think about the subjective contract between the individual and their employer that specifies the bundle of benefits that the individual receives from their employment in the orga-nisation, and the bundle of inputs that the individual gives. The organisation will look at the benefits of employing the individual (the inputs from the individual), but the individual will think of some of these as costs and others as benefits. Each party will look at the implicit contract from their own point of view; when deciding whether to employ the individual (employer's view point), or whether to accept, or continue to accept, the job (employee's view point). The psychological contract captures some of what we think of as the informal or enacted culture of the organisation. The essence of psychological or implicit contracts is that many of the elements of inputs and rewards (as partially listed in Table 4.1) are not in the explicit, "printed on paper", contract of employment that the employer and employee sign. In the implicit contract there are additional elements about fair and reasonable behaviour on the part of the employee and the employer. If either of the parties feels that their implicit elements are not being met, then the implicit contract is not being fulfilled, and this may result in explicit renegotiation, or either one or both parties terminating the contract through resignation or termination of employment. For a more detailed discussion of psychological contracts see Herriot et al. (1997).

Notice that we wrote of the subjective costs and benefits. Some elements of the benefits of work can be quantified, like the salary that the worker will receive, but how do you put anything but a subjective value on the status that flows from a job, or evaluate the stress that results from a job. The individual may be able to put a monetary value on their costs and benefits in order to compare total costs and benefits, but these figures are inevitably subjective in the main.

In the Leadership chapter we will discuss how part of the leadership process is setting and manipulating implicit contracts, just as they may try and set and manage organisational culture (see the Organisational Culture chapter).

Watson (2006) argues that we can see the process of motivation as being the manipulation, by the employer, of the implicit contract.

Goal setting theory

This theory evolves from the work of Locke in the late 1960s (Locke and Latham, 2002). The basic idea is that "it seems a simple fact that human behaviour is affected by conscious purposes, plans, intentions, tasks and the like" Ryan (1970); that an individual's conscious goals and intentions are the most important determinants of their behaviour.

Research suggests that:

- The more difficult the goal, the better the performance, unless the goal is seen as impossible.

- Feedback is important so that the individual knows how they are progressing towards their target.

- The goal needs to be specific and detailed, not just "do your best".

- In certain circumstances it matters how the targets are set, whether imposed, self-set goals, or participatively set goals.

In considering motivation using goal setting, it is clearly important that the individual is committed to the goal. Without commitment, the goal would be meaningless. Part of being a leader who can motivate is getting an individual to commit to a challenging goal. This will be part of manipulating the implicit contract between the organisation or leader and the individual, and part of managing the organisational culture.

Another important factor if goal setting is to succeed is the existence of an individual's sense of self-efficacy (an individual's self-belief in their ability to achieve); the belief that they can make things happen, as opposed to a belief that things "happen to them".

GROUP MOTIVATION

We can expect that theories of individual motivation are important in countries with a high level of individualism (as defined by Hofstede (2001) in Chapter 3). In collectivist societies, such as those in much of Asia, where group or collectivist working is the normal mode of organisation of work, then the motivation theory that we need to examine is about motivating groups. Group motivation is also becoming more important in individualistic countries as group and team working becomes increasingly common. Engineering, both at a professional level and at the student level, is also very much a group activity and has been for a long time.

We may speculate that the failure of some group and team initiatives (like Quality Circles) in European, North American and other individualistic countries is a result of trying to impose something that is against the culture of the country.

The Hawthorne experiments in the 1920s (Mayo, 1949) showed that when a group was recognised to exist by its members, as a result of social interaction, then that group begins to develop group norms or rules about how individual members of the group will behave.

The three main group norms that came out of the Hawthorne studies, were that:

- A group member was not to work harder than the group norm (they were not to be "rate busters");

- They were not to work less hard then the group norm (they were not to be "chisellers"); and

- They were not to inform supervisors about what was happening in the group (they were not to be "squealers").

These rules, or norms, amounted to an agreement between the group members on what was a reasonable level of effort by members of the group (the notion of a "fair day's work for a fair day's pay") and that the group norms would be the group's secret, to be kept from the supervisors and managers. We should note that the supervisor is not a member of the group. The existence of a group norm concerning output and effort implies that trying to get a group of workers to increase their output or their input (to be more motivated) would require delicate renegotiation of the implicit contract.

Tuckman (1965) showed that as groups develop through the stages of forming, storming, norming and performing, an essential stage in the development is the formation of group norms or rules, exactly what was observed in the Hawthorne experiments. Thus, we can see that Tuckman provided a theoretical explanation for the observations in the Hawthorne experiments.

Matsui et al. (1987) clearly showed that individual goal setting motivation theory could be applied to groups.

What follows sets out the research findings about group motivation, of the last two decades.

We remember from earlier in this chapter that research shows that:

- The more difficult the goal, the better the performance, unless the goal is seen as impossible.

- Feedback is important so that the individual knows how they are progressing towards their target.

- The goal needs to be specific and detailed, not just "do your best".

- In certain circumstances, it matters how the targets are set, whether imposed, self-set goals or participatively set goals.

Before we can look at applying these bullet points to group motivation we need to start by discussing the idea of self-categorisation (Haslam et al, 2000). This is to examine how we define ourselves; are we individuals, or are we defined by the group to which we feel that we belong? Clearly this is going to vary between nations (Individualistic or Collectivist societies (Hofstede, 2001), as discussed in Chapter 3) and between individuals.

To complicate matters, we are likely to feel that we belong to a number of groups, each of which will have its own norms. We may feel that we belong to a family group and also to one or more work groups. At work we may feel that we belong to a large group called engineers, where we accept the norms of the engineering profession as a result of our education, our work experience with other engineers and our membership of professional engineering institutes. We may also feel that we belong to the task group that we work in each day, which is struggling with a particular engineering or product problem. Each of these groups will have norms, and they may be conflicting. What we can be sure of is that the norms and behaviours that we are

conforming to when we are at work may well not correspond to what the organisation would really like. As we said earlier in this chapter, getting individuals and
groups to conform to the organisation's needs may well be a delicate renegotiation of
the implicit contract between the organisation and the group to which the individual
currently feels they belong.

The strength of feeling about belonging to a group is described as group cohesiveness, where cohesiveness can be defined as the "Strength of group members' desires to
remain in the group and their commitment to the group." (Gibson et al., 2000, p. 208).
There have been a number of studies about the impact of cohesiveness on the group
motivation. Significantly, given our discussion of the Hawthorne studies and cohesiveness, Podsalnoff et al. (1997) found that group cohesiveness had a positive impact on
group productivity, but only when the group accepted the organisation's goals. Klien
and Mulvey (1995) found that group cohesiveness was positively related to self-set goal
difficulty and goal commitment, and that goal difficulty and goal commitment were
positively related to group performance, but, in this last study, the direction of causation
is not clear. Other studies, and the general theory of goal setting, would suggest that the
direction of causation was from cohesiveness to goal setting, to commitment, to
performance. Reflection suggests that the causation may be circular, in the sense that
improved group performance may increase cohesiveness, and that then cohesiveness
may add to goal setting and so on.

We can now look at each of the four bullet point elements of goal setting and look at
what the research into group motivation shows:

- The more difficult the goal the better the performance, unless the goal is seen as
impossible.

Papers in the early 1990s showed that challenging goals produced better planning
and performance than "do your best" (Smith et al., 1990), and that group performance
rose as the group goal rose (Weldon et al., 1991)

- Feedback is important so that the individuals know how they are progressing
towards their target.

Weldon et al. (1991) found that if the performance of a group was monitored,
so that there was the possibility of feedback, then the group's performance was
boosted. It is not clear whether this effect was about being monitored, or whether
the positive impact was about feedback. What Weldon et al. (1991) did observe
about performance monitoring was that it did not increase the level of communication
within the group, nor did it boost non-task related talking and similar activities.
Mesch et al. (1994) found that groups that were given negative feedback (feedback
that was critical of group performance) became less satisfied, but that the group
subsequently set themselves higher goals, developed more strategies and performed
at a higher level. We may speculate that the lowered level of satisfaction might act
rather like Herzberg's dissatisfiers, and result in an increased level of staff leaving the
organisation, Herzberg (1966).

- The goal needs to be specific and detailed, not just "do your best".

Smith et al. (1990) found that specific challenging group goals produced better
planning and performance than if the goal was simply set as "do your best".

Mitchell and Silver (1990) managed to demonstrate that group goals, when combined with individual group-centred goals, produced results that were 38% better than when the goal set was "do your best", and were superior to all other combinations of goals.

They also found that individual goals set for group members tended to undermine the performance of the group where the group was an interdependent task group, that is, where each individual interacts with other members of the group to ensure the group's success.

Further, they found that individual goals produced intra-group competition – that is individual members competed rather than co-operated with other team members in the pursuit of team goals.

One final result of Mitchell's and Silver's work was to show that group goals that deliberately encouraged strategy development lead to increased group performance.

- In certain circumstances it matters how the targets are set, whether imposed, self-set goals or participatively set goals.

O'Leary-Kelly et al. (1994) conducted a meta-analysis (an analysis of the combined results of a number of research studies) on published papers concerning group motivation. They looked at the impact of how group goals were set, comparing performance when goals were assigned to the group (that is, imposed on the group), compared with when the goals were set participatively (that is, when the group was involved in the setting of the goals). They found that when goals were assigned, then in 78% of the studies they examined the group performance was improved, compared with no goals being set. However, when group goals were set participatively, they found that 100% of studies showed improvements in group performance, compared with no goals being set.

In a related study, Durham et al. (1997) showed that when a group had a participative leader, then the group developed more effective group tactics than those groups with an autocratic leader.

If there is an important conclusion to be drawn from the literature on group motivation, it would seem to be that participatively set goals are better than assigned goals, which are better than "do your best", when we try to motivate groups. This also has implications for organisational culture and leadership style.

REFERENCES

Adams, J.S., 1963. Toward an understanding of inequity. Journal of Abnormal and Social Psychology 67, 422–436.

Alderfer, 1972. Existence, Relatedness, and Growth; Human Needs in Organizational Settings. Free Press.

Buchanan, D., Huczynski, A., 2004. Organizational Behaviour: An Introductory Text. Prentice Hall.

Donne, J., 1624. Meditation XVII, <isu.indstate.edu/ilnprof/ENG451?ISLAND/text.html>.

Durham, C.C., Knight, D., Locke, E.A., 1997. Effects of leader role, team-set goal difficulty, efficacy and tactics on team effectiveness. Organizational Behaviour and Human Decision Processes 72, 203–231.

Gibson, J.L., Ivancevich, J.M., Donnelly, J.H., 2000. Organizations: Behaviour Structure Processes, tenth ed. McGraw-Hill.

Hackman, J.R., Oldham, G., 1980. Work Redesign. Addison-Wesley.

Haslam, S.A., Powell, C., Turner, J.C., 2000. Social identity, self-categorization and work motivation: rethinking the contribution of the group to positive and sustainable organisational outcomes. Applied Psychology: An International Review 49 (3), 319-339.

Herriot, P., Manning, W.E.G., Kidd, J.M., 1997. The content of the psychological contract. British Journal of Management 8 (2), 151-162.

Herzberg, F., 1966. Work and the Nature of Man. Staples Press.

Hofstede, G.H., 2001. Culture's Consequences: Comparing Values, Behaviours, Institutions and Organizations Across Nations, second ed. Sage.

Klein, H.J., Mulvey, P.W., 1995. Two investigations of the relationships among group goals, goal commitment, cohesion and performance. Organizational Behaviour and Human Decision Processes 61, 44-53.

Locke, A.E., Latham, G.P., 2002. Building a practically useful theory of goal setting and task motivation. American Psychologist 57, 705-717.

Maslow, A.H., 1943. A theory of human motivation. Psychology Review 50 (4), 370-396.

Matsui, T., Kakuyama, T., Onglatco, M.L.U., 1987. Effects of goals and feedback on performance in groups. Journal of Applied Psychology 72, 407-415.

Mayo, E., 1949. Hawthorne and the Western Electric Company. In: Pugh, D.S. (Ed.), (1990), Organizational Theory: Selected Readings. Penguin Books.

McClelland, D., 1961. The Achieving Society. Van Norstrand.

Mesch, D.J., Farh, J., Podsakoff, P.M., 1994. Effects of feedback sign on group goal setting, strategies and performance. Group and Organization Management 19, 309-333.

Mitchell, T.R., Silver, W.S., 1990. Individual and group goals when workers are interdependent: effects on task strategies and performance. Journal of Applied Psychology 75, 185-193.

Noon, M., Blyton, P., 1997. (Chapter 3), The meaning of work. The Realities of Work. Palgrave Macmillan.

O'Leary-Kelly, A.M., Martocchio, J.J., Frink, D.D., 1994. A review of the influence of group goals on group performance. Academy of Management Journal 37, 1285-1301.

Pugh, D.S., 1990. Organizational Theory: Selected Readings. Penguin Books.

Podsakoff, P.M., MacKenzie, S.B., Ahearne, M., 1997. Moderating effects of goal acceptance on the relationship between group cohesiveness and productivity. Journal of Applied Psychology 82, 974-983.

Ryan, T.A., 1970. Intentional Behaviour. Roland Press.

Seivers, B., 1986. Beyond the surrogate of motivation. Organization Studies 7 (4), 353-367.

Skinner, B.F., 1947. "Superstition" in the pigeon. Journal of Experimental Psychology 38, 168-172.

Smith, K.G., Locke, E.A., Barry, D., 1990. Goal setting, planning and organizational performance: an experimental simulation. Organizational Behaviour and Human Decision Processes 46, 118-134.

Thrash, T.M., Elliot., A.J., 2002. Implicit and self-attributed achievement motives: concordance and predictive validity. Journal of Personality 70 (5), 729-755.

Tuckman, B.W., 1965. Developmental sequences in small groups. Psychological Bulletin 63 (6), 384-399.

Vroom, V.H., 1964. Work and Motivation. Wiley.

Watson, T., 2006. Organising and Managing Work, second ed. Pearson Longman.

Weldon, E., Jehn, K.A., Pradhan, P., 1991. Processes that mediate the relationship between a group goal and improved group performance. Journal of Personality and Social Psychology 61, 555-569.

Stress

5

Why should there be a chapter about stress? The answer is brief and easy. Research shows that the result of excessive stress is that organisations experience higher levels of sick leave, staff turnover and lower levels of motivation, morale and productivity, with the consequences that organisations are less profitable, efficient and effective. In addition, you, as an individual, need to be able to recognise when you are suffering from stress, and be able to recognise the causes, so that you can keep yourself healthy and able to live life to the fullest. The UK Health and Safety Executive estimates the level of self-reported stress each year, and the following list outlines the scale of stress-related problems in UK organisations:

- About one in five people say that they find their work either very or extremely stressful.

- Over half a million people report experiencing work-related stress at a level they believe has actually made them ill.

- Each case of stress-related illness leads to an average of 29 working days lost.

- A total of 13.4 million working days were lost due to stress, depression and anxiety in 2001.

- Work-related stress costs society between £3.7 thousand million (billion) and £3.8 billion a year (1995/1996 prices).
  (http://www.hse.gov.uk/stress/standards/).

Case Study 5.1: Stress-related sickness in a company HQ

When the author was working at the company headquarters of Unilever, at that time it was the eighth biggest company in Europe and the fifth biggest company in the UK. The doctor who headed the company medical department had kept a check on the people who came to consult him over the course of 1 year. His conclusion was that one-third of the patients were suffering from stress (with no related physiological illness caused by the stress), one-third were ill and the cause was stress and one-third had medical problems that were unrelated to stress. Two-thirds of medical self-referrals were stress-related, although the source of the stress was not obvious; it could have been stressors within the company or in the patient's private life.

Before we can discuss stress in organisations, we need to define what we mean by stress; and, by implication, what we do not mean by stress.

Some people will complain that having too much work to do in their organisation is *causing* them stress, whilst others will say that the excessive workloads are stress. We need to be clear whether stress is the *cause*, too much work, or whether it is the *consequence* of having too much work to do, for example, the inability to concentrate, or disturbed sleep after work. Is stress the cause or the effect?

To resolve this dilemma, social science has defined stress as the consequences of stressors – having too much work to do is a stressor for some people. Thus, social scientists define stress as:

> *The reaction of a person to their perceived environment.*

What exactly does this mean? Let us use an example. Two of you are walking to work when a large dog comes bounding towards you. You both see a large dog, but perhaps you both perceive it differently. The perception of one of you is "This is a big dangerous dog that is going to bite me." That person's heart begins to beat quicker, they breathe quicker, their blood pressure rises and their palms begin to perspire and they feel frightened. The other person thinks, "What a nice dog. I bet this is the nicest thing that happens to me today; I hope that it comes near enough that I will be able to pat and stroke it." The only obvious effect on this second person is that they are smiling. The physiological, cognitive and psychological reaction of both these people is stress – their reaction to their perceived environment. The only time you have no stress is when you are in your coffin, dead – unless you hear them screwing down the lid of your coffin!

The consequence of defining stress in this way, as a consequence and not a cause, is that stress is a very individual subject. For any one unique person, we cannot be certain of how they will perceive their environment, and thus how they will respond to that perceived environment.

Another important consequence of defining stress in this way is that we have not defined stress as a bad thing, or as a good thing; we can only say that stress is a bad thing if the physiological, cognitive or psychological effects are dysfunctional – that they serve no useful purpose or are even harmful or counterproductive.

A SIMPLE MODEL OF STRESS

Let us apply a simple model to our "big dog" example. The *Event* is seeing a big dog, the *Perception* is the way that an individual makes sense of what they see (is it a frightening dog or is it a fun dog) and the *Reaction* is their response to their perception. In our

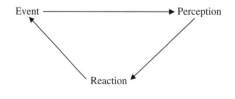

FIGURE 5.1

Stress model

model there is a causative link that leads from *Reaction* back to event. This link may be that if you perceive the dog as threatening, and cross the road to avoid it, then the dog may follow you across the road (because it knows that it wants to lick you!). The event has changed; it is now a dog that is following you. Your perception is now that it really does want to bite you. So you begin to run in order to get away. The dog starts to run, because it still wants to lick you and chasing is fun. And so you race round and round the model from *Event* to *Perception* to *Reaction*. It may alternatively be that there is no link that goes from Reaction back to Event.

An organisation application of the model might be: you are writing a report against a deadline; at some point your *Perception* changes from "I do have time to complete this report" to "I may not have time". Your *Reaction* to this changed perception is, "How am I going to explain to my boss this failure to meet the deadline?" In spending the time worrying that you may miss the deadline, the *Event* changes – you are more likely to miss the deadline because you are wasting time worrying rather than preparing the report. Again you may race round and round the model. An alternative scenario is that your perception is, "My boss will just have to accept that the report is going to be late." If this is your perception, then you will not race round and round the model, and the report will be completed, and in better time than if you spend time worrying about failure. Again we see that perception is a very individual thing that tells us that individuals are different.

A more general point about stress, the reaction, is that it is on a spectrum that runs from functional and useful, right through to dysfunctional and harmful. For one person, their reaction to their perception may be that it does make their heart beat quicker, and they do have elevated levels of adrenalin, but that this acts as a stimulus that motives them to get on with the activity and bring it to a successful conclusion. A general model that has been put forward is that, as the level of perceived stimulus rises, so does the level of performance, up to some optimum level. If the perception produces a level of stimulus or arousal above this optimum performance level, then the level of performance begins to fall as the level of stress becomes excessive and dysfunctional. If the level of stress/arousal/stimulus rises too much, then the person may not be able to function at all, and the level of performance at that point falls to zero. If a person is too stressed, then they may become ill, or they may give up and resign from their job. This situation is illustrated in Figure 5.2, where there is an optimum level of performance as a response to an optimum level of stress. Beyond that optimum level of stress, the level of performance declines until stress reaches a critical level at which point all performance ceases.

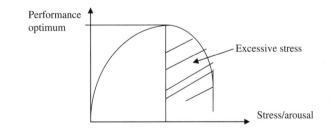

FIGURE 5.2

Performance as a function of stress

Each human activity, and each individual person, will have a unique curve, with the optimum level of stress situated at a different level. In Figure 5.3, we suggest, that the optimum level of stress needed to sleep successfully is lower than that to eat, and that is lower than to read, write or lecture.

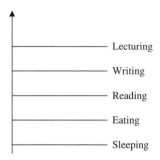

FIGURE 5.3

Optimum levels of stress for a variety of behaviours

On one occasion, the author saw his infant son confuse the optimum level of stress/arousal necessary to eat, with that to sleep. His son was fast asleep in his high chair, with his face in a plate of uneaten food! You need to be more aroused/stressed to eat than you do to sleep.

The art of self-management, or the management of staff in an organisation, is to manage the level of stress so that performance of the chosen task is at an optimum level. Within the organisational setting this is a difficult task, as it means that the level of stress has to be optimised individually – each individual may need to be managed differently as stress is the individual's personal reaction to their perceived environment. One stress management policy does not fit all.

THE FLIGHT OR FIGHT SYNDROME

We have referred to the individual response to the perceived environment, but how does the individual respond? The individual's physiological response to his/her environment is called the *Flight or Fight Syndrome*. The syndrome is the ancient way that our body ensured that we survived a threatening environment. Long ago, when wild beasts roamed the earth, it was possible that a man would meet a sabre-toothed tiger that would attack, with a view to eat the man. The two obvious life-saving reactions would be to run away, or to fight the tiger. Both required an unusual level of physical action, to be able to run extraordinarily fast or to fight with great power and savagery. For either of these courses of action man gradually evolved so that when he perceived himself to be threatened, a range of physiological changes occurs that enables extreme *flight* or *fight*. All that is needed to initiate the Flight or Fight Syndrome is that a person has to feel threatened by what they perceive of their environment. The basic responses of the Flight or Fight Syndrome are:

- Adrenalin and a number of other hormones and chemicals are released into the bloodstream. These chemicals enable people to be stronger and faster than they usually are.

- Speeding up of the heart rate, as a result of the adrenalin.

- Speed of respiration rises; that is, the increased speed of breathing gets more oxygen into the body, and the raised heart rate pumps the extra oxygen in the blood more quickly to the muscles, allowing more extreme physical exertion.

- Blood pressure rises because the heart is beating quicker in order that the richly oxygenated blood is pumped to the muscles.

- The blood sugar level rises, providing a source of energy for the body as it runs or fights more vigorously.

- Serum cholesterol is precipitated out in the bloodstream. This means that the body can more easily burn the cholesterol as a source of energy.

- Waste products are evacuated – an urge to go to the toilet. You can run faster if you weigh less, and it may put off the pursuers. Police officers (on management courses) have told the author that sometimes when an officer surprises a criminal, who is at that moment breaking the law, the immediate response is that sometimes the criminal empties their bladder and bowels spontaneously – not a nice experience!

- *Heightened awareness*: this response is as though the brain becomes turbo-charged and can evaluate the environment, and make judgments as to appropriate responses to the perceived threat, at greatly increased speed. If you ask people about their experience of being in a car crash, when they had a brief moment when they knew that there was going to be a crash, they will tell you that their life didn't flash before their eyes, it crept past; they have the experience that they could think many things and make many decisions in the fraction of time before the crash. Climbers, who fall, will relate similar stories, as do police officers who have had to shoot at someone during their professional police duties. Crash victims, climbers and police officers have all related these experiences to the author.

- Digestive acids and enzymes flood the stomach. This ensures that any food in the stomach is fully digested and all energy is extracted from it, for fighting and running away.

All of these elements of the Flight or Fight Syndrome occur to assist the body in running or fighting in the perceived threatening environment. These are the physiological things that are happening to the person earlier in this chapter, who saw a dog and perceived it as threatening.

The syndrome sounds really useful if you are faced by a perceived threat where flight or fight is an appropriate response, but what if the threat is of losing your job, being reprimanded by your boss, failing to do yourself justice in a university or professional examination, being ridiculed in front of your colleagues or having your departmental budget cut? Because you see the environment as threatening, the Flight or Fight Syndrome kicks in; this is what we meant about the level of arousal when we discussed the idea that there is an optimum level of stress for each activity. If you are too aroused in a threatening negotiating situation in a departmental meeting, then you are too aroused to successfully negotiate; you are ready, perhaps, to fight or run away, but neither is appropriate.

If fighting or flight is impossible or inappropriate, then there are a number of displacement activities, alternate actions that somehow serve the same purpose. Instead of fighting, an employee may lose his/her temper and start to shout, they may stand up and adopt a physically threatening pose, make rude or insulting comments or make threatening gestures like shaking their fists. All of these are clearly displacements for fighting and defence. There are also some displacement activities for flight; withdrawing from the scene for feeling unwell is a way to take flight, as is resigning from your employment, going silent or being unable to think. Some extremely stressed examination candidates have their mind go blank.

THE PERSON–ENVIRONMENT-FIT MODEL OF ORGANISATIONAL STRESS

Much of the research on organisational stress has been done using the "Environment-Person-Fit" model. This model hypothesises that excessive stress is caused if a person does not fit their environment, or the environment does not fit the person. The Person-Environment-Fit model seems to imply that the person has to somehow cope with the organisational environment, whereas the Environment–Person model implies that the organisation (the environment) should be adjusted to accommodate the people in the organisation. These two perspectives imply very different approaches to coping with, and managing, stress in organisations.

The other major stress model that underlies research is the load model, which hypothesises that excessive stress is caused when the individual is overloaded, when the demands placed on them exceed their coping ability or resources.

To begin with, we will look at the organisational stressors that research suggests underlie organisational stress problems. Much of the work on the basic causes of stress in organisations was done in the 1970s and the 1980s and is nicely summarised in Burke (1988) and Wallace et al. (1988). Subsequent works have looked at case studies and more detailed research into the findings of the 1970s and 1980s. The following sections on organisational stressors draw heavily on Burke (1988) and Wallace et al. (1988).

Organisational stressors

Organisational stressors cause stress. As we have already discussed, this only matters if the level of stress is so high as to be dysfunctional, in the sense that performance is reduced below the optimum level. Logically, performance is also suboptimum if the level of stress is too low, but this is usually not a problem in organisations and it is the excessive levels of stress that have been researched in organisations. To the extent that dysfunctional low levels of stress have been studied, this comes under the heading of job design and motivation, and not stress. Below, we set out the main stressors that research has shown lead to excessive and dysfunctional levels of stress for managerial and white-collar employees:

■ *Poor working conditions*: excessive stress has been shown to result from unpleasant working conditions, where there is noise, dirt, inadequate lighting, excessive physical demands on workers (e.g., heavy materials to be lifted or excessive speed of repetitive jobs), crowding (social density), temperature extremes, poor ventilation, excessive periods of time at computer screens and excessive and inconvenient hours. Shift working has also been shown to be stressful, especially when the shifts are constantly changing so that the body never fully adjusts to the hours that are being worked (Taylor et al., 1997). Constant night or late evening shifts, and long 12-hour shifts, have also been shown to be stressful and result in reduced worker efficiency, increased errors and accidents and harmful effects on maternity and family life (Spurgeon and Cooper, 2000). Open plan offices can often be stressful, if poorly designed, because of constant sounds and visual distractions, and it is well known that the colour of the decorations affects workers sometimes negatively and sometimes positively, depending on the colour. It is not for nothing that "red light districts" (sex industry districts) are red!

■ *Excessive workloads*: much research has shown that excessive workload leads to excessive stress. This has been broken down into quantitative (excessive working hours) and qualitative excessive workload (work that it is too difficult for the worker because of lack of ability, experience, education or training). Numbers of telephone calls, meetings and office visits per unit of time are amongst ways that quantitative overload has been measured. It has been demonstrated that hours of work and early deaths from coronary heart disease (CHD) are linked. One American study of men working in light industry under the age of 48 showed that those working more than 48 hours per week were twice as likely to die of CHD as those working less than 40 hours per week. In Japan, there is even a condition called karoshi, where people literally work themselves to death through heart failure and other heart conditions (Kanai, 2007). Work overload in quantitative terms has also been shown to be related to escapist drinking, absenteeism, low motivation at work, lowered self-esteem and an absence of suggestions to employers.

Case Study 5.2: The overworked engineer

I was asked by the head of a university engineering department to visit one of his "star" academics in the cancer ward of the local hospital, because of my interest in stress and illness. I asked the engineer, "tell me about your life". The answer told me of a life of 12-hour days, 7 days per week. My response was to explain that excessive stress from overly long hours resulted in the immune system being less effective, with the result that the engineer was vulnerable to illness, in his case cancer, for the second time in 18 months. The engineer recovered from the cancer and cut back his working week to 8 hours per day, 5 days per week. Shortly after, he was promoted to professor. A few years later, I met him in the street. He told me

Continued

that he still worked the short weeks, and that whenever he was tempted to break his 8-hour day rule he remembered the cancer ward. I asked how work was progressing, and the answer was "the funny thing is that now I only work 8 hours per day, 5 days per week, I have never been so creative or so productive in my life. When I worked long hours I was tired, I made errors, I fouled up relationships, all of which were counterproductive." Last week I met him again, and he said that he was working cleverer, not longer, than when he made himself vulnerable through excessive hours. In his field he is now one of the most cited engineers in the world.

Case Study 5.3: The academic who was saving the university

I was asked to go and visit a senior university academic who was in hospital after having had a heart attack. I asked, "Why are you here?" The answer was "I don't know; I'm not overweight (true), I don't smoke, I take exercise (he walked to and from the university), CHD doesn't run in the family and I take time off." I asked what "taking time off" meant, and I was told that he worked 12 hours per day, but he didn't work on Sundays. I also asked why he was working so hard, and the answer was "because I am helping to save the university" (the university had financial problems at that time). After some more discussion he said, "I suppose the reason that I've had a heart attack is because at 58, I am behaving as though I am 38." Sadly his insight came too late, as he died a few days later.

In both the above cases, some details have been changed or omitted to protect the identity of the individual.

Case Study 5.4: The overworked pro-vice-chancellors

Some years ago, the author worked in a university where there were a number of pro-vice-chancellors, who were in effect deputies for the vice-chancellor (VC). Their duties were to take on particular senior leadership responsibilities and to represent the VC in his absence. After 5 years in the post, the individual became the Senior Pro-VC, the first deputy VC; this post was particularly onerous. There was a sequence of five successive years when, in the year after stepping down from the post, the immediate ex-senior pro-VC had a heart attack. The person who broke the sequence was single, not in relationship and lived with his parents.

Questions

1. What lessons are there to be learnt from these three cases?
2. If you could have met these people, what questions would you have asked them?
3. What happens to you when *you* try and work very long hours?

When a job is too difficult, there is some evidence that this is a source of stress, particularly resulting in lowered self-esteem.

Research has shown that both qualitative and quantitative overload produce job dissatisfaction, job tension, lowered self-esteem, threat, embarrassment, high cholesterol levels and increased heart rate.

An important point is that people may work very long hours, not because they have too much work, but for some other reasons. It may be that they are perfectionists, for whom there will never be enough time; or it may be that they are Type-A personalities (of this more later) who are prone to take on more and more work because of their insecure and competitive personality and not because the job demands that they do.

Finally, in some firms, the "overworked manager" is part of the culture of the company. Employees come to feel that long hours and excessive workloads are expected of them, leading to what has been termed "presenteeism" (Hemp, 2004), behaviour that, it is hoped, demonstrates how committed they are to the organisation when either redundancies are a possibility, or where hard work and long hours are a company criteria for promotion at least in the enacted or informal organisational culture.

■ *Role ambiguity and role conflict*

Role ambiguity exists when an individual has inadequate information about their work role, that is, where there is lack of clarity about the work objectives associated with the role, about work colleagues' expectations of the work role and about the scope and responsibilities of the job.

Research suggests that there is a significant but weak relationship between role ambiguity and the following stress indicators – depressed mood, lowered self-esteem, life dissatisfaction, job dissatisfaction, low motivation to work and intention to leave the job.

Role conflict exists when an individual in a particular work role is torn by conflicting job demands, or doing things they really do not want to do or does not think are part of the job specification.

Various studies have shown that role conflict is positively related to CHD and stomach ulcers. People particularly at risk are those whose organisational role is at a boundary, for example, between departments or between the firm and the outside world or between one level of staff and another. First-line supervisory or first-line managers are particularly prone to role conflict-generated excessive stress, thus people who have been promoted once are in danger; for example, team leaders and supervisors. People in these positions will have a number of roles that represent the way that they relate to the various people in their organisational life. They have a role in relation to their subordinates, and they have a different role in relation to their line manager. The actions and behaviours necessary to fulfil the role in relation to their subordinates may well be very different from those necessary to fulfil their role in relation to their line manager; managing that conflict can be very stressful.

To get some sense of role conflict, try the following little exercise. List all the relationships that you have, and for each of them think what your role is. Your list may include your boss, your subordinates, parents, friends, a society for whom you are the treasurer, your girlfriend or boyfriend, your cat or dog and so on. When you start to examine their expectations of you then it soon becomes obvious how the roles conflict, even if it is only in terms of the amount of time that these people expect of you in order to meet their expectations of you.

■ *Responsibility*: evidence suggests that being responsible for people is more stressful than being responsible for things, and is linked to CHD. It is worth noting that responsibility is stressful even if we seek responsibility. Stress does not only result from circumstances that we would like to avoid.

It has been found that responsibility for people is significantly related to diastolic blood pressure and serum cholesterol levels – both of these being known CHD risk factors.

There is circumstantial and anecdotal material suggesting that too little work, undemanding work and too little responsibility may all be stressful.

■ *Relationships*: this is a difficult area for research to produce clear results. What work has been done is suggestive rather than clear-cut. It seems that poor relations with the boss and poor relations with subordinates both produce excessive stress. Also implicated are poor ability to delegate and failure to allow participation, and participation.

Case Study 5.5: The man who could not delegate

One of my former students became the practice manager of a large engineering consultancy. As a feature of his personality, he found it very difficult to delegate, with the consequence that he became more and more overloaded with work that he felt *he* had to do, as no one else could be trusted to do it to the appropriate standard. One Monday he did not arrive at work. He disappeared and could not be traced for several months, until someone took him to a hospital, having found this disorientated man wading into the Pacific Ocean, 5000 miles from his workplace. He had been triggered by his work pattern into a mental illness called Dissociative Fugue, which is usually brought on by "…traumatic, stressful or overwhelming life events" (American Psychiatric Association, DSM-IV™, 1994) (some details have been changed to protect the identity of this individual).

If people are excluded from management participation, it is stressful for them, and, for insecure and non-adaptive managers, participation by those at lower management levels may be threatening. Managers may find being accountable and allowing participation may cause personal conflict.

Ivancevich (1979) found that a sample of 154 project engineers, with managerial responsibilities, who were excluded from decision making, reported greater physical symptoms and job tension, but they reported no greater role conflict, ambiguity or fatigue than those who were involved in decision making.

Morris (1975) has neatly summarised some of these problems in what he calls the "cross of relationships", Figure 5.4.

Very competitive management cultures will result in each manager being very isolated and unsupported, subject to office politics and colleagues' rivalry.

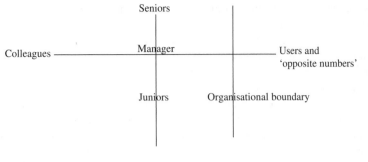

FIGURE 5.4

The cross of relationships

Problems cannot be discussed for fear of appearing weak or inadequate. American literature often notes the isolated life of a top executive as being stressful.

Emotionally demanding interactions with others have also been shown to lead to *Burn Out* as a result of excessive interactions over too long a period of time. *Burn Out* is a state of being physically, intellectually and emotionally exhausted, and is found particularly in industries with a lot of emotional interactions, like social work and teaching (Maslach, 1982).

■ *Career development*: a useful framework for viewing career-related stressors is to look at the career life cycle with four phases:

  □ *Starting a career*, with stress arising from having to learn the organisation's culture and structures, and having no support structure.

  □ *Career development*, where choices may have to be made between career and family.

  □ *Maintaining a career*, where the individual may have to come to terms with how successful or not their career is going to be, and increasing conflict between career and family.

  □ Career ending.

Three major clusters of potential stressors are observed:

  □ *Lack of job security*: this is clearly stressful, as losing a job, especially in times of economic recession, may lead to other problems like debt and losing one's house. Doctors' waiting rooms are full of managers with sleeping problems, depression and anxiety as a result of job insecurity. Some years ago a mature student in one of the author's classes brought to the author the summary medical records of the student's former organisation, which had announced that there would be major redundancies at the year-end. They showed a major increase in almost every medical condition compared with the previous year.

  □ *Status incongruity* (a mismatch between qualifications and job demands), which can manifest itself as under- or over-promotion, frustration at reaching a career ceiling or adjustment to new positions. The Peter Principle (Peter and Hull, 1969) suggests, not entirely humorously, that in hierarchies, every time someone is good at a job they are promoted, until they end up in a job that is one promotion too many, and there they remain, unhappy and incompetent. The shorthand version is that everyone is promoted to their level of incompetence! Over-promotion is really qualitative overload in another guise. If we accept that the Peter Principle has some element of truth, then it implies an interesting paradox. Often the author has heard people arguing that everyone senior to them has been promoted at least once too often, but they have been under-promoted. How is it that these people are the only people *under*-promoted?

Clarkson (1995) talks of the Achilles Syndrome, where each time someone is promoted they feel insecure, because they know that they can do their previous job, but they do not know whether they can do their new job. This insecurity starts the Flight or Fight Syndrome as the promoted person feels threatened. A further complication is that, having been promoted, they may keep going back to their previous responsibilities, where they feel secure. This behaviour delays them mastering their new job and delays their successor from mastering their new job.

Middle-aged middle management, it is suggested, is particularly subject to stress: job opportunities are fewer as you rise up through the organisation; new jobs take longer to master, being more complex and responsible; past errors cannot be undone; and new techniques and ideas must be mastered just as mind and body may be flagging and family commitments are particularly onerous. Some writers have referred to this syndrome as the "male menopause". At the time of writing, the author has a client, a director of an international company, who comments that at their level of seniority they cannot look to their subordinates for support, and there are fewer peers to whom they can turn. Additionally, to turn to peers for support may be to show weakness, and thus blights further career progress. These problems of the loneliness at the top of organisations are discussed in Kitchin (1998).

☐ *Two-career household*: a third element of career development that has been researched is the two-career household, where both the people in a relationship are working and have careers. For a review of this literature, see Eby et al. (2005). There may then arise the problem that if the career development of one partner requires them to relocate, what happens to the other partner's career or the partnership. There is an additional problem of the two-career household, and that is the difficulty of managing the family; how are the children looked after, who goes to the school open days, who does the housework? Both people in a two-career household tend to have paid employment *and* domestic/family duties – there is a danger of overload, equivalent to working excessive hours. Additionally, family commitments may make career development more difficult.

Mobility may be a source of stress. A manager moving locations every few years to further their career may never put down roots and may never acquire friends and foundations. There is some evidence to suggest that such mobility results in marital problems and problems for the family, for example, delinquency, teenage violence and drug taking.

- *Status inconsistency*: there is a growing body of research work showing that the risk of CHD is greatly increased by the presence of status *inconsistency*, that is when, for managers, their social class in childhood, or their partner's social class in their childhood, was higher or lower than the class level that they presently share. Clearly this may be a factor in considering candidates for promotion.

- *Organisational structure and climate*: simply being in an organisation is a source of potential stress, as it may threaten the individual's freedom, autonomy and identity.

  Principal problems flow from exclusion from participation in decision making, no sense of belonging, lack of effective consultation, poor communications, restrictions on behaviour and office politics.

  Studies have shown that participation in decision making results in greater job satisfaction, reduced job-related feelings of being threatened, greater self-esteem, high productivity and reduced staff turnover. It has also been found that exclusion from decision making was significantly a cause of overall poor physical health, escapist drinking, depression, low self-esteem, low life and job satisfaction, low work motivation, intention to leave the job and absenteeism from work.

- *Organisational change*: in Chapters 2 and 6, we make repeated references to peoples' reluctance to change, or more especially, peoples' reluctance to have change imposed upon them. Change means uncertainty, even if you are the managers and initiators of the change, and uncertainty leads to excessive levels of stress. People worry whether they will lose power and influence, whether they will be able to learn new skills and expertise and whether they will have a job after the changes; all of these are stressors that may lead to excessive stress which will be dysfunctional for organisations and the individuals who make up the organisations.

- *Contemporary sources of management and professional stress*: there are a number of stressors that seem to have become more prevalent in recent years:

  □ *Mergers and acquisitions*: whether an organisation takes over another, is taken over or they merge, the result is usually a reduction in the number of staff, a rise in the level of uncertainty and a new culture to learn or develop, all very stressful. Some estimates suggest that no more than 50% of mergers are even commercially successful.

  □ *Retrenchment and budget cut backs*: both of these factors are regular events in organisations, especially in times of recession and credit crunches, and generate a great deal of uncertainty amongst the staff, and thus stress.

  □ *Reorganisations*: the author's sister worked for the UK National Health service, and during her career there were six major reorganisations of at least her part of the NHS. Every time uncertainty was generated, and on most occasions she had to apply for a job in the new structure, and on occasions she had to re-apply for her own existing job, even if it had survived the reorganisation. Her experience was typical of the impact of reorganisations.

Readers may have noticed that a number of the organisational stressors are hygiene factors in Herzberg's theory of individual motivation, which was discussed in Chapter 4.

EXTRA-ORGANISATIONAL STRESSORS

For most people, work and non-work life cannot be kept in two separate boxes where what happens in one has no impact on the other. If you have had an argument at home before leaving for work, then you are likely to arrive at work in a different mood than if home was peaceful and calm. Conversely, if work has been excessively stressful then one's mood at home is likely to be changed, which in turn may generate stress at home, which is then carried over to the workplace. There can easily be a vicious circle of stress combining work and home.

THE PERSON IN THE ENVIRONMENT

The Person–Environment-Fit models of organisational stress emphasise that stress is a result of the impact of the environment on the individual. When we discussed stress earlier in this chapter, we emphasised that how a person perceives their environment determines how they respond to it, and thus the degree to which they are stressed. How a person perceives their environment is to a major extent a result of their personality, which is a result of their genes and their life experiences and the interaction of the two. Research on stress has investigated a number of mediating factors between stressors and the manifestations of stress. Research concludes that the following mediating factors are important (Burke, 2002) in the sense that individuals who exhibit a higher level of hardiness, and the other mediating factors listed below, are able to cope better, or worse, with stressors:

- *Hardiness*: this factor is a combination of commitment (a tendency to involve oneself fully in one's total life situation), control (a tendency to believe and act as if one can influence the course of events within reasonable limits) and challenge (a belief that change rather than stability is the norm of life, and is seen as an opportunity for personal growth).

- *Locus of control*: this factor essentially means that the individual who displays a high level of *locus of control* feels that they control their life rather than being controlled by their environment.

- *Self-esteem*: this is the level of regard or value that we have for ourselves – how we feel about ourselves, what image we have of ourselves and what we believe we are capable of.

- *Self-efficacy*: this is our belief in our own capacity to organise and execute courses of action required to manage prospective situations.

- *Perfectionism*: people suffering with *perfectionism* will often feel that they are unable to complete a task to the standard that they wish, and that they do not have the time or resources necessary, thus leading to an ongoing sense of personal failure and guilt.

- *Sense of coherence*: a person with a *sense of coherence* experiences the world as comprehensive, meaningful and manageable.

- *Neuroticism*: someone who has a high level of *neuroticism* has an enduring tendency to experience negative emotional states and will experience high levels of anxiety, anger, guilt and depression. Clearly a neurotic person is likely to find life very stressful.

- *Extroversion*: someone who is extrovert will be gregarious, assertive and seek out excitement and new experience as they are easily bored. An introverted person will score lower on each of the dimensions. Extroverts will tend to become stressed if the environment is boring, unchanging and allows low levels of social interaction. Conversely, introverts will become stressed if the environment consists of change and high levels of social interaction.

- *Type-A personality*: this is a personality syndrome, that is, a number of inter-related symptoms, characteristics or behaviours. As every organisation seems to have some Type-A personalities, whose behaviour can be difficult to understand and disturbing for people who are not Type-A, we will present a fuller discussion of Type-A.

Type-A personality

This syndrome was first defined by Friedman and Rosenman (1974), who were cardiologists seeking to understand whether there was a particular personality type that was prone to CHD. Their research suggested that there is a personality syndrome that makes people prone to CHD. People with Type-A personalities are characterised by:

- *Low self-esteem* – they tend to think that they are not very clever or creative and that the only way they can succeed is to work harder than other people.

- *Free-floating hostility* – they tend to be aggressive and hostile, and make colleagues uncomfortable.

- *Competitive* – they make everything a competition that they can win, so that observers will not realise that they are not very good (low self-esteem). This means that they may be very good employees where individual competition (for example, sales) leads to success for the company.

- *Numeration* – everything is turned into numbers, so that they can demonstrate that they have won the competition that *they* have set up with their colleagues. If you ask Type-A engineers how they are, they will tell you how many projects they have completed this year, and how many more that is than any other colleague, or how quickly they completed the project. Type-A academics will tell you how many papers they have had published this year, and Type-A surgeons will tell you how many operations they have performed and how much greater that is than any of their colleagues. They have to win the competition they have set up, and numbers let them demonstrate that.

- *Self-destructive* – it is as though there is some driving force that causes Type-A's to self-destruct so that their low ability and creativity are no longer a secret. There are many examples, particularly US politicians, who are eager to tell the world how many points they are ahead in the opinion polls and how many dollars they have raised, who then destroy their campaign with some public indiscretion. Lester Piggott, one of the most successful, and aggressive, horse racing jockeys ever to live was sent to prison for tax evasion, an act of self-destruction of someone who was almost certainly a Type-A individual.

Working with Type-A colleagues is rarely going to be easy, and may well be very stressful, as they are poor team players (as they have to win as an individual), and they make poor managers, as they are drawn to hard work and competition rather than reflecting and planning. Ironically, Type-A's may well be promoted into management positions if the criteria for promotion are that the individual is very successful at meeting and fulfilling targets and being the individual who outperforms their colleagues.

The mediating factors that cause people to be particularly prone to stressors can all be tested for, but the evidence is too weak to allow such tests to be accurate criteria for selecting staff to work in stressful environments, but at least they may offer some guidance that will prevent wholly inappropriate individuals being appointed.

CONSEQUENCES OF EXCESSIVE STRESS

The impact of sustained excessive stress, whatever its source, organisational or extra-organisational, is manifested in individuals in one of three main ways, each of which can have a profound effect on the organisation within which the individual is employed:

- Physiological, medical consequences

- Cognitive changes

- Behavioural manifestations

Physiological consequences of excessive stress for individuals

When we discussed the Flight or Fight Syndrome earlier in this chapter, we saw that stress results in a number of key physiological changes at the time that the individual is excessively stressed as a result of perceiving them-self to be threatened. In summary, the key changes are the rise in the level of serum cholesterol precipitated out in the bloodstream and the increase in the acids and enzymes released into the digestive system.

If the person, who perceives them-self to be threatened does not fight or run away in a physical way, then the cholesterol is not burnt up by vigorous activity, and some of it attaches to the walls of the blood vessels. If this happens repeatedly, then the blood vessels gradually "fur up" and become narrowed. The consequence of the gradual narrowing is that in order to pump a given amount of blood round the body, the heart has to pump harder, and thus the blood pressure rises on a permanent basis (not only an extra rise at the time of a perceived a threat). This gradual rise in the blood pressure over the years means that people become more prone to strokes, haemorrhages (including cerebral haemorrhages), kidney disease and CHDs. These illnesses are serious, and can cause long-term sick leave from work, or even premature death.

If there is no food in the stomach to be digested, then the excessive digestive juices resulting from the Flight or Fight Syndrome digest what is present, that is they begin to digest the digestive system, with the well-known result that excessive stress can lead to stomach or duodenal ulcers; again these are both conditions that can result in sick leave or even death.

If we look at the physiological consequences of excessive stress, we can present these in a general framework that lists the major physiological systems of the body and comments on how each might manifest the consequences of excessive stress. If we rewrite the word disease as DIS EASE then it nicely suggests how a lack of ease (excessive stress) can manifest itself as disease. Medical science has long recognised the existence of psychosomatic diseases, and indeed there are several leading journals of Psychosomatic Medicine, for example, the Journal of Psychosomatic Research.

Each person seems to have some part of their physiology through which they manifest their dis ease. If we are a manager, then we may observe the illnesses of our staff as a message about their level of excessive stress, and thus the need to make some adjustments to the level of the stressors to which they are subjected. Managers who know their staff well will begin to recognise recurrence of the particular medical condition that is that employee's manifestation of excessive stress.

We will now list the body's main systems and the major illnesses that might be the manifestation of excessive stress. Not only do we manifest our stress through our physiological systems in the form of acute episodes (short-term illnesses) but major traumas may also trigger the onset of chronic (long-term) conditions. The trauma could be the loss of a job, retirement, demotion, death of a loved one and so on. We can say that what constitutes a trauma is about how the individual perceives an event, just as they define stressors in an individual perceptual way.

Excessive stress may make pre-existing conditions worse, or may initiate chronic conditions.

Skin problems, e.g. rashes, eczema, psoriasis, mouth ulcers and urticaria.

Bladder problems, e.g., cystitis.

Nerves, e.g., shingles.

Stomach problems, including ulcers, indigestion and heartburn.

Skeletons, e.g., arthritis.

Bowels, e.g., looseness, constipation, irritable bowel syndrome and colitis.

Blood circulation, e.g., high blood pressure, strokes, haemorrhages and kidney disease.

Hearts, e.g., all manner of CHD, including heart attacks, arrhythmia and angina.

Immune system, e.g., frequent minor medical problems, colds flu, etc.

Glands, e.g., diabetes and tonsillitis.

Lungs, e.g., asthma, emphysema, bronchitis and hay fever.

Reproductive organs, e.g., sexual dysfunction, impotence and infertility.

Brain, e.g., failure of three-dimensional perception, other perceptual problems, memory problems and data processing problems.

Psychological/mental health consequences of excessive stress for individuals

We have already presented a case study in this chapter about one possible psychological consequence of excessive stress brought on by working excessive hours ("The man who could not delegate"). We also presented a case study showing how productivity, creativity and effectiveness can be affected by excessive work hours ("The overworking engineer").

The author has also come across a number of cases where excessive hours of work and the resulting fatigue have resulted in a variety of mental illnesses, including depression, psychosis, eating disorders, panic and anxiety attacks, agoraphobia and obsessive compulsive disorder, and research literature also indicates that fatigue can trigger a wide variety of mental illnesses. In effect, fatigue can make, or trigger, the mental illness that is the way that the individual manifests their "dis ease". It has also been argued that conflicting roles or responsibilities can trigger schizophrenic episodes when the individual finds that they cannot resolve the conflicts (Laing, 1965). We also know that about 25% of the population will at some point suffer from depression, and that very many are reactive depressions (a reaction/response to life events) (American Psychiatric Association, DSM-IV™, 1994).

Other research shows that concentration, creativity, decision-making ability, memory and motivation are all potentially diminished by excessive levels of stress.

It could be argued that a way of taking flight (the Flight or Fight Syndrome) from excessive stress resulting from perceived excessive threat is to take flight into physiological and psychological ill-health. If you are sufficiently ill then you have to withdraw from work until you are fit enough to resume.

Behavioural consequences of excessive stress for individuals

One way to observe excessive stress is to look for inappropriate, or otherwise inexplicable, changes in behaviour.

Patterns of eating, drinking and smoking change when people are under increasing stress. In all three cases, consumption tends to rise (although for some people eating diminishes under excessive stress). We may speculate that increased food consumption at times of excessive stress is a response to the increase of digestive juices (Flight or Fight Syndrome), or is an example of comfort eating. If parents comfort their anxious or distressed children by giving them something to eat (a common parental pattern) then it is not surprising if people grow up with a conditioned response to eat more at times of dis ease.

We also observe that some people's timekeeping changes when stress levels rise.

An officer from a police force training school once remarked to the author that you could sometimes tell when police recruits were struggling with excessive stress, because they often became sexually promiscuous, or more promiscuous – they were in effect taking flight from their excessively stressful training. In addition, he observed that personal hygiene and care of uniform also deteriorated when recruits were struggling with excessive stress.

On one occasion the author, whilst playing cricket, accidentally split open the eyebrow of a member of the rival team – I could not stop giggling – a wholly inappropriate response that indicated my level of stress. Often we may observe inappropriate laughter that tells us of stress.

As we listed and examined organisational stressors in the early part of this chapter, we reported a number of behavioural/psychological changes, which clearly have impacts on the organisation. In the next section, we will list these individual impacts of excessive stress and then show how the organisation is impacted.

ORGANISATIONAL SYMPTOMS OF EXCESSIVE STRESS

Individual responses to excessive stress that we noted when discussing stressors included reduced worker efficiency, increased incidence of errors and accidents, illness, escapist consumption of alcohol, absenteeism, reduced motivation and self-esteem, a reduction in creativity, job dissatisfaction, depressed mood, increased intention to change jobs, burnout, reduced concentration, absentmindedness and deterioration in memory function, reduced decision-making ability and an increase in prevarication.

When we look at this list of individual responses, we can see that there are a number of impacts on organisations, which flow from these individual responses that will reduce the effectiveness and increase the costs of organisations:

■ Efficiency, motivation and productivity are reduced, with a resulting reduction in profits and increased prices so that organisations are less competitive.

■ Absenteeism is increased, with the consequence that a larger staff has to be maintained to ensure any given level of production.

■ Staff turnover is increased, with the consequence that more staff have to be recruited and trained, thus requiring increased human resource and training budgets. Increased staff turnover also means that the average level of training and experience is lower.

■ Sick leave is raised as a consequence of excessive stress, and thus the workforce has to be increased, resulting in a higher wage and salary bill and again an increase in the recruitment and training budgets.

■ Raised levels or accidents and errors lead to increased costs.

COPING WITH EXCESSIVE STRESS

Organisations have a number of ways that they can cope with the consequences of individual excessive stress. These may be stand-alone or can be used in combination:

■ *Individuals can learn, or be taught, how to cope with the consequences of stressors*: in order to do this, the individuals may be taught time management, or relaxation skills, or they can be encouraged to take the vigorous exercise for which the Flight or Fight Syndrome prepares them. The reaction of some organisations has been to have in-house gyms or to provide or subsidise gym membership. Taking part in vigorous exercise burns up the products that undermine health that are produced as part of the Flight or Fight Syndrome. An additional advantage of physical fitness is that it means that people can cope more easily with stressful situations. Increased fitness also strengthens the immune system, and thus time spent in the gym means that not only can people continue to thrive in stressful situations, but also they are less likely to become unwell.

■ *Organisations can seek to reduce the level of stressors*: earlier in this chapter, when we looked at organisational stressors, we saw that these stressors are manifestations, or parts of, the organisational culture. In Chapter 2 we saw that to make fundamental changes to culture can take 5–10 years, so obviously organisational cultural change is not a "quick fix" for the consequences of excessive stress. When we look in detail at the stressors we see that often they are manifestations of an overall organisational culture, meaning that individual stressors cannot be changed without affecting other manifestations of the culture.

As an example of the inter-relatedness of cultural elements we can look at the culture of excessive working hours, which is typical of many British organisations. Note that we say British; if we look at Germany, for example, we find that the attitude and practice concerning long working hours are very different. If a British manager tries to telephone their colleague in German after 5.00 p.m., they will probably find that they are not there, they have gone home. The German attitude to long hours is "why are you not able to complete your job within normal working hours?" If you insist that UK managers go home at 5.00 p.m., they are likely to worry about how they can prove that they should be promoted, as the informal culture around suitability for promotion is often that the workers voluntarily puts in long hours to show their commitment to their job and the organisation. They will also often worry that if there are to be redundancies then the people who go home at 5.00 p.m. will be the people who are made redundant. Simply announcing that people are to go home at 5.00 p.m. will not work so long as people believe that hours of work influence promotion (part of the enacted culture of many British organisations). Even if there is a ban on working after 5.00 p.m. this may just mean that people take work home.

■ *Employee Assistance Providers (EAP) provision*: if organisations cannot reduce the level of stressors (requiring cultural change), or teach people how to be better prepared for high levels of stressors (time management, delegating skills, etc.), then an alternative is to help them cope with the consequences of excessive stress through the provision of psychological, career or financial counselling. Such counselling services are usually subcontracted to external counselling services called EAP's. The psychological counselling is usually provided in the form of five or six one-hour private, confidential counselling sessions. The sessions need to be confidential so that the stressors and the stress can be examined in detail, without the client fearing that what they say will be reported back to their employer, with the possibility that their promotion or career prospects will be damaged as a result of the counselling. The only exception to this confidentiality rule is when the counsellor's judgment is that the stressed client is a danger to them-self or to others. Clearly an oil refinery needs to know that an employee is so angry that they might start a fire at the refinery, or that they may be drunk, or under the influence of drugs, when working in the dangerous environment of the refinery. The company has a duty of care for other employees and people who live and work in the area surrounding the refinery. The source of the stressor that has led to dysfunctional stress does not have to be within the organisation; for example, marital problems that result in stress that reduces a person's ability to work effectively within their employing organisation are as important to the organisation as stressors internal to the organisation, as both result in a reduction of organisational effectiveness.

There have been studies completed on the commercial cost-benefit of counselling services. For example, United Airlines found a benefit-cost ratio for every dollar spent on their counselling services of 16:1, Equitable Life found a ratio of 3:1 and General Motors 2:1. The General Motors study showed that counselling cut lost time by 40% , accidents by 50% and sickness benefits by 60% (Ross, 1996).

- *Organisations can change their recruitment and selection processes* so that they only employ people who can cope with the organisational pattern and level of stressors. Clearly, recruiting people who need control and structure in their working lives to a job, which is characterised by role ambiguity and change, is bound to lead to stress problems.

- *Ignore the problem*: a brutal alternative is that the organisation does not worry about the consequences of excessive stress on its staff and simply replaces those people who leave or become ill, and recruits substitutes. Increasingly, in a range of countries, laws have been passed that specify that an organisation has duty of care to its staff, that is that the organisation has to care for the health, safety and welfare of its staff, and failure to do this entitles the suffering employee to sue the organisation for compensation. Organisations that do not exercise a duty of care may try and insure themselves against being sued, but an organisation that does not exercise a duty of care will find that their insurance premiums will rise to the point where it would be cheaper to look after the health, safety and welfare of their staff – ignoring the problem ceases to be a solution to stress within organisations.

CONCLUSION

The cost of excessive stress can be very high both for individual employees and for employing organisations.

Organisations that ignore the whole issue of stress are likely to be less profitable and less successful. The material in this chapter is meant to help in the design of organisational environments so that stress levels are not dysfunctionally high, and/or to help design systems (such as EAPs) that will help individual employees cope with the levels of stress experienced in the organisation.

Individuals need to understand stress so that they recognise what is happening to them, and the way that they may be endangering their health and so that they make more reflective and successful managers.

REFERENCES

http://www.hse.gov.uk/stress/standards/.

American Psychiatric Association, DSM-IV™, 1994. In: Diagnostic and Statistical Manual of Mental Disorders, fourth ed.

Burke, R.J., 1988. Sources of managerial and professional stress in large organisations. In: Cooper, C.L., Payne, R. (Eds.), Causes, Coping and Consequences of Stress at Work. John Wiley and Sons Ltd.

Burke, R.J., 2002. Work stress and coping in organizations: progress and prospects. In: Frydenberg, E. (Ed.), Beyond Coping: Meeting Goals, Visions and Challenges. Oxford University Press.

Clarkson, C., 1995. Change in Organisations. Athenaeum Press.

Eby, L.T., Casper, W.J., Lockwood, A., 2005. Work and family research in IO/OB: content analysis and review of the literature (1980–2002). Journal of Vocational Behavior 66 (1), 124–197.

Friedman, M., Rosenman, R.H., 1974. Type-A Behaviour and Your Heart. Wildwood House.

Hemp, P., 2004. Presenteeism: at work – but out of it. Harvard Business Review.

Ivancevich, J.M., 1979. An analysis of participation in decision-making among project engineers. Academy of Management Journal 22, 253–269.

Journal of Psychosomatic Research, Elsevier.

Kanai, A., 2007. Economic and employment condition, karoshi (work to death) and the trend of studies on workaholism in Japan. In: Burke, R.J. (Ed.), Research Companion to Working Time and Work Addiction. Edward Elgar.

Kitchin, D., 1998. The higher you go, the harder it gets. Professional Manager 7 (2), 3.

Laing, R.D., 1965. The Divided Self. Penguin Books.

Maslach, C., 1982. Burnout: The Cost of Caring. Prentice Hall.

Morris, J., 1975. Managerial stress and the "Cross of Relationships". In: Gowler, D., Legge, K. (Eds.), Managerial Stress. Gower Press.

Peter, L.J., Hull, R., 1969. The Peter Principle: Why Things Always Go Wrong. William Morrow & Company, Inc.

Ross, P., 1996. Counselling and accountability. In: Palmer, S., Dainow, S., Milner, P. (Eds.), Counselling: The BAC Counselling Reader. Sage.

Spurgeon, A., Cooper, C.L., 2000. Worktime, health and performance. In: Cooper, C.L., Robertson, I.T. (Eds.), International Review of Industrial and Organizational Psychology, vol. 15. John Wiley.

Taylor, E., Folkard, S., Shapiro, D., 1997. Shiftwork advantages as predictors of health. International Journal of Occupational and Environmental Health 3 (2), 20–29.

Wallace, M., Levens, M., Singer, 1988. Blue collar stress. In: Cooper, C.L., Payne, R. (Eds.), Causes, Coping and Consequences of Stress at Work. John Wiley and Sons Ltd.

Organisational Politics

6

There tend to be strong overlaps and interconnections between all topics in organisational behaviour, but this is particularly so when we come to look at organisational politics.

Organisational politics arises when people think differently and want to act differently.

(Morgan, 1997, p. 160)

Politics is the process by which these differences are resolved. People think and want to act differently because they come from different national cultures and different subcultures within organisations. There are other reasons why people want to act differently within the process of decision making: decisions can change who benefits and who loses from the organisational changes which result from decisions about changing the organisation's structure, systems, strategy, products, markets or production process. We can already see that this chapter should be read together with the chapters on Groups and Group Processes, Organisational Culture, Leadership and International Cultural Differences. Organisational politics is about the processes that change organisations, and the processes that try and prevent change or resist change.

There are two broad schools of thought about organisational politics. One approach is to say that politics within organisations is undesirable and tends to lead to chaotic situations within organisations, and to increase stress levels, see for example Fandt and Ferris (1990). The second approach is to say that organisational politics is not only inevitable, but can also be functional rather than dysfunctional, see for example Ammeter et al. (2002) and Huff (1988). Ammeter et al. (2002) said "...politics... [is]... neither inherently good nor bad but rather a fact of life and a feature woven into the very fabric of organisations." (p. 752)

THE ESSENCE OF ORGANISATIONAL POLITICS

In this chapter we draw extensively, but not wholly, on the approach to organisational politics that is presented by Gareth Morgan in a chapter of his fascinating book Images of Organization (Morgan, 1997).

We can define organisational political processes as:

...the interaction of interests, conflict and power within organisations.

People in organisations will have differing interests, which inevitably leads to conflicts, and these conflicts are resolved by the exercise of power.

Interests…are…about predispositions, embracing goals, values, desires, expectations and other orientations and inclinations that lead a person to act in one way rather than another.

(Morgan, 1997, p. 161)

Conflict arises whenever interests collide.

(Morgan, 1997, p. 167)

Power is the medium through which conflicts of interest are ultimately resolved. Power influences who gets what, when and how.

(Morgan, 1997, p. 170)

What should already be clear to the reader is that politics is inevitable in organisations. We cannot imagine an organisation where every member of the organisation wanted the same things and agreed about the best way to achieve these things; such an organisation is called a unitary organisation. So, politics is inevitable. We might also ask whether organisational politics is functional, that is, does an organisation function better because there are organisational politics? Later in this chapter, we will argue that organisations that have internal conflicts, and the resulting political processes, will actually function better, and be more successful, than organisations where there are no conflicts.

Now we will look in some detail at the three concepts of interests, conflict and power, and then go on to look at the processes where the three concepts interact.

INTERESTS

Individual interests: when we wrote about the garbage-can theory of decision making in Chapter 1, we noted how each of the individuals in a decision-making process had their own agenda. One person might want a decision because it will make their professional life easier; another may want a decision because it will help them gain promotion; another will see it as a means of increasing their income; and another may see it as a way to work fewer hours, or fewer days, so that the quality of their work-life balance is improved. Each person has their own interests that they are trying to further. Life would be easy if each person only had one interest, but most people will have a number of conflicting interests. A woman or man with a family may want to maximize their income, and reduce their working hours, further their career and increase the flexibility of their working life. There is going to be an internal decision-making process as they balance the trade-offs between the conflicting options; to maximize their income may mean working longer hours; to maximize career progress may mean sacrificing flexibility of working hours.

Group interests: a group of employees may have resolved their individual internally conflicting interests and found a group of other individuals with whom they can pursue shared interests. If there are a number of people with shared interests then they will be a more powerful voice to pursue their shared interests.

…the political metaphor encourages us to see organisations as loose networks of people with divergent interests who gather together for the sake of expediency.

(Morgan, 1997, p. 166)

People need one another, to meet at least some of their individual interests. And,

Organisations are coalitions and are made up of coalitions, and coalition building is an important dimension of almost all organisational life.

(Morgan, 1997, p. 166)

We may also expect that there will be conflicts between groups that represent subcultures in the organisation. The Finance Department may well have very differing priorities than the Marketing Department or the engineers in Research and Development.

Whole organisation interests: within the whole organisation there may well be conflicting interests. It is easy to see that increased profits might be in conflict with reducing the organisation's carbon footprint or maintaining the current level and pattern of employment. A UK manufacturer who moves its production to China will reduce its UK carbon footprint and increase profits, but reduce UK employment.

Those people who are involved with making decisions for the organisation as a whole will be influenced by individual, group and organisation-wide conflicting interests throughout the organisation.

Conflict between internal and external stakeholders: the policies and behaviours of organisations are not just a result of the resolution of internal conflicting interests, but are also the result of the interests of external stakeholders. Stakeholders are any individuals, groups or organisations who are influenced by the organisation, or who can have an impact on the organisation. So far we have looked at internal stakeholders and their conflicting interests, but we also need to take into consideration the external stakeholders and their interests. In many countries, local government and the national government will potentially have interests that may be expressed in the form of local and national laws, leading to a potential conflict between what the organisation wants to do, and what the law says that it can do. Non-governmental organisations (NGOs) will also have interests. An example of a powerful NGO, with a particular interest, is the movement called Greenpeace that pursues environmental issues including the pollution of seas, rivers and air.

We will be using the idea of stakeholders later in this chapter, when we examine the way that interest groups ensure that their interests are fulfilled by an organisation of which they are stakeholders.

Now we go on to examine how interests can be in conflict, the second element of organisational political processes (interests, conflict and power).

CONFLICT

Conflict arises whenever interests collide.

(Morgan, 1997, p. 167)

We have already demonstrated how there are conflicts of interests at a variety of levels, but for the sake of clarity we will list them, and elaborate the list:

- *Intra-personal conflicts*: the conflicts that are internal to an individual; do I further my career or my family responsibilities?

■ *Inter-personal conflicts*: the conflicting interests between two or more individuals; individual A wants the organisation to maximize profits through reducing the number of employees, and individual B wants to maintain employment levels (one is sure of their job, the other fears for their job, fearing that they will be made redundant if profits are maximized).

■ *Intra-group conflicts*: these are conflicting interests within a group. There may be conflicts within a group, for example where an engineering task/project group cannot agree on which proposal to support. Students who are members of engineering project groups will be familiar with this conflict.

■ *Inter-group conflicts*: we discussed in-group and out-group conflicts in Chapter 1 when we discussed decision making (Sherif and Sherif, 1953). In this case the members of one group "rubbish" another group just because they are another group. Additionally, the Accounting and Finance Department may view the organisation's problems in a very different way than the members of the Marketing or Engineering Departments because each department analyses the organisation from its own professional standpoint, and may not understand the competing perspective.

■ Conflict may be built into:

☐ *Organisational structures*: when we look at the abbreviated organisational structure, Figure 6.1, we see how conflict is built into the organisation, as the directors of Accounting (A/C), Marketing (Market), Manufacturing (Manu), etc. fight with one another for the limited finances and resources. It may well be that the directors are also in conflict as each of them fight to become the Chief Executive Officer (CEO). Within the Marketing Department there will be conflict between the heads of the UK, USA, EU and Asian sections, again for resources and promotion. Within the EU Section of the Marketing Department there will be conflict between the heads of the Atlantic, Mediterranean and German speaking subsections, also over resources and promotion. There is conflict over resources and promotion because of the organisational structure.

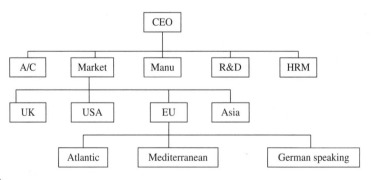

FIGURE 6.1

Organisational structure as a basis for conflict

☐ *Roles*: it is inevitable that the Marketing Department will concern itself with marketing problems, both because that is their job, and because marketing peoples' training and experience means that they make sense of the organisational world in a marketing way, and not as engineers or finance people do. When the organisation is structured into functional roles, with Marketing Department, Engineering Department, etc. then conflict is inevitable.

☐ *Attitudes and stereotypes*: when people believe in stereotypes then conflict is inevitable. When we hear people saying, "isn't that typical of a woman manager/marketing manager, etc.", then we know that conflict is implicit. This is the individual version of the in-group/out-group ideas of Sherif and Sherif (1953) who looked at the way that out-groups and in-groups were stereotyped (see Chapter 1).

■ Conflict is inevitable in the presence of scarce resources. It is hard to imagine an organisation that has limitless resources such that everyone in the organisation can have all of the resources that they want for their departments, their sections or their individual organisational responsibility.

■ Organisational conflict may be covert or explicit. Depending on the culture of the organisation it may be very difficult to be aware of internal conflict, or it may be very obvious.

■ Conflict can be functional or dysfunctional. It has long been suggested that whether conflict is functional or dysfunctional depends on the level of conflict. This argument suggests that as the level of conflict raises from zero, as in Figure 6.2, then the organisation benefits, until some optimum level of conflict is reached, and that any further increases in the level of conflict will be dysfunctional and the level of performance of the organisation will decline. This argument suggests that, up to a certain level, conflict produces better decisions, and beyond that point the organisation moves towards a dysfunctional state of conflict more akin to continuous war, where time and resources are consumed in conflict without any reward (Taffinder, 1998). Task conflict tends to improve performance as the conflict within a group leads to the consideration of more ideas, stimulating discussion and the integration of differing views (Jehn, 1997; Pelled et al., 1999).

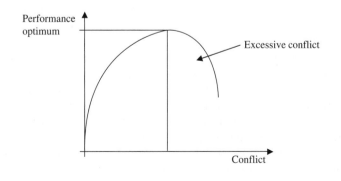

FIGURE 6.2

Performance as a function of conflict

Having looked at the first two elements of organisational politics, interests and conflict, we now move on to discuss power, the resource that resolves the conflicts of interests.

POWER

Power is the medium through which conflicts of interest are ultimately resolved. Power influences who gets what, when and how.

(Morgan, 1997, p. 170)

Power is quite a complex concept, so we will look at a number of the key parts to the concept before going on to discuss the sources of power within organisations, and how power can be used to change organisations or to keep them unchanged. What is being changed – structure, strategy, production methods, etc.? All these can be seen to be about changing culture that is then expressed as changes in strategy, structure, production methods, etc. Another viewpoint is that if you change structure, strategy or production methods, then you will be changing the culture.

Chaos theory and the butterfly effect (Morgan, 1997, pp. 261-265, and pp. 43-44 of this book) can be used to show how a very small change to one element of the system and subsystems that are within an organisation may ultimately result in large and unpredictable changes to the system. This view suggests that the use of power may result in an unpredictable change where there is no prediction of "…who gets what, when and how" (Morgan, 1997, p. 170).

Power involves an ability to get another person, or group of people, to do something that they would not otherwise do. In a way this sounds like power enables the powerful to abuse those with less power, in the sense that abusing people is to get them to do something that they do not wish to do. We might suggest that there is something morally evil about using power to get the result that we want without accepting responsibility for the welfare of others. These problems of political philosophy take us away from the central thrust of this book, and are thus left for the reader to follow if they are so minded (try Googling "political philosophy").

Power is a resource that we do or do not have, or have to varying degrees. Within an organisation an individual may have lots of power or very little, but a central part of the concept is that power is relative. If I have more power than you, then it does not matter whether I have a lot of powers or a little. If I have more power than you, then I can make you do what I want.

But it is not enough to *have* power; we have to *know* that we have power, or *believe* that we have power, if we are to be able to use it to get what we want. If I believe that you have more power than me, and I believe that there is no way that I can gain more power than you, then I will let any conflict of interests be resolved in your favour. This is based on belief, even if the reality (unknown to you) is that you have more power than the other person (Lipman-Blumen in Leavitt et al., 1989).

Now as we understand more about the nature of power, we go on to look at the sources of power, so that we can understand what power we have as political entities in an organisation, and how we can increase our power so that we are more powerful and effective operators to further our interests.

Sources of power

The most important of the early writers on power, as applied to organisational politics, were French and Raven (1960). They argued that there were five main sources of social power, by which they meant the power that can be exercised among people. These sources are:

- Referent

- Coercive

- Reward

- Legitimate

- Expert

Subsequently they added two further sources:

- Informational

- Connectional

Subsequent writings on power have often started from these ideas of French and Raven, so we will look at their 5/7 sources of power before going on to look at some elaborations of them:

- *Referent power:* this is where power essentially flows from the charisma that the person has. People want to follow this leader because they are impressed by them and feel that they are trustworthy and a good person, whose analysis, ideas and interests are right and appropriate and should be followed. This source of power is clearly about the belief that the follower has about the leader.

- *Coercive power:* this is the power to make others conform to interests, other than the ones that they would personally have chosen, because they believe that the person can punish them if they do not conform. The punishment might be about withholding resources, or ending employment, not promoting or even demoting. Again note that we use the word *believe*. Implicit is the belief, or knowledge, that the punishment can be administered, and the potentially punished person has no way of preventing the punishment. The punisher is believed to have the legal right to inflict the punishment.

- *Reward power:* this source of power flows from the *belief* (that word again), that if the follower accepts what the leader wants, then the follower will be rewarded for their conformance, and that the reward is great enough to make it worth giving up the pursuit of their own interests. We might think at this point of Chapter 4 and the expectancy theory of motivation, where the person has to work out whether the expected net present value of the future benefits is greater than zero. That motivation theory required that the person looked at the gains and losses of changing their behaviour.

- *Legitimate power:* this source of power depends on the belief that the leader can legitimately request conformance to their instructions. Ultimately this amounts to the belief that the leader has the legal right to command conformance. Legitimate power clearly overlaps very much onto coercive power. The person who is being overpowered needs to believe that the other person has the legal right to punish them or to withhold rewards. This source of power is not just about the legal framework of the organisation and society. Just imagine what it would be like working with a boss who you had successfully taken to court to prevent some of their actions, or where you had threatened to take them to court when it was clear that you had the law on your side.

■ *Expert power:* this power flows from expertise. If you have the ability, training and experience to analyse better than another person, then they are likely to accept what you say. If you know how the IT system works, and they do not, then they may feel that you can punish them (coercive power) by refusing to help them in using the IT system unless they accept what you want.

We can see that the five sources of power that we have looked at are not free standing, and often there are overlaps. Expertise can be used coercively or in a rewarding way. Coercive power may be useless if the wielder of the power does not have legitimate power as well.

■ *Informational power:* nothing weakens as much as ignorance. We can see in organisations that there are often disputes about access to information. This is often presented as "need to know" - you may only access the information that you need to complete your narrowly defined job. Organisations that are functionally structured into departments of marketing, research and development, production and so on, often ensure that the staff within a department are restricted to know only the information that they need for their department to function. This ensures that the people who have access to all of the information in all of the departments, can almost always win the arguments about strategy and structure. This may mean that it is the CEO who is the most powerful person in the organisation, as they are likely to be the only person with access to all of the information within the organisation - it is difficult to win an argument if you do not have *all* of the necessary information.

■ *Connectional power:* who you know can be a source of power, as long as people believe that you have powerful friends and acquaintances within the organisation.

Case Study 6.1: The power that comes from who you know

Many years ago, the author worked briefly in the Economics Department of Unilever, which, at the time (and may still), dominated the production of margarine in Europe. The author was forecasting the prices of edible oils and fats (the ingredients of margarine). I noticed that even very senior people who I met in the course of my work were very helpful and supportive, and almost deferential. Then I heard that the head of all of Unilever's margarine interests in Europe was a man called Ford Kitchen. My surname is Kitchin. I foolishly pointed out that we were not related, and that our surnames were even spelt differently. The deference disappeared immediately!

Whilst French and Raven started off with five sources of power, Morgan (1997) suggested that we could easily recognise 14 sources of power in organisations. As is to be expected, these are often elaborations and subdivisions of the sources delineated by French and Raven, but we will look at some of the 14 where they are clearly quite distinct and new.

- *Control of scarce resources*: when, earlier in this chapter, we wrote about organisational structures having conflict designed into them as people fought for promotion and scarce resources, we were anticipating the view that if you control scarce resources then this gives you power. You are in a position to use coercive and reward power, as described by French and Raven, by withholding or providing resources.

- *The use of organisational structure, rules, regulations and procedures*: the structure of an organisation determines how much power each post in the structure has; thus, if you have the power to restructure the organisation, whether it is the whole organisation or just a department or section, then you can change who has power and how much. Splitting a department into two separate departments will reduce the power of the existing head of the department. There will be fewer resources under the control of the former head of the department, fewer employees and fewer areas of strategy for which they are responsible. As organisations have both formal structure and cultures, and informal ones that develop as the organisation evolves, changes and responds to the changing environment, we can see that to enforce the formal structure and systems may cause the organisation to become dysfunctional. People may insist that the formal systems must be used, as a powerful lever against others in the organisation – "let me have what I want or I will disrupt the organisation by insisting that every formal rule has to be used." Trade unions used to use such a "work-to-rule", where all work practices were according to the formal rules rather than the informal practices that had developed, to put pressure on the management. (Google "work-to-rule" for a number of good discussions of how a "work-to-rule" can be used as a source of power.) Silvester (2008) shows how the Human Resource (HR) Department in organisations is often a seat of power as they are responsible for setting lots of regulations around organisational structure, appointments, behaviour, rewards and other HR issues.

- *Control of the decision process*: if you have power over what decisions are made and how they are made, then you have lot of power. The decision-making structure of an organisation powerfully influences decision making. An organisation can be any of the following:

  - *Technocracy*: where science and rationality determine the best decision. We are unlikely to ever find this type of organisation, if only because individual behaviour in organisations is rarely rational.

  - *Autocracy*: where a single person or a few people at the top of the organisation make all of the decisions.

  - *Democracy*: where every person in the organisation has an equal vote when decisions are made, and the decisions are accepted if the majority vote for them.

☐ *Consensus*: where for a decision to be made, everyone has to agree – the vote has to be unanimous. This process of decision making clearly may take a very long time, and that is unhelpful when a speedy decision is required. There are a number of modified consensus rules, the strongest of which is that everyone agrees with the proposal except the dissenters, who agree not to resist the decision and to co-operate in its implementation.

☐ *Bureaucracy*: where rules and regulations are used to make decisions. This results in an organisation that is rather machine-like, but does mean that the rules still have to be made to cover all decisions, and there have to be decisions made about these rules, giving the need for political processes.

If you can control which of the above decision-making processes are used, then you can have a certain amount of political power.

There are other ways that you can exercise power over decision making. If you can control the agenda of the decision-making group, then you can influence the outcome. Two examples of this control are:

☐ If you can control what items are on the agenda, then you can have power. If you do not allow a decision proposal to appear on the agenda of the decision-making body, then you can ensure that a decision is not made on that proposal.

☐ If you can control the order of the agenda, then you can have power. If you do not want a decision made about a matter, then you can have that proposal put at the end of the agenda, so that the meeting runs out of time and has to end before the proposal can be discussed.

A full discussion of many of the complexities of using agendas and agenda building, as part of a political process can be found in Dutton (1988).

If a decision is to be based on a report or enquiry, then the decisions that result can be greatly influenced by the terms under which the enquiry is set up. In effect, the decision agenda is set at that point in time. In 1963, there was a government report, the Beeching Report, published. The enquiry had been set up to look at making the UK railways profitable. If the terms had been to look at an integrated transport system, then it seems certain that the UK railway network in the twenty-first century would have been very different than the actual twenty-first century railway network that resulted from the implementation of the Beeching Report.

■ *Gatekeepers*: gatekeepers are people who control the flow of information between people and parts of an organisation and can be liaison roles. Gatekeepers may control the flow of information and people to those higher up in the organisation. The author had an Executive MBA student some years ago, who was the CEO of a large firm that made glass light bulbs for the whole of the UK market. This CEO said that the time that he had felt most powerful in the organisation was when he was the Personal Assistant (PA) to the CEO, and not when he was the CEO. In the role of PA he was able to control the flow of information to and from the CEO, and control who actually got to meet with the CEO (source: personal discussion). A similar role for Adolf Hitler was played by Martin Boorman (Speer, 1970).

■ *Control of counter organisations*: by counter organisations we mean those stake-holders who are in conflict with the central organisation. These can be trade unions, or any group that represents opposing stakeholders. In the UK, the ecology group GreenPeace is a good example of a counter organisation. In the USA, in 1965, Ralph Nader published a book called Unsafe at Any Speed (Nader, 1965). Almost single-handedly Nader took on the USA automobile industry and eventually forced it to stop designing unsafe cars. This was a powerful example of a counter organisation.

■ *Symbolism*: symbolism is a complex source of power. We may ask, "What is the function of big cars, large offices, imposing office furniture and fittings?" for the senior and powerful people in an organisation. The answer is that they symbolise power, and make those with less imposing cars and offices feel less powerful. In Hitler's Chancellery, visitors to Hitler had to walk through a large room where the floor was kept very highly polished and sloped very gently to one side (although not visible to the visitor's eye) so that the visitor arrived feeling physi-cally insecure, disconcerted and less powerful. The room was deliberately designed by Hitler's architect, Albert Speer, to have this effect (Speer, 1970).

Part of the reason for delineating so many sources of power is to encourage the readers to reflect on how they can increase their power, or alternatively, how they can reduce the power of their organisational opponents – how the readers' relative power can be increased.

The use of power

In Chapter 2, we looked at a number of strategies for changing organisational culture. Now that we have discussed the nature of political processes in organisations, the reader might benefit from going back to Chapter 2, Organisational culture, and apply the lessons of this chapter about political processes.

Whether you go back Chapter 2, or not, we are going to look at a number of ways that political processes can be used to bring about organisational change.

An early way of looking at changing organisations was discussed by Kurt Lewin, within the framework of his Force Field model (Lewin, 1951).

This approach has been very seminal. Lewin argued that for there to be change, the total power of the forces *for* change had to be greater than the total power of the forces *against* change (or resisting change). Any decision is going to result in change, and there are usually people who gain from the change and people who will lose from the change. It is enough for people to *believe* that they will be gainers and losers. If we do a stake-holder analysis, we can examine which of the organisational stakeholders will gain and which will lose from the decision. The theory argues that the summation of the power of the gaining stakeholders is set against the summation of the losing stakeholders' power. Even if all the potential gainers form a coalition to push for change, it does not follow that they will all gain in the same way, each may be fulfilling their own different individual interests.

Earlier in this chapter, we suggested that what mattered was the relative power of the opposing coalitions, but Lewin makes a crucial extra prediction, namely, the harder the coalitions for change push for change, the greater will be the resistance to change, so instead of pushing more and more powerfully for change, the change agents are better advised to try and reduce the resistance to change, and change the relative power of the coalitions in this way.

In Figure 6.3 the stakeholders who will benefit from the changes that will flow from a decision are the shareholders, the company directors and the suppliers of parts, services and resources. The stakeholders who are opposed to the decision/change are the bankers, the workforce and the environmental counter organisation, GreenPeace. The direction and length of the arrows indicate the direction of change (for or against the decision and change) and the amount of power available to the stakeholders.

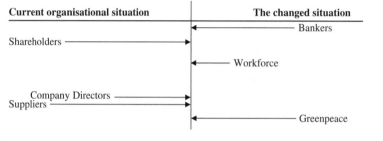

FIGURE 6.3

Lewin's Force–Field analysis

To get the decision made and the change accepted and implemented, the gaining stakeholders need to reduce the power with which the opponents are resisting. The stakeholders who want the change need to examine how the resistance of the resisting stakeholders can be reduced to enable the decision to be made and the change implemented. For example, we might know that the workforce believes that if the decision is made, and the changes are implemented, then there will be redundancies, with job loses for the workforce. A way of weakening their resistance is to give an undertaking that there will be no compulsory redundancies.

Johnson and Scholes (1994) elaborated the Force-Field analysis by suggesting that what mattered was not just the potential power of the stakeholders, but also their degree of interest in the proposal. If a stakeholder has a lot of power but does not feel strongly about the proposal then they will choose not to have much influence on the decision, and their effective political power will be small.

This approach can be expressed as an equation:

$$\text{Effective political power} = \text{power} \times \text{interest}$$

The interest can be positive or negative and thus the effective power can be positive or negative, for the proposal or against the proposal. If we represented this as a diagram, then the effective power of a stakeholder is the area represented by power times interest. The proposal will succeed or fail depending on whether the total positive effective political power is greater or less than the total negative effective political power.

If you are trying to get a proposal accepted, then you need the maximum positive effective political power when it is summed for all of the stakeholders who support the proposal, and you need the minimum negative effective political power when it is summed for all of the stakeholders who are against the proposal. The implication is that you try to increase the power and/or interest of the stakeholders supporting the proposal, and minimize the power and/or interest of those stakeholders opposing the proposal. The proposers need to ask themselves how they can change the levels of interest and power of the stakeholders.

Political games

There are many "games" that people play to get the result that they want in the political process. Two examples are "log-rolling" and "pork-barrelling", which can be seen being used in legislative bodies, but they can clearly be used within commercial organisations. These two tactics are described by Johnson (www.auburn.edu/~johnspm/gloss/logrolling):

> *"Log-rolling: A practice common in the US Congress and in many other legislative assemblies in which two (or more) legislators agree for each to trade his vote on one bill he cares little about in exchange for the other's vote on a bill that is personally much more important to him."*

Clearly log-rolling can be used in any decision-making body, including those committees and working parties that make decisions in organisations.

and,

> *"Pork-barrel legislation: Appropriations of public funds by Congress (or other legislative assemblies) for projects that do not serve the interests of any large portion of the country's citizenry but are nevertheless vigorously promoted by a small group of legislators because they will pump outside taxpayers' money and resources into the local districts these legislators represent. Successful promotion of such pork-barrel legislation (often through skillful log-rolling) is very likely to get the legislator re-elected by his constituents."*

> *Pork-barrelling is about someone seeking to win the support of their subordinates by working for a proposal that will benefit their subordinates. This is a way of increasing personal power within the organisation by getting the support of subordinates.*

Handy (1987) discusses a long list of political "games" that are not discussed here, but are easily available to the reader in Charles Handy's popular book "Understanding Organisations". In the fifteenth century, Niccolo Machiavelli produced what is perhaps the definitive account of how to win at politics, in his book "The Prince". Machiavelli (1961) covered every way of winning in politics from the gentle to the brutal and vicious. Modern readers of "The Prince" may be shocked by some of Machiavelli's writing, but he was just interested in winning, whatever you needed to do.

RESISTANCE TO CHANGE

In this section we are going to look at why people resist change in organisations, and, by implication, what the advocates of change need to do to ensure that appropriate decisions about change are made and successfully implemented.

As we discussed earlier in this chapter, groups and individuals within organisations have their own interests that they try and satisfy. These interests may be the same for everyone in the organisation (a unitary organisation), but this is very unlikely.

We need to examine in detail why people resist the proposals put forward by others in their organisation. There are a number of main reasons, which we will list and then discuss in more detail within the organisational politics framework:

■ Differing interests (or values);

■ Different theoretical analysis about how to reach shared interests;

■ Different information held by the stakeholders in the decision situation;

■ Low tolerance for change;

■ Stakeholders may resist changes that they perceive as harming the organisation; and

■ Stakeholders may not accept or trust the reasons that are given for the change.

Differing interests: it is obvious that if the interests of the stakeholders in a decision situation differ, there will be conflict. One solution can be to resort to power to resolve the conflict. Another solution is the one discussed under Lewin's Force–Field and Johnson and Scholes' approaches, where the resistance of the resistors to the proposal is lessened through reducing their interests, reducing their power or by finding something that can be offered to them to reduce their resistance (see log-rolling, earlier in this chapter).

The differences in value might be that one stakeholder's main priority is to maintain the level of employment in the organisation, whilst for another stakeholder the important priority is to maintain income levels.

Differing theoretical analysis: understanding and predicting the consequences of any change in an organisation requires a theoretical model of how organisations work. There are no generally agreed theoretical models of organisations that everyone can agree are correct. Everyone tends to have their own theory of organisations, so there is likely to be disagreement about the consequences of any change, or the way to cause a change. Some of these theories will have been developed in the academic literature, but others will be the way that individuals have come to make sense of what they observe, based on what they have read and have experienced. These "personal" theories are called implicit theories. We have already seen that Lewin believed that resolving conflict by the exertion of overwhelming power simply results in increasing resistance. If overwhelming power is used to resolve the conflict, then the "losers" may well remember what happened and look for a future opportunity for revenge. When we think in terms of organisational culture, and the critical perspective, then we may want to ask what the "losers" will have learnt by being overwhelmed. The lessons will become part of the organisational culture, and that change in culture may not be in the long-term interests of the stakeholders who used their overwhelming power.

So, if using overwhelming power may not be a good solution to conflict, what can be done when the conflict is based in differing theoretical models? A humble approach by the proposers that says "We think we are right, and this is how we arrived at our proposal" may help by educating the stakeholders who are resisting. An additional action that may be of further assistance is to ask the resistors to explain their thinking and their theoretical model. These discussions about the theoretical models may lead to learning, or an even better model that is agreed by all. An organisational culture where the senior and powerful people assume that they have nothing to learn from their subordinates is likely to struggle with a lot of conflicts, with all the costs that conflicts bring.

Differing information: in putting forward a proposal for a decision, the inputs are not only interests and theories, but also information. There may be conflicts that have to be resolved, even when interests and theories are the same, because the information that is used differs among the stakeholders. What each stakeholder knows about the organisation is likely to differ between one stakeholder and another. In a motor assembly plant, the beliefs, attitudes and experiences of the assembly-line workers are likely to be very different that those of their managers, even if those managers used to be assembly-line workers. As organisations change their processes, and culture is constantly evolving and changing, the knowledge of the assembly-line managers is likely to become increasingly out of date – they used to know what it was like to be an assembly-line worker, but with the passage of time this knowledge becomes outdated. The solution to this problem of differing knowledge bases is to share the knowledge. Again, it is dangerous for senior and powerful stakeholders to assume that they have all the knowledge that they need in order to make a good decision.

Low tolerance for change: change in an organisation can have a major impact on how people do their jobs, what jobs they have to do, what skills they have to exercise to do their job and what power, status and kudos they have. Many people may not like change, and they may not like the uncertainty that comes with change (remember in Chapter 3 we discussed how the level of uncertainty avoidance differed not only between individuals, but also between nations). The consequence is that change may be resisted just because it is change. Even if we know what the change will mean, we may resist, because we don't want to change. In addition, there is often uncertainty around the consequences of change, and thus the *beliefs* that people have about what change will mean may also cause them to resist. In Chapter 2, we presented two mini cases of the response of people to change, and you might benefit by re-reading these cases of how some machinists chose to retire or resign rather than learn how to use computer controlled machines, and how, in another organisation, process workers were prepared to risk being sacked rather than to sign up to a compulsory educational course (even though the course was to be of their own choosing).

Resisting change that harms the organisation: people will resist change that harms an organisation that they care about. They may care because the organisation looks after their interests or because they have developed a sense of belonging, of being a part of the organisation. This alternative way of thinking about conflict, as a result of believing that the proposers of change do not understand the consequences of their proposed change, suggests that people can develop a sense of "ownership" of the organisation, even a sense of pride in the organisation of which they are a member.

Lack of trust: here the opposing stakeholders do not trust the proposers of change. They may not trust that the proposers have the appropriate theories and information to get the analysis correct, or they may not trust the motives of the proposers. A frequent example would be where there is a proposal to merge two organisations so that "…the joint organisation will be more competitive." Often the opponents will believe that what the proposal actually means is that duplication will be removed from the merged organisation to cut costs, and this will lead to unemployment.

Conclusions from resistance to change

The previous discussion on resistance draws heavily on the work of Kotter and Schlesinger (1989) and Nevis (1987). Perhaps the most important idea is that stakeholders have many reasons to resist change in addition to the difference of interests emphasised in the treatment of organisational politics in the early part of this chapter. Nevis (1987) argues that organisation should not try and use power to overwhelm resistance to change, but should use the resistance to learn more about the organisation, its staff and stakeholders, and thus make fewer errors flowing from poor theory and analysis and ignorance about the organisation, to its staff and the culture of the organisation.

THE FUNCTIONALITY OF ORGANISATIONAL POLITICS

Many people believe that organisational politics is a "bad thing", and should be discouraged. Huff (1988) argues that so long as the political process operates within a functional framework, then the political process has a number of positive advantages to offer the organisations. These advantages will not occur in organisations without a political process. Not least among these advantages is that the political process will reduce the danger of Group Think (see Chapter 1).

Huff (1988) makes five assertions:

- "Organisational politics provides an arena for identifying and assessing new strategic alternatives which draws upon the varied experiences of organisation members." (p. 80). A fund of ideas is tapped by the political process. This idea complements the idea of Nevis (1987), where he argues that resistance should be welcomed and embraced by the proposers of change, as a source of ideas and analysis and information from the people in the organisation who are not part of the change planning, but who are impacted, and who are repositories of information, experience and insight. Here Huff writes not of resistance as a response to proposals, but of politics as a source of proposals.

- "Politics challenges organisation leaders to clarify and modify their thinking about strategic issues. In general, politics is more effective at this task than formal planning systems." (p. 80). Ideas are tested and improved through political argument. In the process of argument, the weak points of a proposal are highlighted and can be amended or abandoned, and strong proposals can be confirmed as such and can be shared and understood by all of the stakeholders, thus making implementation easier.

- "Organisation politics identifies the individual and group commitments necessary for designing and implementing new strategy." (p. 80). In order to design and implement change, the initiators need to build support for the proposals and they need to know why individuals and groups are opposing the changes. The political processes allow these individuals and groups to be identified. This idea is comparable to the stakeholder analysis used by Johnson and Scholes (1994) when they looked at the management of change.

- "Political diversity facilitates the succession of individual leaders and promotes adaptation in the practices and beliefs which contribute to organisational culture."

(p. 80). Politics helps the process of changing leaders, strategy and culture. Existing leaders often are attached to current strategy and culture, which they helped to develop, and the development of new strategies and culture may require a change of leadership that will emerge from political conflict between the existing leadership and their potential successors.

- "While organisation politics can be disruptive, routine decision cycles can channel potentially disrupting differences of opinion into manageable cycles of debate." (p. 80). An anxiety that many people have about the existence of organisational politics is that decisions will never be made, as a result of endless political struggles. Agreement between stakeholders over a timetable for decision making can prevent this endless political warfare. Warfare would result in the organisation being unable to evolve and change and would result in the organisation becoming an increasingly poor fit in the evolving external environment, with the consequence that the organisation would fail or become bankrupt.

A slightly different and additional point about the functionality of politics is made by Kirk and Broussine (2000) (in Silvester, 2008), when they argue that "…political activity can create consensus and shape shared beliefs between different groups". This is making the point that politics has a role in shaping the culture of an organisation through the interactions of people within the political process.

CONCLUSIONS

Part of the intent of this chapter was to make the case that politics is inevitable in organisations, and that because this is so, it is advisable for people within organisations to understand why politics exist and how political processes work. If you understand political processes then you have more power than if you do not, it is less likely that you will be abused and more likely that you will get what you want from the organisation within which you are an employee or for which you are an external stakeholder.

Many people expect that organisations are, or should be, rational optimisers. The discussion of organisational political processes makes clear some of the reasons why organisations may not appear to be logical and rational optimisers. Because organisations can be understood as the summation of all the internal and external stakeholders, and "…political activity as a constant process of negotiating shared organizational realities." (Silvester, 2008, p. 110) there are certain to be conflicts which will have to be resolved by political processes.

REFERENCES

Ammeter, A.P., Douglas, C., Gardner, W.L., Hochwarter, W.A., Ferris, G.R., 2002. Towards a political theory of leadership. The Leadership Quarterly 13, 751–796.

Andrews, P.H., Baird, J.E., 2000. In: Communication for Business and the Professions, seventh ed. McGraw Hill, New York, NY, pp. 371–373.

Dutton, J., 1988. Understanding strategic agenda building and its implications for managing change. In: Pondy, L.R., Boland, R.J., Thomas, H. (Eds.), Managing Ambiguity and Change. John Wiley & Sons.

Fandt, P.M., Ferris, G.R., 1990. The management of information and impressions: when employees behave opportunistically. Organizational Behaviour and Human Decision Processes 45, 140–158.

French Jr., J.P.R., Raven, B., 1960. The bases of social power. In: Cartwright, D., Zander, A. (Eds.), Group Dynamics. Harper and Row, pp. 607–623.

Handy, C.W., 1987. In: Understanding Organizations, third ed. Penguin Business.

Huff, A.S., 1988. Politics and argument as a means of coping with ambiguity and change. In: Pondy, L.R., Boland Jr., R.J., Thomas, H. (Eds.), Managing Ambiguity and Change. John Wiley & Sons.

Jehn, K.A., 1997. Qualitative analysis of conflict types and dimensions in organizational groups. Administrative Science Quarterly 42 (3).

Johnson, G.F., Scholes, K., 1994. Exploring Corporate Strategy. Prentice-Hall International.

Kirk, P., Broussine, M., 2000. The politics of facilitation. Journal of Workplace Learning 12 (1), 13–22.

Kotter, J.P., Schlesinger, L.A., 1989. Choosing strategies for change. In: Leavitt, H.J., Pondy, L.R., Boje, D.M. (Eds.), Readings in Managerial Psychology, fourth ed. University of Chicago Press.

Lipman-Blumen, J., 1989. Why the powerless do not revolt. In: Leavitt, H.J., Boje, D.M., Pondy, L.R. (Eds.), Readings in Managerial Psychology, fourth ed. University of Chicago Press.

Lewin, K., 1951. In: Cartwright, D. (Ed.), Field Theory in Social Science; selected theoretical papers. Harper & Row.

Machiavelli, P., 1961. The Prince. Penguin Classics.

Morgan, G., 1997. Images of Organization. Sage.

Nader, R., 1965. Unsafe at Any Speed: The Designed-in Dangers Of The American Automobile. Grossman Publishers, LC.

Nevis, E.C., 1987. Organisational Consulting. Gardner Press.

Pelled, L.H., Eisenhardt, K.M., Xin, K.R., 1999. Exploring the black box: an analysis of work group diversity, conflict and performance. Administrative Science Quarterly 44 (1).

Sherif, M., Sherif, C.W., 1953. Groups in Harmony and Tension: An Integration of Studies on Intergroup Relations. Octagon Books.

Silvester, J., 2008. The good, the bad and the ugly: politics and politicians at work. International Review of Industrial and Organisational Psychology 23.

Speer, A., 1970. Inside the Third Reich. Simon & Schuster Inc., Macmillan, New York, NY.

Taffinder, P., 1998. Conflict is not always a bad thing, Personnel Today. http://www.auburn.edu/~johnspm/gloss/logrolling.

Leadership

7

Leadership is a topic which has been discussed for almost as long as we have written literature, and indeed Burke (2006) reported that by 2006, he could find over 15,000 articles and books on leadership. He also noted that $50 thousand million a year is spent on the development of leaders. However, this level of interest is not, in itself, a reason to include a chapter on the topic in this book. It has also been a topic in almost every book on organisational behaviour that has ever been written, but that is also a poor reason to include a chapter in this book. So why have we included a chapter for your delectation?

In all organisations, teams and groups, it seems that leaders emerge and have an important role in the success or failure of the organisation, group or team, and as you are going to be working in organisations, you will be in a more powerful position if you know something about leadership behaviour and the emergence of leaders. You may remember that in Chapter 1 we discussed the work of Belbin (1981), who examined why some teams won and others lost in competitive interactive decision-making games. His conclusion, as you may remember, was that winning teams needed a number of roles, and that all of these roles had to be filled if the team was to be sure of success. One of the roles that was necessary was that of Chair, which we may well think of as being the leadership role. Thus we may conclude that at least *teams* need a leader if they have to succeed. So, if teams need leaders, then perhaps we should look at Belbin's description of what qualities a Chair needs in order to lead a successful team. Briefly, he described the typical features as "calm, self-confident and controlled"; the positive qualities as "A capacity for treating and welcoming all potential contributions on their merits and without prejudice. A strong sense of objectives"; and allowable weaknesses as "No more than ordinary in terms of intellect or creative ability" (Belbin, 1981, p. 78). We can say that we need a chapter on leadership because Belbin suggests that teams need leaders if they are to succeed.

Another reason to study leadership is that many studies of group behaviour show that a leader will emerge, even in groups that are set up as leaderless groups (Brown, 2000). If we are to understand what leaders contribute and why they seem to be necessary, then we may feel that we need to be able to recognise potential good leaders so that we can appoint them to this important role, and so that we can recognise poor leaders so that we can beneficially remove them. It is also important that we do not appoint to leadership positions people who are good managers but who do not have the potential to be good-enough leaders. As you can see, we are assuming that managers and leaders are not the same. We will discuss this distinction shortly. We also have problems that revolve around the question of whether leaders

Case Study 7.1: Leadership by default

Many years ago when the author was a very young academic, I was invited to attend a major international conference that was to take place over 14 days. The conference was about foreign aid for developing countries. A number of task groups were set up, each with about eight members, and each with an appointed Chairperson and a Rapporteur. The Rapporteur's job was to keep a written record of the group's discussion and conclusions. I was a Rapporteur. The Chairman of my group was a very distinguished professor of economics who was also, at that time, the Minister of Finance of his country. The Chairman of my group was very brilliant, but his command of English left something to be desired, making it difficult for him to control the group and get the best out of the equally distinguished participants. Gradually, over the fortnight, I adopted the role of Chairperson. It was only towards the end of the fortnight that I realised that I had taken over as Chairman. My, out of awareness, motive was that I could not bear to see the group struggling because of the Chair's language difficulties. When I realised what I had done, I apologised and was told not to worry, as I had been doing a better job of chairing than he had been able to!

are born or made. If they are not born, then we may need to learn how to train people to be better leaders.

Groups usually need leadership, and leadership will normally emerge if no one is appointed as Chair, and sometimes there may be a power struggle if a poor leader has been appointed.

As with all organisational behaviour topics, the literature has a history of ideas and theories that have developed through time. It could be argued that we should only examine the current state of theory about leadership, but that would be to run the danger of readers making the same mistakes as the early writers on this subject, as a result of ignorance. To help avoid making old errors, we will look through the development of leadership theories, starting with the *great man* theories of leadership, but only after defining what we mean by leaders and leadership.

DEFINING LEADERS AND LEADERSHIP

An obvious place to start this discussion is with the word leader. Leader implies that there must be followers. There cannot be a leader if they do not lead their followers. *Leader* also implies the person who chooses the route, although that does not necessarily mean that they choose the destination or the target. *Follower* seems to imply that not only you don't lead, but you also don't choose the destination, the target or the route.

John Bray of FORUM Consulting of Boston, in the late 1980s, used to distinguish between leaders and managers in the following way:

■ Leaders manage change; and

■ Managers manage stability.

The implication seems to be that a leaderless organisation will be stable and unchanging, and that managers are not concerned with change, evolution or revolution. These are the managers that we will write about when we discuss bureaucracies in Chapter 8. John Bray's distinction comes from a FORUM video in the late 1980s, when the author was working as an associate consultant for FORUM.

Bray's view is supported by Schein (1992, p. 5), who says "If one wishes to distinguish leadership from management or administration, one can argue that leaders create and change cultures, whilst managers and administrators live within them."

Brown (2000) defines leadership and leaders as:

- "…those occupying high-status positions – otherwise known as leaders – and their interactions with the rest of the group – the leadership process." (p. 91).

- "…they have a tendency to initiate ideas and activities…" (p. 91).

- "…they have some means of influencing others to change their behaviour." (p. 91).

- "…what really characterises leaders is that they can influence others in the group more than they themselves are influenced." (p. 91).

The last of Brown's defining statements implies that leaders have more power than followers, so that they are influenced less than they influence. In Chapter 6, we looked at sources of power. French and Raven suggested that there were five sources of power that leaders had in greater amounts than their followers. The ones we might expect to be most important in terms of leadership might be legitimate power and referent or charismatic power, but the other sources of power, reward, expert, informational and connectional power can all be seen to help leaders have more influence.

Schein (1992, p. 5) suggests that "…the only thing of real importance that leaders do is to create and manage culture and that the unique talent of leaders is their ability to understand work with culture."

These definitions by Bray, Schein and Brown seem to capture the essence of many writers' definitions, and we will look no further to define leadership.

GREAT MAN OR TRAIT THEORIES

These theories were amongst the first theories on leadership and seem to have an abiding attraction; we find that much recent research on leadership has returned to Trait Theory. Essentially, they say that there are some characteristics that leaders need to have, that mark them out as special and destined to lead. The theories imply that these characteristics are either genetically determined, or as a result of upbringing and early socialisation. Avollo et al. (2009, p. 331) recently reported that "Preliminary leadership research evidence using a behavioural genetics approach suggests that approximately 30% of the variation in leadership style and emergence into leadership roles is accounted for by genetic factors, while the remaining variation is attributed to nonshared environmental influences, such as individuals being exposed to different role models and early opportunities for leadership development" (Arvey et al., 2006, 2007; Llies et al., 2004).

The obvious way to test the Trait Theory that leaders share common characteristics (traits) is to look at the personal characteristics of leaders who are generally agreed to be good or even great leaders; what personality and physical characteristics or traits they all share. The trouble with this approach is that the list of characteristics grows longer and longer and there always seem to be exceptions.

It has been noted that in USA presidential elections, the tallest candidate almost always seems to win (even in the presidential election of 2009), and yet Gandhi, who everyone agrees was a great leader, was physically a very little man.

The easy assumption that we all know what makes for a good leader offers us little help in promoting or choosing people for leadership. Stogdill (1974) reviewed a large number of investigations of leadership traits and found very few traits that correlated with successful leadership. He concluded that there was some evidence to support the view that leaders had the following traits: they were more intelligent, sociable and achievement orientated, adaptable to situations, alert to social environment, ambitious, assertive, co-operative, decisive, dependable, dominant (desire to influence others), energetic (high-activity level), persistent, willing to assume responsibility, tolerant of stress and more self-confident than their followers. He also concluded that there was evidence to support the view that leaders also tended to have the following skills: they were conceptually skilled, creative, diplomatic and tactful, able speakers, knowledgeable about group tasks, organisational ability, persuasiveness and social skills.

McCall and Lombardo (1983) identified four primary traits by which leaders could succeed or fail:

- *Emotional stability and composure*: calm, confident and predictable, especially in difficult times.

- *Admitting error*: owning up to mistakes, and not putting energy into concealing errors. Recent research on narcissistic leaders has cast grave doubt on this idea, suggesting that for narcissistic leaders, errors are always the fault of someone else. Recent research suggests that many, if not most, leaders are narcissistic. The whole topic of leaders' personalities will be discussed later in the chapter, starting on page 132.

- *Good interpersonal skills*: able to persuade without using negative or coercive tactics.

- *Intellectual breadth*: having a good general understanding rather than a narrow area of expertise.

If we make a comparison between leadership and motivation theories, then the trait theories can be compared with content theories of motivation, as they ask *what*, "What are good leaders?" If we think of motivational process theories then we are looking for theories about what leaders *do*. Whilst writers struggled to develop successful trait theories, other researchers were developing these process theories that looked at the behaviour of successful leaders – what leaders do.

LEADERS AS MOTIVATORS

As we think of what leaders *do*, as opposed to what they *are* (Trait Theory), it is clear that one of the things that leaders need to do is to motivate their staff to contribute as fully as is possible to the success and effectiveness of the organisation. When discussing leaders, we suggested that leaders manage change; they get employees to change what they do and how they do it – thus leaders need to motivate their staff to change.

An element of what motivates staff is the form that the organisational culture takes. If the culture is one where people feel themselves to be a part of the organisation, and that there is a reward that comes to them if they work hard and creatively, then they will be motivated.

An important role of leaders is to manage employee motivation. If we reread Chapter 4, we see theories that suggest a number of actions that leaders need to enact in order to have a motivated work force. We will list the theories that we covered, and look at what they suggested that leaders need to provide, or what behaviours they need to enact, in order to motivate their employees:

- *Maslow*: only an unsatisfied need can motivate. The needs are physiological, security, social, ego and self-actualisation. The last two of these needs seem to imply that leaders need to provide empowerment to their staff, where staff can feel fulfilled and as though they are contributing. This sounds like Theory Y, or a participative, democratic and person-centred style of leadership. (See the Behavioural Theories of Leadership section of this chapter for definitions of these terms.) The first three needs could be Theory X or Y or any style of leadership. A task-centred bureaucracy could also meet the last two needs through promotion, with its implied leadership style of autocracy.

- *Alderfer's ERG*: this was motivation through allowing people to meet Existence, Relationship and Growth needs. The comparison with Maslow is clear and does not need repeating.

- *Herzberg*: Herzberg distinguished between hygiene and motivating factors. His motivating factors were responsibility, advancement, growth, achievement and recognition. Again, these factors sound like characteristics of organisations led by Theory Y, participative, democratic and employee-centred style leaders, rather than autocratic task-centred leaders.

- *McClelland*: McClelland thought that we learn needs as we grow up, and that the principal ones that motivate are the needs for power, achievement and affiliation. Again, these needs are likely to be met by leaders whose style is Theory Y, participative, employee-centred and democratic. We could argue that a bureaucracy offers the scope for motivating staff through promotion that reflects power and achievement. Later in this chapter we will see that people with narcissistic personalities have a great need for power and achievement, but not affiliation.

- *Expectancy Theory*: to motivate in this way, possible rewards have to be desired and clearly defined, and people need to know the probability that motivated behaviour will result in the fulfilling of needs. This sounds to be a task-orientated style of leadership and a mechanistic or bureaucratic style of organisation, with all that implies.

- *Equity Theory*: this reminds us of Fayol's principle of equity (Chapter 8) where employees are aware of fairness within the organisation. This sounds rather like a bureaucracy where rules and conditions are clearly set out, are enacted and there is an autocratic, task-orientated style of leadership. If there is no equity, then employees may be dissatisfied in the way that Herzberg wrote of dissatisfiers.

■ *Goal setting*: this theory has been used to explain how both individuals and groups can be motivated. The crucial element of this theory is the research finding that employees are most effectively motivated if the goals are set participatively; that the next best is when goals are autocratically imposed on employees; and the poorest is when the employees are simply told to "do your best", as is likely to be the case with laissez-faire leadership. (See the next section of this chapter for a definition of laissez-faire.) The leadership implications of this research are obvious.

We can conclude that Motivation Theory suggests that the most appropriate leadership style in order to ensure the most motivated workforce is a participative style, unless the organisation is most appropriately mechanistic and/or bureaucratic in structure. The implication is that the organisational structure partially determines the style of leadership that is most appropriate.

BEHAVIOURAL THEORIES OF LEADERSHIP
Theories X and Y

We have previously mentioned Macgregor's' Theories X and Y in Chapter 4, and there is an Appendix that sets it out fully. McGregor (1960) suggested that leaders and managers tend to hold one of two extreme beliefs about the people who work in their organisation: people are either lazy and unmotivated, and would do as little work as possible (Theory X), or they enjoy work and will be creative and hard working (Theory Y). Managers and leaders who held a Theory X set of beliefs would manage and lead staff in a distrusting way, where staff were constantly monitored and would be paid by results. That clearly is a leadership style. The alternative leadership style was a result of holding Theory Y beliefs, where staff would be empowered, and authority and responsibility would be devolved or delegated to them. The beliefs of leaders, about their employees, are clearly predicted by McGregor to lead to different leadership styles.

Lipitt and White (1943)

These researchers set up three groups of young schoolboys engaged in after-school activities, each with an imposed adult leader. One group had a leader who was instructed to behave in an autocratic manner, giving orders and remaining generally aloof. The second group had a democratic or participative-styled leader, who allowed the children to discuss decisions and helped them to be involved in making decisions. The third group had a laissez-faire style leader who left the group to their own devices and was largely absent and hands off. The groups ran for 7 weeks, after which they started again with a different leader, who adopted one of the two different leadership styles that the group had not experienced in the first 7 weeks. Some clear results emerged. The democratic leaders were the most popular and their groups tended to be the most friendly, group-orientated, were quite productive and continued to work when the leader was absent. The groups with autocratic leaders were more aggressive, more dependent on the leader and members were self-centred compared with the group-orientated members in the democratic groups. The autocratic-led groups were the most productive of the three groups when the leader was present, but tended to stop working in the leader's absence. The laissez-faire led groups played more than the other groups and tended to work harder and better when the leader was absent.

This research produces seemingly clear conclusions, but we need to bear in mind that it was done a long time ago, not with adults, and in the USA. Having sounded that cautionary note, the author can report that as an associate consultant with FORUM of Boston, I have rerun the exercise, over a period of only a few hours, with adult organisational leaders, and the results of Lipitt and White (1943) were confirmed. I have also run the exercise with innumerable groups of Business Studies undergraduates, and again the results were confirmed. An interesting implication of this experiment, to which we shall return later in this chapter, is that leaders can be trained and encouraged to successfully adopt different styles of leadership. The underlying assumption of the FORUM Leadership courses that the author co-facilitated in the late 1980s was that people can chose which leadership style to adopt.

The Universities of Ohio and Michigan studies

At about the same time as Lippitt and White were working, researchers at the Universities of Ohio and Michigan were both looking at the behaviour of leaders in successful organisa-tions (Ohio: Stogdill, 1950, and Michigan: Katz et al., 1950). They came to the conclusion that there were two basic types of leadership behaviours in successful organisations. Leaders of successful organisations were found to be either Consideration-based or Structure-based (Ohio) or Employee-centred or Production-centred (Michigan). Essentially, consideration-based and employee-centred meant the same thing: the leaders were con-cerned with being employee-centred, working with employees in a mutual and interactive way, interested in team building and a participative style of leadership. We might recognise this style of leadership as appropriate to the organic organisational structures that we have written about in Chapter 8. Structure or production-centred leaders were much more involved with defining roles and structures, tasks and procedures and supervising rather than being participative. This leadership style is likely to be found in the mechanistic workings of bureaucratic organisational structures of Chapter 8. We may also reflect that these leadership styles run parallel with Theories X and Y, with Y being the consideration/employee-centred styles and Theory X being the structure/production-centred styles.

Both studies came to the conclusion that the most successful organisations had leaders who scored highly on both of the leadership styles, leaders who enacted both consideration/employee-centred *and* structure/production-centred behaviours.

The conclusions of the two studies suggested that what was necessary for recruiting and selecting (or internally promoting) leaders, was that lists of characteristics or behaviours of the two leadership styles should be developed from the research findings, so that there was a checklist of behaviours that could be used to evaluate potential leaders.

This approach sounds to be different from the Trait Theory in that it was not about inborn traits (or personality) but was about behaviours – what good leaders do. This distinction again raises the question as to whether possible behaviours and leadership styles can be learnt or taught, or does a person's personality determine and/or limit their possible leadership behaviours? Whatever the answer to this question, the two studies seem to be useful in providing a description of desirable behaviours whether learnt or inherent. Later in this chapter, (page 132) we will look at personality and leadership styles and whether a person's personality means that they can only adopt a limited range of leadership styles. At the extreme, can people with a person-centred leadership style also adopt a task-centred style, or will their personality limit their possible leadership style?

A further question that arises out of the Ohio and Michigan studies is why some organisations are successful with person-centred leadership style and others with a task-centred style; can an organisation succeed with either style, so long as it is enacted to a high standard? This question led researchers on to the next development in the search for successful leadership, namely, situational or contingency theories of leadership.

SITUATIONAL OR CONTINGENCY THEORIES OF LEADERSHIP

Situational and contingency theories essentially propose that the nature of the organisation, and the environment in which it operates, determine which style of leadership is required for the organisation to be successful.

A simple example flows from Chapter 8. In that chapter we demonstrate how in a stable environment, where the market, the product and the production process are unchanging, or only changed slowly and predictably, then the appropriate organisational structure is a bureaucracy, with all that implies about structure, culture and other aspects of the organisation. It is clear that a leader with a structure/production-centred leadership style would be the most suitable. A participative, democratic team-centred leadership style would be inappropriate, and would actually disrupt the smooth mechanistic working of the bureaucracy.

Now we need to ask not only what personal qualities are possessed by good leaders (Trait Theory), and what good and effective leaders *do* (the process theories; person-centred or task-centred, or preferably both), but we also need to look at the organisational environment both within the organisation, and its external environment. We need to find a leader whose traits and behaviours fit the organisational and external environments.

One of the most important theorists who examined the organisational environment, and developed the first Situational or Contingency, Theory of leadership, was Fiedler (1964). He suggested that there were essentially two principal leadership styles, which he called relationship-centred and task-centred. These two styles really follow on from the Ohio and Michigan studies and reflect Theories X and Y leadership beliefs. The leadership styles were assessed using a Least-preferred Co-worker Scale. Leaders were asked to recall the worker with whom they had least enjoyed working, and then to describe them by answering 16 or 18 questions, each of which had an 8-point scale that ran from, for example, friendly to unfriendly, and co-operative to unco-operative. After assessing leadership style, the organisational environment or context was evaluated in terms of three variables:

- *Leader–member relations*: this is about how well leaders and followers relate – whether they are respected and trusted or not respected and distrusted. This was ranked from good to poor.

- *Task structure*: "…the task is clear-cut, structured, and identifies the goals, procedures and progress of the work …" (Fiedler, 1978, p. 421). This was ranked from high to low.

- *Position power*: "...the leader has the ability to reward and punish, and thus to obtain compliance through organisational sanctions..." (Fiedler, 1978, p. 421). This was ranked from strong to weak. Interestingly, Fiedler only looks at rewards and punishment as sources of power, with no reference to legitimate power, charismatic power, or any of the other sources of leadership power that other writers have identified (see the Chapter 6).

Fiedler concluded that:

- When leader–member relations were good, task structure high, and leader position power strong, then the most appropriate leadership style was task-motivated.

- When the context variables were at the opposite extreme (leader–member relations were poor, task structure low and leader position power weak), then the appropriate leadership style was also task-orientated.

- With any other situational combination of the three context variables, then the appropriate leadership style was relationship-motivated.

The reader is left to work out the logic of Fielder's conclusions, before perhaps resorting to reading Fiedler's paper to check their conclusions or confusion!

Fiedler was convinced that leaders could not vary their leadership style, which he felt was a function of their personality, and then rather strangely concluded that the only way to ensure a fit between the leader and the organisation was to change the organisation's three contextual factors so that they fitted the leader. This implies that these three factors are relatively easy to change. As these three factors could be argued to be facets, or manifestations, of the organisational culture. We would argue, as we did in Chapter 2, that organisational culture is very difficult and slow to change, taking between 5 and 10 years for a radical change of culture. We would also argue that the three factors are only part of the organisational culture and that they cannot be changed by themselves without all the other manifestations of culture also changing, so that there is a coherent culture where all the elements fit together.

A further implication of Fiedler's work is that it implies that if the external environment changes so that the internal culture has to change in order to ensure an appropriate fit between the organisational culture and the external environment, then the leadership style may need to change. That is, a new leader will have to be appointed.

There are many situational leadership theories, but it seems unnecessary to try and cover them all in an introductory book, so only one other traditional Situational Theory will be discussed. This is the Hersey–Blanchard (1996) Theory. Fiedler looked at leader–member relations, task structure and position power as the situational variable, but Hersey and Blanchard saw the important variables as relating to the employees and their readiness and ability:

- *Readiness*: this employee variable was about the *willingness* of followers to direct their own behaviour - their job readiness and psychological readiness; their motivation and desire to do quality work.

- Ability: how *able* is the staff to work without direction, further coaching or training.

These two dimensions mean that there are four possible situational states for the employees.

Table 7.1 Hersey and Blanchard situations	
Ready and Able	Ready and Unable
Unready and Able	Unready and Unable

Adapted from Hersey and Blanchard (1996)

Hersey and Blanchard suggested that there were four possible styles of leadership, one for each of the four situational states:

- *Telling/directing*: this is a style where the leader defines for the employees what will be done, how it will be done, when it will be done and how it will be supervised. This is the leadership style for the situation where the employees are Unready and Unable.

- *Selling/coaching*: this is the appropriate style when the employees are Unable and Willing.

- *Participating/supporting*: when the employees are Able and Unwilling, this is the appropriate leadership style.

- *Delegating/observing*: when employees are able and willing, then the leader can delegate responsibility to the employees, as they do not require leading, supervising, teaching or motivating.

CONTEMPORARY THEORIES OF LEADERSHIP
Transformational leadership

Theories labelled as Transformational leadership theories began to emerge in the 1980s and 1990s, as a result of the perceived failure of heroic or Great Man leaders and the rather simplistic situational leadership theories up to that point in time. In the 1990s, writers began to write of the emergence of post-heroic leaders.

The economic and financial crisis of 2007–2009 had produced a fresh crop of celebrated heroic leaders who have fallen from grace and have been observed to have feet of clay. We only have to reflect on a number of leading USA and UK banks, and the American automobile industry, where lauded, heroic, predominately male and very highly rewarded CEO's are now recognised to have led their organisations into bankruptcy. The CEO of Lehman Brothers, Richard Fuld, was voted in 2006 the "Number-1 CEO in the Brokers and Asset Managers Category" by the Institutional Investors Magazine, and then 2 years later was listed as the "Worst American CEO of all time" by CNBC.

The development of the ideas around transformational leadership was as a result of a number of factors, including the environmental changes that occurred in the business world, in the last 20–30 years. The development of transformational theories is partly an extension of the situational/contingency theories to look at specific changes in the environment, and have started to ask what qualities would a leader need to succeed in this new environment.

The most important changes have been about the increase in globalism, and the reengineering of organisations where the number of employees was cut drastically, and organisational structures were made much lower, with many fewer levels of hierarchy. With these changes came a need to change the culture of organisations. As headcounts were cut and organisations delayered, the remaining staff found that their jobs had become much broader and they required many more skills, and they were empowered and less closely supervised. These changes meant that for staff to be motivated, they needed to be led rather than managed and supervised, and the leadership needed to be about vision and charisma, hence the growth of inspirational and motivating leaders (and the theory that went with that, namely Transformational Leadership), that managed the culture of the organisation.

Research around the theories of transformational leaders has also resulted from a dissatisfaction with the unidimensional theory of the Great Man, and the dyad (two-dimensional) theories of leadership that included Consideration/Structure (Ohio), Employee-centred/Production-centred (Michigan) and Relationship-centred/Task-centred (Fiedler) (Yukl,1999). Even the triad (3-dimensional) theory of Lippitt and White, Autocratic/Democratic/Laissez-faire, and the 4-dimensional theory of Hersey and Blanchard, Telling/Selling/Participating/Delegating, were found to be too simplistic to explain what was actually observed in case studies and qualitative research on effective and identified successful leaders (identified by followers – colleagues and subordinates).

Transformational leaders have been defined as:

> *"...those who inspire confidence, communicate a positive vision and emphasize their followers' strengths".*
>
> **(Pederson et al., 2009, p. 349)**

> *"Transformational leadership includes individualized consideration, intellectual stimulation, idealized influence (charisma) and inspirational motivation."*
>
> **(Yukl, 1999, p. 36)**

A rather different development of transformational theories comes from gender studies and is based on the work of Rosener (1990). This approach emphasises the role of leaders in motivating staff through:

> *"...persuading them to commit to group/organizational goals; encouraging them to participate in decision making; managing through personal qualities rather than by using one's position; and trying to make staff feel good about themselves."*
>
> **(Brewis and Linstead, 2004, p. 72)**

Supportive of this last quoted comment is the work of Wang and Huang (2009), who, using a sample of Taiwan textile firms, found that emotional intelligence was a positive indicator of transformational leadership, and that seemed to lead to increased levels of group cohesiveness.

The Peterson and Yukl definitions make it clear that this approach has evolved from the Great Man and Trait Theories and have, by some writers, been labelled as Heroic Theories. The new factor is the emphasis on motivation and the role of leaders as the managers of organisational culture (Schein, 1992), as we observed in page 123 of this chapter.

The definition that flows from the work of Rosner (Brewis and Linstead, 2004) and gender studies is importantly different from the other two definitions that we quote, and has led to a discussion about the way that women manage and lead in a different way than men. This different approach, it is argued, is particularly suited to the times of turbulence and change that characterize late twentieth and early twenty-first century organisational environments, where the ability to change rapidly gives an organisation an advantage over male led organisations.

The style of leadership adopted by men has been called transactional leadership in the leadership and gender leadership literature. A typical definition is:

> *"[Transactional leadership]…which focuses on leadership being essentially a matter of supporting, directing and co-ordinating work or efforts towards a known goal or purpose. Transactional leadership is not focused on initiating radical or dramatic change, rather fine-tuning what goes on in the organisation."*
> **(Fulop et al., 2004, p. 339)**

Transactional leadership is thought of as being typical of male leaders, as reflecting the stereotype of male characteristics, with a more autocratic, individualistic and competitive style, based on a transactional approach of rewards and punishments for set and defined tasks.

It is clear that both transactional and transformational leadership fits nicely within the historical development of leadership theory. Transactional leadership sounds to be well suited to industries where change is slow and predictable and the emphasis needs to be on efficiency and effectiveness, and the structures are likely to be mechanistic and bureaucratic. In contrast, the transformational leaders are the ones who will succeed in environments of rapid change and uncertainty, where employees have to share a vision of what the organisation is trying to do, and where they work co-operatively towards this shared vision in organisational structures that are organic and flexible with few levels of hierarchy and where empowered staff are motivated and coached by a leadership that both manages and enacts the culture.

A topic that we have not yet addressed, although we have made a number of passing references to it, is whether the styles of leadership which individual leaders can adopt are limited by their personality, or whether leadership of any style is something that can be taught.

PERSONALITY AND LEADERSHIP

The author's position on personality comes from his training, practice and experience as a psychotherapist. It also comes from his personal experience of being a psychotherapy client. I state this as a starting position so that the reader can be wary in reading this section as there are very differing theories and conclusions about the development of personality and the extent to which personality can be changed in adulthood.

The author's position is that our personality is formed from a combination of the genes that we inherit from our parents and the formative experiences that we have as we grow up, and that it is also a reflection of our biological experience through the course of our mother's pregnancy. The importance of the pregnancy experience and the experience of being a baby is accessibly discussed in Gerhardt (2004).

Widely agreed theory suggests that with the passing years, life experiences have less and less change impact on our personality, and that the younger we are the more formative of our personality are the life experiences. The major impact on our personality is as a result of the years from conception up to our early teens.

Implicit in this general agreement is the thesis that it is very difficult or impossible to significantly change our personality once we are beyond our teens. If there is a connection between personality and leadership styles, then we conclude that leadership courses may have little or no impact on the styles of leadership that people can adopt. We recall, from earlier in this chapter, that Fiedler (1964) believed that leadership style cannot be changed. Fiedler clearly believed that personality cannot be significantly changed, and that personality determines what possible leadership styles can be adopted by an individual leader.

Psychotherapy theory is more or less agreed that if personality can be changed at all, as adults, then it is only as the result of years of psychotherapy. The sought for Holy Grail of a form of therapy that changes our personality in a short time appears to be an illusion; certainly something that we have not yet developed.

There is a growing literature that suggests that some personality disorders are more prevalent in senior business managers than in the general public, and that some personality disorders are more prevalent amongst senior managers than even in the criminal population. Board and Fritzon (2005) found that histrionic (characterised by superficial charm, insincerity, egocentricity and manipulativeness), narcissistic (grandiosity, self-focused, lack of empathy, exploitativeness and independence) and compulsive (perfectionism, excessive devotion to work, rigidity, stubbornness and dictatorial tendencies) personality disorders were particularly found amongst senior managers. They also commented that research shows the prevalence of so-called "successful" psychopaths in the senior management population.

Research quoted by James (2005) suggests that one-third of people who are recognised as high achievers have lost a parent by the age of 14 years, compared with only 8% of the general population. Why loss of a parent leads to high achievement is not clear, but we can speculate that the bereaved child may have to accept responsibilities at an unusually young age, or they are determined to be in control of their life, having had the experience of dramatically not being in control as a victim of early parental death.

A recent paper by Avolio et al. (2009) has looked at the role of parenting style on the emergence of children into leadership roles. Their conclusion was that authoritative parenting led children to leadership as adults. They defined authoritative parenting "... as being demanding (challenging), responsive, rational, considerate, consistent and assertive yet not restrictive", and setting "...clear standards of conduct..." p. 334. Their alternative style was authoritarian parents, who were "...controlling, lacking in warmth, support and consistency..." p. 334. Avolio et al.'s (2009) research shows that some of the qualities of leaders include having a sense of agency (that they can make things happen and that things do not just happen to them), a belief in their own capabilities, motivation, and a striving to accomplish. All of these qualities can be seen to be developed as a result of parenting style and life experiences in the teen years. We should note that this research is about people emerging into leadership roles, and does not address the issue of whether, having emerged into leadership roles, they make effective leaders.

Much of current research is about emergence into leadership roles and not about the effectiveness of leaders. At the time of writing we still do not seem to have a clear answer as to whether appropriate parenting, life experiences and training can produce effective leaders, although it does now seem to be clearer as to what qualities leaders have and how they come to have them.

Narcissism and leadership

What we do know is that there does seem to be a particular connection between a feature of personality called narcissism and emergence into leadership. This finding is reflected in the recent and growing literature on the emergence of leaders, which is really a revisiting of Trait Theory. When we examine the definition of narcissism we can understand why it might lead to leadership. Listed below are the diagnostic criteria for Narcissistic Personality Disorder as set out by the American Psychiatric Association (1994). The diagnosis requires five or more of the following to be present:

- "Has a grandiose sense of self importance (e.g. exaggerates achievements and talents, expects to be recognised as superior without commensurate achievements).

- Is preoccupied with fantasies of unlimited success, power, brilliance, beauty or ideal love.

- Believes that he or she is special and unique and can only be understood by, or should associate with, other special or high-status people (or institutions).

- Requires excessive admiration.

- Has a sense of entitlement, i.e. unreasonable expectations of especially favourable treatment or automatic compliance with his or her expectations.

- Is interpersonally exploitative, i.e. takes advantage of others to achieve his or her own ends.

- Lacks empathy; is unwilling to recognise or identify with the feelings or needs of others.

- Is often envious of others or believes that others are envious of him or her.

- Shows arrogant, haughty behaviours or attitudes."
    American Psychiatric Association (1994, p. 661)

The psychiatric discussion of narcissism has a characteristic that does not appear in the diagnostic criteria above, and that is that underlying the diagnostic criteria is a fragile sense of self-esteem. In effect, the narcissist fears that they are not very good or able and that others will notice this unless they work very hard to be successful and in control. We may speculate that narcissism underlies the Type-A Syndrome that we wrote about in Chapter 5.

Much modern literature, see for example Rosenthal and Pittinsky (2006), suggests that surveys show that people who emerge into leadership roles are characterised by their narcissistic personalities. They are people who need and seek, achievement, power and admiration. People with these qualities are often seen as charismatic people who achieve great success, although they do it for their own benefit and are uncaring for others. It is easy to see how narcissistic people rise to positions of power through seeking to get to these positions, as it is only in positions of leadership that they can truly satisfy their characteristic needs. The literature, see for example Rosenthal and Pittinsky (2006), draws a comparison between transformational leadership and narcissistic personality disorders. Whether narcissism is useful or not, and whether it results in effective leadership may well depend on how narcissistic the leader is on a scale from slightly to strongly narcissistic.

Rosenthal and Pittinsky (2006) give as examples of narcissistic leaders, Hitler, Stalin, Saddam Hussein, Steve Job (of Apple), Kenneth Lay (of Enron) and Michael Eisner (of Disney), amongst others. A reading of almost any brief biography of Richard Fuld, the former CEO of Lehman Brothers, would add his name to the list of narcissistic leaders who have risen to power and had then crashed their career and/or their organisations, exactly because of their personality traits.

When we wrote about Type-A Syndrome in Chapter 5, we noted that one of the characteristics was that the Type-A personality was often ultimately self-destructive, and if we look at the histories of the named examples of narcissists in the previous paragraph we see that they have all been self-destructive and are remembered as much for their ultimate disaster as their earlier great success. The road to ruin may be seen as lying in their inability to cope with criticism and their need to be praised and lauded, both characteristics resulting in them being ultimately surrounded by "yes men" and syco-phants, so that errors and misjudgments are not pointed out and reflected on in time. Part of the character of the narcissist is that they cannot bring themselves to admit that they may be wrong or have made a mistake.

Narcissistic leaders may not at first sound like transformational leaders, but at times of crisis when organisations need visions of massive change and success, the narcissistic leader is exactly the person who can inspire and drive change, although it is in fact entirely for their own benefit. When the organisation is changing and succeeding, then it is easy for them to appear to be charismatic and inspirational leaders to their followers. An alternative view is put forward by Koo and Burch (2008), whose research suggests that narcissistic personality is a negative predictor of transformational leadership (as assessed by followers), compared with avoidant (cautious) and histrionic (colourful) personalities, which were seen by followers to be characteristic of transformational leaders.

The second type of transformational leader, the one from the gender literature is clearly much less likely to have a narcissistic personality, as the type is about trans-forming by working *with* people and coaching and supporting in a cohesive style.

NEUROTIC ORGANISATIONS

This topic brings together material about the personality of leaders and the topic of organisational culture and the impact of leaders on that culture. Earlier in this chapter, we briefly discussed the idea that one of the functions of leadership in modern orga-nisations is to manage the organisational culture. In this section we look at the way that leaders do not so much manage culture, as to form it in their own image, out of their awareness. Our principal hypothesis is that the culture of an organisation is a function of the CEO's personality.

The initial discussion of neurotic organisations was in the work of Kets de Vries and Miller (1984). Their hypothesis was that neurotic leaders of organisations formed organisations that reflected the neurosis of those leaders. They examined five neuroses, or personality disorders, and suggested that each of the five could be encapsulated in the form of a fantasy that reflected the personality of the CEO. We now set out the five neuroses and their companion fantasies that encapsulated the way that the CEO made sense of their world:

- *Paranoid*: i cannot really trust anybody; a menacing superior force exists that is "out to get me"; I had better be on my guard.

- *Compulsive (obsessive/compulsive)*: i do not want to be at the mercy of events; I have to master and control all the things affecting me.

- *Dramatic (or Histrionic)*: i want to get attention from and impress the people who count in my life.

- *Depressive*: it is hopeless to change the course of events in my life; I am just not good enough.

- *Schizoid*: the world of reality does not offer any satisfaction to me; my interactions with others will eventually fail and cause harm, so it is safer to remain distant and withdrawn.

We all have various elements of neurosis in our personality, and that only matters if our personality is dominated by one of them.

The next element of Kets de Vries and Miller's argument is that the CEO will develop an organisation that reflects their fantasy of the world. Thus a paranoid CEO will develop an organisation that is paranoid in all the manifestations of its organisational culture.

We may wonder how the employees come to share the neuroses of the CEO. Kets de Vries and Miller suggest that there are three mechanisms:

- Staff are recruited who share the CEO's neurosis. In the case study that follows we note that sales staff wanted to be paid on a commission basis even though they knew that commission rates were adjusted so that total earnings remained more or less stable and did not rise even if sales were greatly increased. Perhaps the sales staff did not trust themselves (paranoia) to work hard without performance-related pay.

- Staff who do not share the neurosis leave the organisation, thus the only survivors are employees who share the neurosis.

- Staff are slowly converted by the CEO until they share the neurosis. At one time the author worked in a department where the head was paranoid, and really did seem to believe that everyone was "out to get me". A manifestation of the head's paranoia was their belief that the University Centre was taking advantage of the department, and they kept on presenting evidence in departmental meetings that indicated exploitation. In the end, almost all of the staff of the department believed that we were being exploited, but we never saw all of the documents from the Centre, only those that the Head of Department chose to share with us.

In Chapter 2 we suggested, after Bate (1994), that organisations did not have cultures, but that organisations were cultures; every aspect of the organisation being a manifestation of the culture or an element of the culture. We can list at least some of the major cultural manifestations of an organisation's culture:

- Organisational structure;

- Payment schemes;

- Management style;

- The artefacts; the look of the building, the way that the company building is furnished, the look of offices, the style of dress of employees;

- Decision-making systems; how are decisions made, who has power;

- Strategy;

- Management information systems; and who has access to information; and

- What types of people are recruited by the organisation.

Before we go on to give an example of one of the neuroses and what an organisation having that neurosis would look like, we will quote the diagnostic criteria of two of the neuroses, taken from the American Psychiatric Association (1994).

Obsessive–compulsive:

☐ "Is preoccupied with details, rules, lists, order, organisation or schedules to the extent that the major point of the activity is lost.

☐ Shows perfectionism that interferes with task completion (e.g. is unable to complete a project because his or her overly strict standards are not being met).

☐ Is excessively devoted to work and productivity to the exclusion of leisure activities and friendships (not accounted for by obvious economic necessity).

☐ Is overconscientious, scrupulous and inflexible about matters of morality, ethics or values (not accounted for by cultural or religious identification).

☐ Is unable to discard worn-out or worthless objects even when they have no sentimental value.

☐ Is reluctant to delegate tasks, or to work with others, unless they submit to exactly his or her way of doing things.

☐ Adopts a miserly spending style both towards self and others; money is viewed as something to be hoarded for future catastrophes.

☐ Shows rigidity and stubbornness." (pp. 672, 673).

Paranoid:

- ☐ "Suspects, without sufficient basis, that others are exploiting, harming or deceiving him or her.

- ☐ Is preoccupied with unjustified doubts about the loyalty or trustworthiness of friends and associates.

- ☐ Is reluctant to confide in others because of unwarranted fear that the information will be used maliciously against him or her.

- ☐ Reads hidden demeaning or threatening meanings into benign remarks or events.

- ☐ Persistently bears grudges, i.e., is unforgiving of insults, injuries or slights.

- ☐ Perceives attacks on his or her character or reputation that are not apparent to others and is quick to react angrily or to counterattack." (pp. 637, 638).

Before we go on to a case study of a paranoid organisation, the reader may like to think what an obsessive compulsive organisation might be like in terms of organisational structure, payments schemes, management style, the artefacts, decision-making systems, strategy and strategy formation, management information systems and the people who are recruited into the organisation.

Let us make general comments about each of the main cultural elements found in a paranoid organisation, and then we will go on to a case study:

- ■ *Organisational structure*: as the staff will not be trusted, the structure is likely to be quite bureaucratic with clear lines of communications, high levels of supervision and narrowly defined jobs and operating systems.

- ■ *Payment schemes*: if the CEO does not trust their employees then they will try and pay them by results as much as possible, thus commission on sales, or payment per piece produced.

- ■ *Management style*: a paranoid CEO would want to monitor staff in great detail and would want to have a very detailed style of management. This would be about Theory X management and not Theory Y.

- ■ *Artefacts*: the organisation would have a lot of security concerning entry to the building and movement around the building, and closed-circuit TV.

- ■ *Decision making*: what we would expect to see would be very restricted and centralised decision making, and certainly not a system where decision making was devolved.

- ■ *Strategy*: because of the lack of trust there would tend to be a strategy that was reactive, in the sense of following and responding to company competitors. There are also likely to be diversified products and markets so that "all the company eggs are not in one basket". There will be lots of market research about customers, suppliers, product outlets (agents and shops) and rivals, as these are some of the very people that the CEO does not trust.

- *Management information system*: within the organisation, access to information will be on a strictly "need to know" basis, with restricted access and lots of passwords. Much information will be collected, employees' emails may well be checked by senior management, and telephone calls monitored.

- *Staff recruitment*: recruitment will check applicant's CV's, and educational qualifications, and there may be a high level of psychometric testing so that the organisations knows all about their staff.

Case Study 7.2: A paranoid organisation

The author did a piece of consulting about staff turnover in the UK headquarters (HQ) of a Japanese computer and telecommunications firm enough years ago that even if the reader can recognise the organisation, it will tell them nothing reliable about how the firm is currently.

I drove to my first appointment to meet the European head of Human Resources, who had invited me to consult in one of the firm's sales departments. I arrived at a barrier at the entrance to the car park and had to explain to an intercom who I was and who I had come to see. The car park was neatly set out with each parking bay having a car registration attached to it, except for the most senior executives, where the label read Chairman, Managing Director, and so on. I parked in a marked "visitor's" bay, and exited the car park to the front door of the HQ building. The door was locked and I had to explain to another intercom who I was and who I had come to see. The door clicked open and I entered the Reception and filled in a form specifying who I was, who I had come to see, what my company name was and my car registration number. I was then given a "Visitor" badge to wear.

The Reception was rather bland with little in the way of artefacts except some Queen's Awards for Exporting.

My contact had told me how to get to his office so I went to leave Reception, but found that the exit door was locked. I was told that someone would come and escort me to my meeting.

So far I knew little about the organisation except that they were very security conscious and didn't give away information about the organisation.

I was escorted to my meeting with my contact, passing a series of open plan offices. Each department that we walked past had a small private office for the head of the department. There were a series of small private meeting rooms. There was no sign of the offices of the most senior executives, all of whom were Japanese; these I was told were all located on the top floor of the building (why is it that Directors and senior executives nearly always seem to have their offices on the top floor where none of the rest of the staff will ever pass by, unless sent for? This surely is some clue to the symbolism of power and the culture of the organisation).

My contact's first act was to say that the organisation did not use outside consultants, as a matter of policy, and that if any Japanese member of staff spoke to me then I was to present myself as a client who had come to meet with a member

Continued

of a Sales Team. I was introduced to the head of the sales department where I was to work, and a series of meetings were arranged where I could interview a cross-section of the non-Japanese staff.

As I left the building, I was escorted to Reception, deposited my visitor's badge and let out of the locked front door.

On my return to conduct interviews, I went through all the same security processes and was again escorted through the building, despite my protestations that I knew my way.

The one-on-one interviews were with a large cross-section of staff. Each was remarkably the same. We would go to an interview room with only social chitchat, never business, as we walked there. My interviewee would shut the door, draw the blinds, so that no one in the corridor passing the room could see who was in the room and then proceed to answer my questions in such a quiet voice that I would repeatedly have to ask them to repeat what they had just said. When I asked why they were speaking so quietly, the answer was that they did not want to be overheard. At times it was appropriate for the interviewee to draw or write something on a flip chart. At the end of each interview the interviewee would always ask to take with them what they had written or drawn, no way were they going to leave it in the room.

When I asked about future products that were to be launched in the next few months the answer was always the same; the senior Japanese executives would not trust the sales staff with the information, in case they left for a rival and took the information with them. One of the reasons why sales staff turnover was so high was that they resented not being trusted!

As a result of the interviewing, I discovered that the sales staffs' payment scheme was 50% based on sales secured. I thought of this as an aspect of senior management paranoia, and it may have been, but I found that the staff preferred a payment by results system, and none of them wanted a fixed salary.

Questions

1. How many of the diagnostic criteria for paranoia does this organisation tick?
2. Did the organisation need to be paranoid?
3. What extra information would you want to have to confirm or reject a diagnosis of paranoia?

INTERNATIONAL CULTURE AND LEADERSHIP

Most of the research drawn on in this chapter has been based in the USA and Europe, and thus we need to be wary before assuming that the conclusions are applicable to all countries.

If we recall the work of Laurent (1983), discussed in Chapter 3, we remember that beliefs about what managers should be, and how they should act, varied significantly between nationalities, even within Europe; for example, in response to the statement:

"Most organisations would be better off if conflict could be eliminated forever", only 4% of Swedish senior managers agreed, but 41% of Italian managers agreed. This would seem to indicate that in relation to strategy and decision making, leadership style might be quite different in these two countries.

Recalling the work of Hofstede (2001), discussed in Chapter 3, we remember the marked differences between countries in their cultural beliefs around five dimensions; masculinity/feminism, individualism/collectivism, uncertainty avoidance, power distance and long-term orientation. As an example of the impact that these differences might make to leadership, we can reflect on the masculinity/feminism dimension. We have seen that transformational leadership has a feminine version that is characterised by feminine characteristic. This style of leadership is likely to be observed less often in very masculine countries as leaders are likely to be uncomfortable with the behaviours that constitute this style of leadership, and feminine style transactional managers are less likely to have been promoted to leadership positions. We may also expect that in masculine cultures there is likely to be a bias in terms of transactional leadership and the organisational structures that go with that leadership style.

A paper by Yancey and Watanabe (2009) found that a sample of Japanese workers believed that, for an effective leader, skills and behaviours were more important than personality characteristics, whereas a sample of USA workers believed that personality characteristics were more important than skills and behaviours; two differing views of what makes an effective leader.

We do not intend to go any further with this discussion of international leadership differences, but the reader is warned to be wary of accepting Western-based leadership theory and applying it to different countries with differing national cultures.

CONCLUSIONS

It is difficult to draw simple conclusions from this chapter. If there is a simple conclusion that will be useful to the reader when they are working in an organisation, it is perhaps the importance of the situational models that suggest that the appropriate style of leadership for an organisation depends on that organisation's environment and situation. An organisation that needs to change rapidly needs a different form of leadership from one where there is little or no need for change. There is no leadership style that is best for all situations.

We think that we have presented a reasonable case that the personality of the leader restricts the range of leadership styles that they can adopt, and thus the range of situations where they are going to be the most effective leader.

Leaders emerge, are appointed and promoted, and thus those charged with appointing and promoting need to reflect on what theory has to say about effective leaders. Recent collapses of massive organisations (Lehman Brothers, Enron and General Motors, for example) clearly show the importance of effective leaders and the cost of appointing inappropriate leaders.

REFERENCES

Avolio, B.J., Rotundo, M., Walumbwa, F.O., 2009. Early life experiences as determinants of leadership role occupancy: the importance of parental influence and rule breaking behaviour. The Leadership Quarterly 20 (3), June 2009.

Arvey, R.D., Rotundo, M., Johnson, W., Zhang, Z., McGue, M., 2006. The determinants of leadership role occupancy: genetic and personality factors,. The Leadership Quarterly 17.

Arvey, R.D., Zhang, Z., Avolio, B.J., Krueger, R., 2007. Understanding the developmental and genetic determinants among females. Journal of Applied Psychology 92.

Bate, S.P., 1994. Strategies for Cultural Change. Butterworth-Heinemann.

Belbin, R.M., 1981. Management Teams: Why They Succeed or Fail. Heinemann Professional Publishing.

Board, B.J., Fritzon, K., 2005. Disordered personalities at work. Psychology Crime and Law 11 (1), 17–32.

Brewis, Linstead, S., 2004. Gender and management. In: Linstead, S., Fulop, L., Lilley, S. (Eds.), Management and Organisation: A Critical Text. MacMillan, Palgrave Chapter 2.

Brown, B., 2000. In: Group Processes: Dynamics Within and Between Groups, second ed. Blackwell.

Burke, R.J., 2006. Why leaders fail: exploring the darkside. International Journal of Manpower 27 (1), 91–100.

Diagnostic and Statistical Manual of Mental Disorders, fourth ed, 1994. American Psychiatric Association, Washington, DC.

Fiedler, F.E., 1964. A contingency model of leadership effectiveness. In: Berkowitz, L. (Ed.), Advances in Experimental Social Psychology, vol. 1. Academic Press.

Fiedler, F.E., 1978. Situational control and a dynamic theory of leadership. In: Pugh, D.S. (Ed.), Organizational Theory: Selected Readings, third ed, 1990. Penguin Books.

Fulop, L., Linstead, S., Dunford, R., 2004. Leading and Managing, in Management and Organisation: A Critical Text. MacMillan, Palgrave. Chapter 10.

Gerhardt, S., 2004. Why Love Matters: How Affection Shapes a Baby's Brain. Brunner-Routledge.

Hersey, P., Blanchard, K., 1996. Management of Organizational Behaviour: Utilizing Human Resources. Prentice Hall.

Hofstede, G.H., 2001. Culture's Consequences; Comparing Values, Behaviours, Institutions, and Organizations Across Nations, 2nd ed. Sage.

James, O., (18 April 2005), Guardian.

Katz, D., Maccoby, N., Morse, N.C., 1950. Productivity, Supervision and Morale in an Office Situation. University of Michigan Institute for Social Research.

Kets de Vries, M.F.R., Miller, D., 1984. Neurotic Organizations. John Wiley and Sons Ltd.

Koo, H.S., Burch, G.S.J., 2008. The "dark side" of leadership personality and transformational leadership: an exploratory study. Personality and Individual Differences 44 (1), 86–97.

Laurent, A., 1983. Cultural diversity of western conceptions of management. International Studies of Management and Organization 13 (1,2), 76–96.

Lippitt, R., White, R., 1943. The "social climate" of children's groups. In: Barker, R.G., Kounin, J.S., Wright, H. (Eds.), Child Behaviour and Development,. McGraw-Hill.

Llies, R., Gerhardt, M.W., Le, H., 2004. Individual differences. In: Leadership Emergence: Integrating Meta-analytical Findings and Behavioural Genetics Estimates, 12. International Journal of Selection and Assessment, pp. 207-219.

McCall Jr., M.W., Lombardo, M.M., 1983. Off the Track: Why and How Successful Executives Get Derailed. Centre for Creative Leadership, Greenboro, NC.

McGregor, D., 1960. The Human Side of Enterprise. In: Pugh, D.S. (Ed.), Organization Theory: Selected Readings, third ed. Penguin.

Pederson, S.J., Walumbwa, F.O., Byron, K., Myrowitz, J., 2009. CEO positive psychological traits, transformational leadership and firm performance in high-technology, start-up and established firms. Journal of Management 35, 348.

Rosenthal, S.A., Pittinsky, T.L., 2006. Narcissistic leadership. The Leadership Quarterly 17, 617–633.

Rosner, J.B., 1990. Ways women lead. Harvard Business Review, 119–125. November–December.

Schein, E.H., 1992. In: Organisational Culture and Leadership, second ed. Jossey-Bass.

Stogdill, R.M., 1950. Leadership, membership and organization. Psychological Bulletin 47, 1–14.

Stogdill, R.M., 1974. Handbook of Leadership. Free Press, New York.

Wang, Y.S., Huang, T.C., 2009. The relationship of transformational leadership with group cohesiveness and emotional intelligence. Social Behaviour and Personality 37 (3), 379–392.

Yancey, G.B., Wantanabe, N., 2009. Differences in perceptions of leadership between US and Japanese workers. The Social Science Journal 46 (2), 268–281.

Yukl, G., 1999. An evaluative essay on current conceptions of effective leadership. European Journal of Work and Organizational Psychology 8 (1), 33–48.

Organisational Structures

8

A one-person organisation does not have a structure. Only if there are two or more people co-operating in the production of a good or service is there a need for a structure that determines who does what, who is the boss (if there is one), who has authority, how decisions are made and by whom and so on.

This chapter is going to look at the structure of organisations. Many books look at the general theories that attempt to explain the logic that underpins, explains and predicts organisations of every size up to and including huge multinationals with businesses and bases in many countries. Whilst these general theories may be intriguing, they are hardly relevant for the readers of an introductory book on organisational behaviour. In this chapter we are going to concentrate on smaller organisations and small parts of organisations where the reader is likely to find the material useful to their everyday experience. It seems unlikely that the readers of this book will need to design or even understand in totality the structure of large organisations; so there will be little discussion of large organisations or multinationals with bases in many countries. We are trying to present an useful and usable theory.

ADAM SMITH AND THE DIVISION OF LABOUR

Why should two or more people come together to produce goods or services? An economics answer is that there are advantages if two or more people work together rather than as individuals. One of the early answers was provided by Adam Smith in 1776 (Smith, 2008) in his seminal book, The Wealth of Nations. Smith argued that if a product had several processes that had to be performed for a complete product to be produced, then there would be advantages in what he called the *division of labour*. His example was the making of a pin, where the series of processes might be, the drawing out of the wire, the forming of the pin head, the sharpening of the pin and the polishing of the pin. If a worker is specialised in just one of these operations then they would become very dextrous, quick and expert at that single operation, and they would not have to spend time putting down the tools necessary for one operation and picking up the next set of tools for the next operation. He argued that if four people, each specialised on one stage of the pin production, then the four people would together produce many more pins in a day than if each of the four people made complete pins.

The next question is why the division of labour means that there has to be an organisation and not four separate one person businesses that each sell their output to the next person in the production process sequence. The answer is again an economics reply. If there are four separate one-person businesses that each produces parts of the finished pins, then there have to be negotiations between the four individuals about how much each of them produces, at what price they buy their inputs and at what price they sell their products. The cost of doing this is essentially the time taken to negotiate, and is called *transaction costs*. A single firm, which is centrally planned by an owner, cuts down on all the negotiations, and thus reduces the transaction costs of producing pins and reduces the price at which they can be sold – division of labour increases efficiency and central organisational planning minimizes transaction costs.

A group of four separate individuals, each producing whole pins, cannot compete with four individuals each of whom specialises in one stage of the production of pins, and they in turn will not be able to compete with a centrally planned organisation where four individuals each specialises in one process in the production of pins.

How are decisions made in the centrally planned firm? If each of the skilled workers is involved in making decisions about production levels and prices then the discussions will be long and complicated, and the internal transaction costs will be high. The economically obvious answer is to have one person who makes the decisions, and the rest specialise on production processes. The cost of democratic (some form of majority voting), or consensus, decision making, is very high and would tend to make the firm uncompetitive because of high costs.

Now we have reached an organisation that the reader may recognise as a conventional firm or organisation, with people specialising in parts of the process in order to let people become specialist producers of goods or services, and in order to minimize transaction costs.

Adam Smith's pin mill was about a particular form of product and particular manufacturing stages and processes, but what if the product being produced was of a very different kind, for example, an engineering design consultancy. In a design consultancy the production process is not a sequence of individual processes but is much more about a team of engineers with differing specialisms co-operating as a team to produce an engineering design, or individual engineering consultants who take responsibility for the complete consultancy project. The consultancy may well need some specialist who concentrates on marketing the consultancy's services (the marketer, or the marketing department), or who looks after billing the customers, collecting the money, borrowing money to pay for the wages of the engineers and to buy the outside services that they may need until the designs are paid for by the clients (the financial expert or the finance department). Even where there is joint production, there may need to be specialisms, as you cannot expect a professional engineer to also be expert in marketing or finance. Here we are beginning to see the emergence of an organisation that is made up of a number of expert departments which provide services to one another. Now we again recognise something that we recognise as a firm, and again it is built on the advantages of specialisation, or the division of labour. Our example of an engineering consultancy is a structure that Minzberg (1983) called a Professional Bureaucracy. Such structures are also found in law firms and educational and training organisations, where the product is produced by professional individuals or teams who need the support of an administrative structure so that they can get on with using their professional skills to produce a service.

Many modern organisations now subcontract the provision of specialist services to outside contractors. The payroll and the payment of staff are often subcontracted, as are marketing and a number of other specialist services. There are at least two reasons why firms subcontract rather than have internal departments within the organisation. We met one reason in Chapter 2 where we mention the work of Peters and Waterman (1982) in their book, In Search of Excellence. One of the ways to excellence was described as "sticking to the knitting", specialising in what your organisation is particularly good at – the core of your business. The second reason is based on another idea that comes from economics, the concept of *economies of scale*.

ECONOMIES OF SCALE

Economies of scale says that if you increase output by a factor of x, where x is a positive number (say a doubling or tripling of output) then it may be possible to do this by increasing the input of productive resources and costs by less than x, thus the unit costs have been reduced. This is arguing that there are cost advantages to being bigger. Karl Marx in 1876 (Marx, 2009) went so far as to argue that larger organisations would always have an economic advantage because of economies of scale, and thus there would be a race between competing firms to be the biggest, until each industry would end up with a single large monopoly firm. Experience, however, has demonstrated that economies of scale are not endlessly available. As organisations get larger and larger they become increasingly complex and difficult to control and the administrative structure may have to grow quicker than the size of the organisation, resulting in a rise in unit overall costs such that we may experience diseconomies of scale. The existence of *dis*economies of scale is one reason why organisations subcontract or adopt a divisional form where the organisation is broken up into smaller semi-autonomous units (divisions), each of which may deal with a single product range, or a single market.

Before the Industrial Revolution in the UK, in the eighteenth and nineteenth centuries workers tended to work as individuals in their homes, and go to market places where they sold what they had produced, whether it was thread for making cloth, or cloth for making clothes. As the Industrial Revolution progressed, bigger and more powerful and productive machines were invented (which offered economies of scale) that needed a major source of power to make them work, so workers migrated to streams that would power large machines, and then to buildings where the owner of the building had installed a large steam engine that was capable of powering many machines on the same site. The large steam engine offered economies of scale in that it provided power at a lower unit cost than many smaller steam engines producing the same total output of power. Again, because of transaction costs, it was cheaper for the owner of the building and the steam engine to *employ* the individual machine operators than to negotiate with them about the supply of power and the rent of space in the building. In addition, individuals might not have been able to finance the purchase of a large, powerful and expensive machine. There was also the benefit of reduced transaction costs in selling the product of each individual machine. Now there were large factories, owned by one person or a small group of people, where the planning was taken out of the hands of individual workers. We can recognise this situation as similar to twenty-first century firms that make double glazing units, furniture, cars, chemicals or any of a range of products that require specialist machinery where the gain of being a firm is the reduction of transaction costs, the specialisation of individuals and the availability of economies of scale.

The ideas of Adam Smith did not have a big intellectual impact on individual factory owners, who arrive at the results implied by Smith by reflection on how to reduce costs and maximize profits, but they were influenced by three twentieth century writers.

Frederick Taylor (Pugh, 1990), writing in the early twentieth century on *scientific management*, Max Weber (Pugh, 1990), writing on *bureaucracies* (although his work was not available in English until the late 1940s) and Fayol (Pugh, 1990), writing on general principles of management (although his ideas were not made familiar to the English speaking world until the late 1930s). Even though these writers were influential, what they did, particularly in the case of Fayol and Weber, was to provide an intellectual justification for organisational structures that had already emerged as a result of economic pressures to minimize cost in a competitive world.

Implicit in the previous paragraph is the statement that people who organise and structure organisations are often ill-educated in business studies (a relatively recent intellectual discipline and form of education), and that people structure their organisations as a result of personal reflection, observing how organisations they have previously worked in have been structured, and how other organisations of which they are aware, are structured. We would argue, however, that better structures could be designed for whole organisations and parts of organisations if the designers know something of the theory of organisational structures, rather than resorting to trial and error and reflection or imitation.

Because of the powerful influence of Frederick Taylor and his ideas about *scientific management*, we will now look at what he had to say and how that was influential in organisational structuring.

SCIENTIFIC MANAGEMENT

Perhaps the best account of scientific management is that given by Frederick Taylor as testimony to the House of Representatives of the USA in 1912 (Pugh, 1990).

Taylor starts by saying that the work of managers and labourers is different and separate, and that managers have four key roles to perform:

1. The managers have to learn everything that labourers have learnt by trial and error over the years, about the best way to perform a particular labouring job, to evaluate that learning and to experiment to see whether there is an even better way to complete the job. One of the examples that Taylor gave was about shovelling materials in the steel-making process. Managers learnt optimum technique by watching men shovelling, and then experimented with different designs and sizes of shovels until they found the optimum combination of shovel and technique.

2. The managers have to select the labourers who were the most suitable to use the optimum tools and techniques, and who could best be trained to use these optimum techniques and tools.

3. They have to put the "best labourers" together with the "best tools and techniques", and train them. Now, together there were the best techniques, the best tools and the best labourers, and thus the most productive workers.

4. The managers have to work with the labourers to manage them, so that the labourers could concentrate just on labouring. Managers managed and labourers laboured. This co-operation was described by Taylor as "…intimate, close, personal co-operation…" and ensured that "…it becomes practically impossible to have a serious quarrel [between manager and worker]" (Pugh, 1990, p. 206).

One of Taylor's ambitions was that, out of the extra productivity that emerged from the application of the principles of scientific management, workers would have increased pay to reflect their greater productivity.

When this scientific management approach is combined with Adam Smith's concept of the division of labour, and the concept of economies of scale, we can see that it seems that a very powerful model of production and management has been evolved.

We have seen the development of the job of the technician who works out the best way to work, the manager who supervises and the labourer who performs manufacturing or assembly actions; here are three elements of an organisational structure.

The contribution of Weber (Pugh, 1990) was when he wrote about bureaucracies, which we may well see as often being organisations that do not produce goods, but produce services, like insurance companies and government services such as the Road Vehicle Licensing Authority that registers cars, that taxes road users and that controls driver's licenses. We know that these types of organisations are all about laws and rules and forms.

BUREAUCRACIES

The key elements of a bureaucracy are set out below as bullet points:

■ Rules govern all actions and decisions within a bureaucracy. For every activity in the organisation, employees will know what they have to do and exactly how to do it; they will have no freedom of action. In this sense, this is rather like scientific management in a service producer rather than a physical goods producer. The rules are designed by the technicians/management. If a situation arises that is not covered by the rules then the technicians/management will decide on the appropriate new rules. Workers are not required to be creative, but just to implement the rules unquestioningly (again like scientific management, where workers work and managers manage). Clearly this structure of rules means that a bureaucracy is very inflexible if the environment changes in such a way that there are no rules to cover the new situation. This inflexibility and inability to react quickly to a changing environment are both good news and bad news. If the environment is unchanging then a bureaucracy is an optimised, cost minimizing organisation, where the best solution has been discovered and incorporated into a set of rules. If the environment is rapidly and unpredictably changing, then the bureaucracy will quickly become inappropriate to the changed environment.

- All workers will be recruited with education, training and experience that are appropriate to their posts.

- Payment will be tailored to employees' competence at carrying out their rules; to the training, education and experience of the employee and to their level of seniority in the organisation.

- Promotion will require competence and training suitable to the next grade.

- Essentially a bureaucracy is a rational logical organisation.

- Bureaucracies are associated with hierarchies – organisations where there are many layers of seniority.

Now that we have discussed division of labour, economies of scale, transactions costs, scientific management and bureaucracy, it is appropriate to look at Fayol's principles of management and organisation, and then we can look at classical organisational structures before going on to look at modern alternative structures, including virtual organisations that have no fixed location, factories or office.

FAYOL'S PRINCIPLES OF MANAGEMENT AND ORGANISATION

Fayol was a French mining engineer by training, who went on to successfully manage a large mining and metallurgical combine. Whilst still a director of the combine, he distilled out what he had learnt about structuring and managing large organisations, in a book, General and Industrial Management, first published in French in 1916. The book was not translated into English until 1949. He developed 14 principles, which we will present below as bullet points with commentary:

- *Division of work*: this is very much the idea to be found in Adam Smith's division of labour, in Taylor's scientific management and in Weber's bureaucracies, but Fayol recognises that there are limits to the division of work, and goes on to say of division of work, "Although its advantages are universally recognised and although possibility of progress is inconceivable without the specialized work of learned men and artists, yet division of work has its limits which experience and a sense of proportion teach us may not be exceeded" (Pugh, 1990, p. 182). What Taylor and Smith failed to recognise, and perhaps Fayol did, was that where the degree of specialisation is excessive people become bored and alienated, with the result that staff turnover may rise, the work process is sabotaged by the workers who may quite literally "drop a spanner in the works" or where a group of specialised workers are working together they may develop group norms that prevent the process being worked at its maximum designed speed (scientific management). The development of group suboptimum norms was first researched in the Hawthorne Studies in the 1930s (E. Mayo in Pugh, 1990). Too high a degree of specialisation makes difficulties if a specialist worker is off sick or leaves, as there may be no-one who can take over the specialist role until a new specialist is recruited. A high degree of specialisation makes an organisation like a machine that will not work if one part is missing or is broken. Flexibility is an important and desirable quality in organisations when they have to respond to changes in the organisational environment in order to survive. We will return to this topic of organisational flexibility.

- *Authority*: Fayol says, "Authority is the right to give orders and the power to exact obedience." (Pugh, 1990, p. 183), and goes on to say that the power must be backed up with the ability to reward or penalise people for following or not following orders. In Chapter 6 we listed many sources of power that are available to leaders, including legitimate power (the legal right to insist on conformance).

- *Discipline*: Fayol says, "Discipline is in essence obedience, application, energy, behaviour and outward marks of respect observed in accordance with the standing agreements between the firm and its employees..." (Pugh, 1990, p. 184) and, "...general opinion is deeply convinced that discipline is absolutely essential for the smooth running of business and that without discipline no enterprise could prosper", (Pugh, 1990, p. 184). The agreements between the firm and its employees may be formally agreed contracts, or they may be a mani-festation of the organisational culture, which has no written existence, but that is agreed and understood by everyone employed in the organisation. These types of contracts, which are based on culture, are sometimes called implicit or psychological contracts (Ring, 1997). For discipline to be effective, Fayol argues that you need good superiors at all levels, clear and fair agreements and judiciously applied sanctions. Clearly Fayol is not advocating a harsh and strict regime.

- *Unity of command*: this essentially means that everyone in the organisation should have only one boss in the organisation, from whom they take orders, and to whom they report and that there is no bypassing of the scalar chain of command; that is, there should be no direct interaction between a subordinate and their boss's boss. In Chapter 3 we noted that one of the ways that countries differ in their national organisational cultures is the extent to which bypassing the hierarchical chain is acceptable. The same chapter showed that when Laurent was writing in 1983, the majority of managers in all countries in his survey believed that organisations should never be structured so that an employee had two bosses. Increasingly, contemporary organisations are resorting to *matrix structures* (Galbraith, 1971) – project groups and task forces, where groups of people from different departments are brought together on a project and will thus have at least two bosses – the head of any project/task group to which they belong and their departmental boss.

- *Unity of direction*: Fayol says "This principle is expressed as: one head and one plan for a group of activities having the same objective. It is the condition essential to unity of action, co-ordination of strength and focus of effort. A body with two heads is in the social as in the animal sphere a monster, and has difficulty in surviving." (Pugh, 1990, p. 187). This principle seems to imply that there needs to be a clear process of making decisions so that only one policy at a time is pursued.

- *Subordination of individual interest to the general decision*: this is clearly an exten-sion of the previous principle of unity of direction, saying, as it does, that there should be unity of purpose, but in Chapter 6 we saw that the possibility, or even the desirability, of a unitary organisation is remote. Huff (1988) made the point that conflict can be functional and will be functional up to a certain level of conflict. Certainly we can agree with Fayol that different agendas need to be resolved, but argue that they should not be structured out of the organisation.

- *Remuneration of personnel*: Fayol discusses the various ways that workers, middle managers and supervisors and senior managers can be paid in terms of payment by time, by output per unit of time, by payment for a completed piece of work, by profit shares and by bonuses, and looks at the motivating or demotivating effects of each of the payment methods. His conclusion is that there needs to be consideration about remuneration so that quantity, quality and effectiveness of labour use are maximized. He suggests that there is no single best remuneration system, and that each organisation needs to find its own best solutions given the nature of the organisation, the production process, the products and the industrial environment.

- *Centralisation*: Fayol says, "The question of centralization or decentralization is a simple question of proportion, it is a matter of finding the optimum degree for the particular concern." (Pugh, 1990, p. 193) and, "Everything which goes to increase the importance of the subordinate's role is decentralisation, everything which goes to reduce it is centralisation." (Pugh, 1990, p.194). Decentralisation stops the people at the top from becoming overloaded, but the extent to which you can decentralise depends on the quality of the staff to whom you delegate decision making, supervision, power, responsibility and authority and the culture of the organisation (the beliefs and values of the people within the organisation).

- *Scalar chain*: this is the direct line of communications both up and down the organisation that runs from the top to the bottom, and bottom to top, with each lower person reporting to their manager, and each manager communicating with their immediate subordinates. At its most extreme, the scalar chain means that two people on the same level in the hierarchy (but reporting to different managers) may not communicate directly with one another, but have to communicate up through the hierarchy until the communication gets to a manager who can communicate down to the second person. Taken to extremes, in organisations with many levels of hierarchy, this can result in very slow communications vertically, horizontally and diagonally. Slow communications mean an organisation responding slowly to the need for new decisions resulting from a new situation or problem for which there is no rule to define appropriate action. This topic is discussed more fully in the Chapter 9.

- *Order*: this is about materials and people – whether the right materials are in the right place, and the right people in the right places. This last implies a structure where each job has a job description (so that the post holder knows what is expected of them), and the right recruitment and training of post holders, so that the person is able to do the described job.

- *Equity*: Fayol says, "For the personnel to be encouraged to carry out its duties with all the devotion and loyalty of which it is capable it must be treated with kindness, and equity results from the combination of kindness and justice" (Pugh, 1990, p. 198). He defines justice as "… putting into execution established conventions…" (Pugh, 1990, p. 198). Clearly Fayol thinks that if people feel that they are not being treated *fairly* then they will not work hard or be committed to the success of the organisation (for a fuller discussion of equity look at the Equity Theory of Motivation in Chapter 4).

- *Stability of tenure of personnel*: one might hope that Fayol meant that offering security of tenure makes staff loyal and hard work, but he actually means that having a stable workforce means that everyone has learnt how to do their job efficiently and effectively, and thus that on average staff are as cost-effective as possible. He even goes as far as to say, "… a mediocre manager who stays is infinitely preferable to outstanding managers who merely come and go" (Pugh, 1990, p. 199).

- *Initiative*: Fayol argues that giving subordinates the possibility of using their initiative to plan, and to ensure the success of their plan, is a good way to motivate staff and ensure the success of the organisation. This is clearly against the implications of scientific management and bureaucratic structuring of organisations. It also implies the need for managers to work from a Theory Y position where workers are believed to be committed and creative (see the Appendix on Theories X and Y).

- *Esprit de corps*: Fayol stresses the importance to an organisation of a sense of harmony and collectiveness amongst the employees. Without these qualities he foresees conflict and discord. He also argues that, wherever it is practical and sensible, communications should be verbal and not written, as he sees written communications leading to misunderstandings and conflict. In these days of emails this is an interesting perspective, when many colleagues never get together, and speak with one another only through email. Fayol would clearly approve of the telephone, SKYPE and video conferencing, rather than written (email) communications. This is an interesting observation by him in the age of virtual organisations where people work spatially remote from one another, with electronics as the principal means of communication.

ORGANOGRAMS

The diagram below is a standard representation of an organisation that shows how some of Fayol's, Weber's and Taylor's principles are enacted in reality. The organogram is only partial, as only the Engineering Department is shown in any detail, for ease of exposition.

As shown in Figure 8.1, the organisation has three levels of hierarchy. The most senior, powerful and central person in the organisation is the Managing Director (MD). The MD supervises the work of the three directors who all have equal status and power, and the three directors all have to report to the MD. The MD may supervise the directors very closely and lay down exactly what they are to do and how, as in a bureaucracy (this is centralisation), or they may give them a great deal of

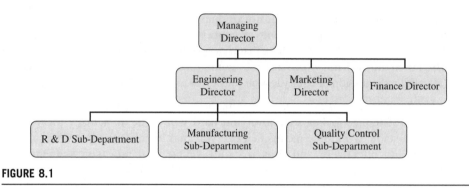

FIGURE 8.1

An organogram: Generated using Microsoft Office

power to accomplish the tasks and policies so long as they meet specified targets (this is decentralisation). The span of control of the MD is three, as they directly control the three directors only.

The organogram then shows in some detail the structure of one of the departments, the Engineering Department. The Marketing and Finance departments will also have structures, but these are not illustrated in order to keep the diagram from becoming too complex. The Engineering Department has three sub-departments, Research and Development (R&D), Manufacturing and Quality Control. Each of these sub-departments will also have a structure, with a Head of Sub-department, and reporting to them, either directly or indirectly, a hierarchy of staff, or perhaps a team of equals or a number of teams of equal individuals. Each sub-department may be centralised or decentralised to varying degrees dependent on how much power and responsibility are given to each employee and post holder, as specified in their job description, or the culture, or their psychological or implicit contract.

The Head of the R&D sub-department communicates with the MD through a scalar chain of command, first to their boss (the Director of Engineering), who then reports to the MD. In the extreme form of the scalar chain of command, if someone in the R&D sub-department wants to speak with someone in the Quality Control sub-department then the communication will have to go up to the head of the sub-department, and that Head will have to communicate with the Director of Engineering, who will then pass the message down to the Head of the Quality Control sub-department, who will then pass it down to the relevant member of their sub-department. Such an organisation is likely to be one where the management do not trust their staff and feel the need to control everything that is happening. This would be the situation where the management was Theory X-based (see the Appendix on Theories X and Y), or where the management were neurotic in a paranoid way (see Chapter 7 and the discussion of Neurotic Organisations). We expect to find these very formalised scalar chains of management in bureaucracies. The scalar chain of command will also be discussed in Chapter 9, as it has obvious implications for communications within organisations.

The organogram also shows the *Span of Control,* that is, the number of people who report directly to a manager, and who are directly controlled by any one manager. Thus the span of control of the Engineering Director is three, as the three Heads of sub-departments in the Engineering Department are directly controlled by the Engineering Director, and report directly to the Engineering Director. The old "rule of thumb" used to be that the span of control should not exceed six as otherwise a manager became overloaded. More recent writing, however, suggests that the span of the control can be much larger if power is decentralised and workers are empowered and trusted. In modern organisations where the culture is to trust and empower workers and to motivate them through targets and goals rather than strict supervision, the span of control can be much greater than six. These sorts of organisations will be short organisations with only a few layers of hierarchy, "organic" rather than "mechanistic" organisations, team- and matrix-based organisations and decentralised organisations with cultures of empowerment and Theory Y management styles.

The case study below is about a small engineering firm and is meant to illustrate a typical small firm which is small, organic and informal.

Case Study 8.1: Anon, an electrical design and manufacturing organisation

Anon (the organisation does not wish to be recognised) is an organisation that designs and assembles electrical components. The company was founded in the early 2000s by its two equal shareholding directors who had a background in the industry. There is no chief executive and the two directors run the company jointly. There are three other shareholders who are engineers but are not directors. The management consists of the five shareholders, plus one or two non-shareholding managers. The remaining 15 employees are shop-floor employees engaged in assembly. The two directors are designated as the Technical Director and the Operations and Sales Director.

Strategy is developed at meetings of the Management Committee attended by the directors and the other managers. Ultimate power is equally in the hands of the two directors. Most communications are informal, aided by the management office being open-plan. Because the organisation is still small and the management is also small there is little in the way of functional specialisation, for example, one of the shareholders and the Technical Director are jointly responsible for R&D and sales.

Approximately 70% of revenue is generated by the design and production of non-standard products that are usually customised versions of standard products, where the creative element comes from the three in-house engineers who form part of the management.

Mid- and small-volume productions take place at the company's UK HQ, but large-scale production uses subcontracted offshore manufacturing. Even a small engineering company has a global aspect, in terms of where it gets some of its output produced, with all the structural and control problems raised by geographically remote production.

Question

If the firm was to double in size, what structural problems do you think the owners would face?

CONTINGENCY THEORY OF ORGANISATIONAL STRUCTURE

An interesting approach to the investigation of organisational structures is to examine the structures that actually exist in reality, that are thus obviously structures that can survive in the harsh realities of the external environment within which the organisations exist. This approach is sometimes referred to as an ecological approach – what species of organisations thrive in the environment. This is about either the "survival of the fittest" – those that survive in a competitive environment are those best adapted to the environment; or may be about the "survival-of-the-fitting". The survival-of-the-fitting seems to imply that more than one species (organisational structural form) can survive, and not just a single "fittest".

The main contingencies that were initially investigated were technology and environment, and they were seminally investigated by Woodward (1965), Burns and Stalker (1968) and Lawrence and Lorsch (1967). Organisational size has also been a major contingency that has been investigated, seminally by Greiner (1972).

In 1965, Woodward published the result of her investigations between 1953 and 1957. She looked at the relationship between production technology and organisational structure. She looked at three technology types: process production (continuous production), large-batch and mass production and unit and small-batch production. Her first main finding in relation to organisational structure was that process producers had the most layers of hierarchy, and that the numbers of layers reduced as the size of the batch reduced. Her second main finding was that spans of control were larger for large-batch and mass production, and relatively smaller for process production and small-batch and unit production. She also found that organisations that conformed to her findings for each of the three technology types were the most efficient. The classical organisational structure theory, that there was a single best structure, was turned on its head. Different types of industries, as defined by their production technology, were best suited by different structures.

Burns and Stalker (1968) examined how Scottish firms were coping with the introduction of electronic technologies and changing market conditions. They ended up suggesting that there were two key organisational structures, and not just the one ideal classical structure that flowed form the work of Weber, Taylor and Adam Smith. They called the two structures the mechanistic and the organic. The classical structure was relabelled the *mechanistic*, and the *organic* organisation was characterised by informality, teams and network-type structures with decision making being delegated to empowered experts. The mechanistic organisations were found in stable, unchanging and predictable external environments, where they were successful, and the organic organisations were found to be successful in industries characterised by dynamic and rapidly changing industrial environments. We have commented earlier in this chapter that the problem with bureaucratic or classical organisations is that they have difficulty adapting to change, where all the rules have to be changed to accommodate the new environment.

Lawrence and Lorsch (1967) investigated in more detail the nature of the external environment that was changing and the impact of the external environments on the organisational structure. Their study was of three US industries: containers, plastics and food. Within each of the firms they examined the structure of three departments or subsystems: Sales, R&D and Manufacturing. Their results showed that the more dynamic and changing the external environment to which the subsystems had to respond, the more the subsystem needed to be organic. Their work showed that within an organisation, different departments would need to adopt a structure that was suitable to their environment. If different departments had different structures, then it raised problems about how the departments would interact together within the organisation. Such differentiated organisations would need more committees and liaison staff to ensure appropriate control and communications.

The size or scale of an organisation is fairly clearly a contingency factor in organisational structure. An early seminal discussion of the scale/size contingency factor was by Greiner (1972) (cited in 317 papers by 2009), who wrote a paper entitled "Evolution and Revolution as Organizations Grow". He developed the idea of organisations having a life cycle through which they passed, one feature of which was the growing size of the organisation as it passed from the initial founding stage, which he called the Creation stage, through five further stages. At the creation stage of the organisation there will be the founder and a very small number of staff who are recruited as the organisation grows from a one-person business. This very small number of employees will be organised in a very organic way with few job descriptions and little in the way of specialisation. People work on whatever needs to be done as they discover the market for their products, how to produce them at the initial level of output, and even discover what products they can produce and whether there is a market for these products. As the organisation grows, with success, there will be a growing number of employees, and people will begin to specialise, and specialist departments will begin to be set up. The structure will then start to change from a very organic and informal structure into a more formalised and bureaucratic structure. The leaders of the organisation will increasingly become specialised on the development of strategy, and will withdraw from daily involvement in all the functions within the organisation. Day-to-day control and management will be devolved to specialist managers who will be selected internally or recruited externally. The factor initiating change at each stage will be some kind of crisis arising from the increasing size of the organisation as it thrives and grows. The following case study demonstrates the impact of scale on structure by looking at an organisation having to restructure as a result of diminishing size due to the economic crisis of 2008/2009. Readers may also find it instructive, at this point, to read the case study *takethatphoto* that appears at page 162 of this chapter; a virtual organisation, which is not only about a virtual organisation but also about a small rapidly growing organisation at the Creation stage of its life cycle.

Case Study 8.2: The international recruitment agency: Change of scale

The recruitment agency, one of the biggest in the world, has offices in very many countries and cities. It is structured so that most offices of any size are run as though they are individual businesses. The international company name is used as a brand for marketing purposes, and top-level strategy comes from Head Office.

The author is familiar with the office in a major US city. Before the international credit crisis of 2008/2009 the office had grown to occupy three floors of a prestige skyscraper, with in excess of 200 recruitment consultants plus the appropriate managers. In late 2008 and early 2009 the recruitment market "fell of a cliff", to quote one of the executive directors. Within months the organisation shrank until

Continued

it occupied only one floor of their building, and the head count was cut by about 65%. As organisations were drastically reducing their recruitment there was very little work for recruitment consultants (the producers of the organisation's services/product), and so consultants were sacked. If they had been the only people to leave, then the organisation would have had a top-heavy structure with lots of managers who were not producing revenue; thus lots of managers were also sacked. The remaining consultants were structured into a smaller number of departments, each of which now covered more segments of the market.

The downsizing meant fewer consultants and managers structured into a smaller number of specialist departments, with managers becoming less specialised. This is an example of restructuring as a function of size. To have continued with the 2008 structure would have been inappropriate and would have resulted in a catastrophic collapse in profitability.

Question

Will the structure revert to its previous structure when the organisation grows back to its former size?

The general conclusion of the contingency approach is that organisations need to be structured in ways that enable them to respond effectively to the environment within which they find themselves.

The early work on contingency implied that the environment was external and had to be responded to by organisations. More recent work has looked at the notion that an organisation may also be at least partially the creator of its environment. New products and new production technology may well be generated within the organisation in their R&D department, thus changing the markets for their products. If we look at PCs and laptops, for example, we see the rapid rate of change of the technology as the result of internal R&D, which means that the specification of the products is constantly and rapidly changing. The development of netbooks has not only meant that there is a differentiated product, but also that there is a new market of buyers, people who want to be in rapid, continuous or frequent communications with friends and colleagues whilst on the move and out of their homes – a new product and a new market.

THE CHANGING EXTERNAL ENVIRONMENT

There are many major factors that have caused the external environment to change in recent decades, and indeed some writers have suggested that the rate of change of the environment is accelerating:

- *Transport costs*
  One of the factors affecting the external environment has been the reduction of transport costs as a result of the development of bulk carriers and containerisation in sea transport, and the falling cost of airfreight with the technical developments in aircraft and the forcing down of air transport prices as competition has grown between airlines.

The reductions in transport costs, amongst other factors, have led to a great growth in globalisation and the sourcing of products in many new manufacturing countries, such as China and India, resulting in companies moving their production to these developing economies, with the consequence that the companies have had to restructure in order to accommodate the new production locations and the problems of controlling operations spread all over the world.

Globalisation has not just affected manufacturing companies but has also affected service providers and the departments within organisations that provide services. Many UK organisations, such as banks, have relocated their telephone customer service departments to India, where educated labour is cheaper than in the UK and English is widely spoken. These changes have also meant that organisations have had to restructure in order to control their globalised form.

■ *Political change*

In both India and China there have been massive political changes in the last 40 years that have meant that the governments in these countries have embraced capitalist free-market economic policies. Similar political philosophy changes have taken place in many other countries, but the massive size of China and India has made them the most important players in the globalisation of the world economy. The changes in both have given a massive boost to the opportunities for globalisation, and have thus put pressure on organisations to develop structures that enable them to benefit from, and control, their globalised form, where both manufacturing and service production are located remotely, often on the other side of the world. Most western organisations that have relocated parts of their operations to China have had to do so as joint operations with Chinese partners (because of Chinese Government policy as enacted in law), thus raising structural problems about controlling and operating international joint ventures and not just organisations with internationally located production divisions.

■ *IT and communication changes*

Developments in the world of IT have meant a revolution in communications as a result of the World Wide Web, emails, web conferencing, cheap long-distance telephone calls and the ease of moving data around the world using electronic means. Increasingly, small and powerful computers, in conjunction with the improved communications and data transfer, have meant that there has been a growing possibility of virtual organisations, where people work from home without the need for central organisational premises. We will devote the next section of this chapter to virtual organisations.

VIRTUAL ORGANISATIONS

Virtual organisations are an organisational form that has become possible, and increasingly frequent, as the result of improved electronic communications and the ability to have electronic data banks that allow remote access. The essence of a virtual organisation is the "...the dispersion of people who have to work together" (Axtell et al., 2004, p. 207). They have also required and encouraged the development of sophisticated communications and data software. These electronic developments have allowed the creation of virtual organisations that have no central office accommodation because employees can all work together whilst being geographically remote from one another. There are also virtual teams or departments, where there is no need for staff to be located together. The industries that are most suited to being virtual appear to be sales, marketing and consultancy. The clear implication is that there can be a virtual marketing organisation, for example, or there can be a virtual marketing department as a part of an otherwise non-virtual organisation.

When information and communications can flow freely through the use of computers, telephones and the Internet, then there are both advantages and disadvantages of creating virtual organisations, or virtual departments.

Advantages of virtual organisations

- A virtual organisation does not need permanent offices and buildings, thus there is a major saving.

- Working from home means that there is no time or financial cost arising from travelling to a central office. When we consider that the cost of a rail ticket to travel daily into central London can run into thousands of pounds per year, this is a considerable saving which may be reflected in lower salary costs, as the salary does not have to cover travel costs.

- Working from home can allow flexitime working, which may enable an organisation to employ good staff who cannot work standard working hours because of their life situation (children and other family commitments, etc.).

- *Increased productivity:* an internal study in IBM showed gains of 15–40% in productivity (Matthes, 1992).

- *Higher sales:* Hewlett-Packard doubled revenue per salesperson after converting its salespeople to a virtual work structure (O'Connell, 1996).

- *Improved customer service:* Anderson Consulting found that their consultants spent 25% more "face time" with clients after changing from permanent offices (O'Connell, 1996).

- Virtual teams can be recruited without having to consider the location of members, but only what they can contribute to the team.

- Virtual project groups or teams can be set up where there is a "relay race". Thus software can be developed 24 hours per day by having team members located in three time zones, so that the work of the first time zone can be sent to the people in the second time zone for them to continue its development, and then their work can be sent on to the third time zone. Such a use of virtual teams allows faster development of software, a very real commercial advantage.

Disadvantages and problems of virtual organisations and teams

- The obvious disadvantage of virtual organisations is that relating between colleagues is much more limited than organisations which are co-located (based in the same building). As we shall discuss in Chapter 9, much of communication lies not just in the words used but also in tone of voice and the emphasising of words, and these two elements are clearly missing when communication is through emails. Electronic chat, gossiping and informal chatter are also less likely when done electronically, and thus it is harder in a virtual organisation to have the informal relating that may be very important in an organisation for developing culture and cohesiveness, and as a channel of communication.

- It takes a particular type of person to succeed in a virtual organisation. Employees of virtual organisations need to be self-motivated (not needing high structure and detailed instructions in order to work effectively), effective communicators (both orally and in writing), adaptable, able to compromise, technically self-sufficient and results-orientated (Cascio, 1999).

- It takes a particular type of manager to manage in a virtual organisation. Perhaps the biggest challenge is to manage performance. This problem is neatly summed up in a quotation (source not given) in Cascio (1999), "If I can't see employees, how do I know that they are working", (p. 9). The management style clearly has to flow from a Theory Y set of beliefs (see the Appendix on Theories X and Y). The first part of the solution is to appoint *appropriate employees*, like those described in the previous list. Next it is important to clearly *define performance*, that is, define what is expected of the employee. This may be about having carefully drawn job descriptions and not just vague statements about "do what is necessary". The next duty of the manager is to *provide resources* that the employee needs in order to be successful in their virtual location. This is about providing all the necessary information in a timely manner, and all the hardware that is needed, such as computers, webcams, modems, sophisticated mobile phones, etc. Finally, the manager needs to *motivate employees*. In virtual organisations Goal Setting would seem to be an appropriate method of motivation, as described in Chapter 4. The key elements are the joint setting of goals and the use of feedback about performance. Both of these elements reduce the out-of-sight out-of-mind sense that employees might experience in a virtual organisation.

- New members of staff, employees or managers, who are newly appointed or newly promoted, may find that it is very difficult to learn the organisational culture and how to operate in a specific virtual organisation.

- The process of group formation, that is discussed in Chapter 1 (Tuckman, 1965), where a group goes through the stages, of Forming, Storming, Norming and Performing, will be slower and more difficult to achieve in a virtual organisation, or team, where members physically spend very little time together.

- The difficulties of working in virtual teams or organisations depend partly on the type of work being conducted – how the employees need to work together to produce the end product or service and the degree and type of interdependence required. Interdependence can be defined as *pooled or additive*, *sequential*, *reciprocal* or *intensive* (Axtell et al., 2004).

☐ *Pooled or additive* interdependence is when tasks are separate and then combined at the end. This is particularly suitable for virtual organisations. The other listed forms of interdependence are progressively less suitable for virtual organisations.

☐ *Sequential* interdependence is when a task flows from one employee to another in one direction. This also fits with virtuality and is an example of the *relay race* that we discussed as the last *advantage* list item above.

☐ *Reciprocal* interdependence is when work flows to and fro between team members, and raises problems for virtual organisations because of the high level of communications between team members that is implied.

☐ *Intensive* interdependence is the least suitable form of interdependence for virtual organisations and is where team members continually and simultaneously need to interact to produce the product.

A more complex discussion of the communications issues present in virtual teams and organisation is to be found in the Communications chapter.

Case Study 8.3: takethat*photo*: A virtual organisation

takethat*photo* (*ttp* subsequently) is a photography business that started in 2006 as an events photography business with two partners who own the business 50% each.

One partner (Dave, the CEO) has a background in marketing, with his two most recent employed jobs being marketing with major photo industry companies. The other partner (Paul) is a professional photographer with a broad knowledge and experience of the technical aspects of photography. The marketing partner had previously part-owned a company (run in his spare time) that organised New Year's Eve Balls and other happenings in the events industry.

This case study is written as the company is just a few months into their third year of trading.

At the time of writing, 2009, *ttp* has five full-time salaried employees and five photographers who work on a daily rate and use a kit (mobile studio, camera, printer, plasma screen and lighting rig) that is provided by *ttp*. At very busy times, such as the Office-party/Dinner-dance season in December, up to an extra 12 photographers have events subcontracted to them and they are paid a percentage of the revenue created by the photographs sold at the event.

Full-time employees and their specialist duties

Dave, the CEO, is chiefly responsible for sales and marketing and jointly responsible for strategy development.

Paul, the other owner, is the operations manager who controls all the technical photographic side of the business and ensures that the photographers know when they are working, where and with what technical equipment. He also contributes to strategy development, especially in terms of what products can technically be offered, as technology develops.

Frank is a full-time salaried photographer.

Kay, controls the administration of *ttp*, making payments, invoicing for jobs done, chasing up unpaid invoices, taking emails and phone calls from clients, fielding enquiries, liaising with clients (past, present and prospective), quoting prices for jobs and dealing with repeat business.

Charlotte assists Kay (3–4 days per week) and assists Dave with marketing, especially to the university market (there are, at the time of writing, 2009, 40+ university student unions as clients).

Currently no one has a formal job description except to the extent that their job is to do whatever is necessary, in their general area of expertise, to grow the business.

Virtual organisation

ttp has no central office facilities. Each of the staff works from their home. If Dave, the CEO, is at the centre, then Paul lives 1 hour and 40 minutes drive away, Frank lives 5 minutes drive away, Kay lives 2 hours and 10 minutes drive away and Charlotte lives about 45 minutes drive away. Having no central office facilities saves about £25000 per year in reduced accommodation costs. The photography takes place at the clients' locations, so photographers have to travel from their home base to deliver the product. The photographed events are spread across England and Wales. No one commutes to a central workplace, thus saving staff commuting time and travelling costs.

Dave speaks by telephone with all employees at least once per day and visits Kay at least once per week. Interaction among staff members is by telephone and email (but not using video conferencing or SKYPE) but there is no regular routine, and other communications are as and when needed for operational reasons.

Each employee is self-motivated and works largely unsupervised, as management supervision is very difficult in a virtual organisation. Company experience is that there is a particular personality that staff need to have if they are to enjoy working in a virtual organisation, and for them to be effective employees.

All the staff meet together in a hotel about three times per year for thanks, feedback, strategy presentation, team building and creation/suggestions.

Computers and mobile phones are provided for the salaried staff.

Some technical photographic editing work is subcontracted to India for cost savings.

Growth

ttp doubled its revenues in the second year of operations and aims to go on growing at that rate for some years, as well as selling events photography franchises where the franchisees buy the right to use the brand name, receive marketing assistance and deliver events photography bookings that are generated centrally by *ttp*.

Continued

Questions

1. What structural changes do you foresee *ttp* having to make in the future as they continue to grow?
2. What extra information would you like in order to analyse this virtual organisation?
3. Would *ttp* benefit from stopping being a virtual organisation?
4. What does *ttp* lose by not having continuous face-to-face communications during the working day?
5. What problems do you think the organisation will already have?
6. What factors might limit the profitable growth of the organisation?
7. Is it possible that *ttp* can grow to the point where they dominate their industry? If not, why?
8. What would be the organisational structure if they rose to industrial domination?

Extra information

You can gain more information about the nature of *ttp*, its products and clients by looking at their website: www.takethatphoto.co.uk, and more information about the nature of the events photography industry by searching the World Wide Web with "events photography" as a search term.

FORMAL AND INFORMAL ORGANISATIONS

So far we have written as though organisations are structured in a rational and logical manner so that they operate in the most effective and efficient way; this is not what actually happens, especially at the micro-level of small organisations, departments and teams.

In Chapter 2 we wrote about the differences between formal and informal cultures, between the espoused and the enacted culture. In a similar way we can write about formal and informal structures, the espoused and the enacted. The culture of an organisation can be seen, in the Critical Perspective, as emerging from the beliefs, values and attitudes of the interacting members of the organisation, contrasted with the efforts of managers to impose a culture on the employees (as viewed through the Managerialist Perspective). The way that a department or small organisation is structured may well be a result of the everyday interactions of the people within the department or organisation, so the structure emerges from interactions and is not deliberately designed. There may be a formal structure, but the enacted structure may be the one that emerges from employee interactions. Viewed in this way, we can say that the structure is a manifestation of the organisation's culture as it develops and emerges.

If we now reflect on Chapter 3, we will remember that one way that organisations differed was in the attitude of staff about whether it was ever permissible to bypass your manager. In countries where bypassing was acceptable, the way that decisions were made would be potentially very different than in a hierarchical bureaucratic organisations. Even if the formal structure was bureaucratic, the reality is that decisions would not be made in the manner expected of a bureaucratic organisation – the informal structure differs from the formal – how things happen is different than how they are supposed to happen. The informal structure that emerges will reflect the beliefs and attitudes of the people within the organisation, and this is likely to differ from one organisation to another, among industries, among different-sized organisations and among different countries.

In Chapter 1 we examine the garbage can theory of decision making, which is the political interacting of the various stakeholders in the organisation. From the interacting comes decisions that are not logical rational decisions to maximize efficiency. This is an example of how the informal structure can differ from the way that the formal structure suggests that decisions should be made.

The final point that we would make in this section is about the influence of founders and long-serving CEOs. There is literature, (see for example the seminal contribution of Kets de Vries and Miller, 1988), that suggests that founders and long-serving CEOs, shape their organisations in a way that reflects their personality. Thus someone who has a personality where order and predictability are important will structure his/her organisation in a very formal and structured way; their organisation is likely to be recognisable as a bureaucracy. Kets de Vries and Miller go further and suggest that if the CEO or founder is neurotic then his/her organisation will also be neurotic with a structure, culture and other subsystems that reflect the neurosis. The ideas of Kets de Vries and Miller were discussed at greater length in Chapter 7.

CONCLUSION

In this chapter we have again, as in a number of other chapters, seen that there is a conflict between the rational and logical and the results that flow from people's interactions and their psychological and personal needs. Organisational structures emerge as a solution to economic imperatives, differing cultures, political processes, personal needs and personalities. There are no easy managerial solutions to what the structure of an organisation should be, and even if the management tries to impose a rational logical solution, the way that it actually turns out will reflect many other interacting forces. We also need to remember that managers, founders and owners also have their own personal agendas that are likely to prevent the design and implementation of a rational logical organisational structure.

REFERENCES

Axtell, C.M., Fleck, S.J., Turner, N., 2004. Virtual teams: collaborating across distance. In: Cooper, C.L., Robertson, I.T. (Eds.), International Review of Industrial and Organisational Psychology. John Wiley & Sons.

Burns, T., Stalker, G.M., 1968. The Management of Innovation. Tavistock Publications.

Cascio, W.F., 1999. Virtual workplaces: implications for organizational behaviour. In: Cooper, C.L., Rousseau, D.M. (Eds.), Trends in Organizational Behaviour. John Wiley & Sons?

Galbraith, J.R., 1971. Matrix organization designs: how to combine functional and project forms. Business Horizons 29–40.

Greiner, L.E., 1972. Evolution and revolution as organizations grow. Harvard Business Review 50.

Huff, A.S., 1988. Politics and argument as a means of coping with ambiguity and change. In: Pondy, L.R., Boland Jr., R.J., Thomas, H. (Eds.), Managing Ambiguity and Change. John Wiley & Sons.

Kets de Vries, M.F.R., Miller, D., 1988. Neurotic Organisation. Jossey-Bass.

Lawrence, P.R., Lorsch, J.W., 1967. Organisation and Environment. Harvard University Press.

Marx, K., 2009. Das Kapital. Shipside, S. (Ed.). Infinite Ideas Limited.

Matthes, K., 1992. Telecommuting: balance business and employee needs. HR Focus 69.

Mintzberg, H., 1983. Structure in Fives: Designing Effective Organizations. Prentice Hall.

O'Connell 1996 In: Casio, R.F.,

Peters, T.J., Waterman, R.H., 1982. Search of Excellence: Lessons from America's Best Run Companies. Harper & Row.

Pugh, D.S. (Ed.), 1990. Organisational Theory: Selected Readings, third ed. Penguin Books, Harmsworth.

Ring, P.S., 1997. Processes facilitating reliance on trust in inter-organizational networks. In: Ebers, M. (Ed.), The Formation of Inter-Organizational Networks. Oxford University Press.

Smith, A., 2008. An enquiry into the nature and causes of the wealth of nations: a selected edition. In: Sutherland, K. (Ed.), Oxford World's Classics.

Tuckman, B.W., 1965. Development sequences in small groups. Psychological Bulletin 63, 384–399.

Woodward, J., 1965. Industrial Organization: Theory and Practice. Oxford University Press.

Communications

9

There is an old story that during the First World War, a message was sent "send rein-forcements, we are going to advance" and having passed along a long chain of communications it arrived as "send three and four pence, we are going to a dance". ("Three and four pence" was a sum of money at that time.) Many readers may have played a children's game, which in the UK is known as "Chinese whispers". In this game a message is spoken to a first recipient who then repeats it to a second recipient, and so on down a long line of recipients. The message that arrives is rarely recognisable from the message that started. In organisations, the importance of good communications, or the cost of poor communications, cannot be exaggerated.

The two illustrations of miscommunications in the previous paragraph show that to discuss communications, it would be helpful to have a formal model of communications so that we can examine both successful and unsuccessful communication.

The most frequently used formal model of communications was developed by Schramm (1953). The process of communication flows from one element to the next. The elements of this model are:

- *Communicator*: someone who wants to communicate some information, whether it is facts, data, opinions, ideas, instructions or questions.

- *Encoding*: the communicator needs to find some symbolic way of turning their ideas, information, data, questions, etc. into a message. They may encode into words, charts, diagrams, facial expressions or any other form of symbols that can embody a communication.

- *Message and medium*: the communicator, having decided what they wish to communicate, and encoding it into appropriate symbols, has to decide how they are going to *send* the symbols into which the message has been encoded. The range of mediums (or media) that are currently available is huge and growing. The communicators could *speak* to the receiver across the space between their two desks, they could use the telephone (land line or cell/mobile phone), they could email, use video-conferencing, they could raise their eye-brows to indicate surprise (in the UK) or they could make a gesture with their hand or their body that communicated their message. They could even print or write their communi-cation on a piece of paper and send it through the surface mail service ("snail mail" as opposed to email).

- *Receiver*: this is the person who receives the communication that the sender encoded into symbols and then sent via a medium. What the receiver now has

An Introduction to Organisational Behaviour for Managers and Engineers

167

to do is to *decode* the message so that they can understand what the communicator wished to communicate.

Whatever the receiver does as a result of receiving the communication will represent a communication back to the originator of the initial communication. We can go so far as to say that:

Whatever is said or not said, done or not done, represents a communication.

This probably sounds like a very obscure statement, so let us give one or two examples. You are about to go on a holiday, and your boss makes no reference to your holiday or to the period that will follow your holiday. You may think "my boss does not care about me, or, they are not interested in me except in the office; or your boss's silence may make you think that they made no reference to your return from holiday because they are going to sack you on your return. In reality your boss's silence may simply reflect that they were too busy to mention your holiday, or that they did not know that you were going on a holiday. Alternatively, your boss may have said "have a great holiday and come back refreshed". What did this communication mean? – "your work has deteriorated recently because you have been obviously tired" or "I really need you to be refreshed and full of life when you return from your holiday because we have to make some critical strategic decisions when you return, and I need you to be involved in these decisions." Everything is a communication.

- *Feedback*: the response of the *receiver* of the original message constitutes *feedback*. They may carry out the order that was communicated, send the information that was requested by the original communicator or they may send a communication saying, "I don't understand what you want me to do". Because "whatever is done or not done, represents a communication" there will always be feedback received by the initiator of the original communication.

- *Perception*: perception can also be called sense making and is clearly crucial to the accuracy of a communication. We need to ask "what does this word(s)/picture/table mean – what does the original communicator think that this word(s)/picture/table means, and/or what do I, the receiver of the communication, think that the word(s)/picture/table means. Communications have perception and sense making at both ends of the process and thus there is scope for confusion at both ends of the communication. Clearly, perception is a part of coding and decoding.

- *Noise*: distortions and errors can appear at each stage of the communication process, and are referred to as *noise*. We have already suggested that perceptual problems about the meaning of words can cause noise at the coding and decoding stages of the process, but we also know that there can be noise at the *medium* stage of the process – we may have a poor telephone connection so that we are not sure what the speaker is saying; or we may have received a fax where the fax machine at the sender's end (or the receiver's end) is faulty and the receiver cannot make out some of the letters, and thus may guess what some of the words are meant to be. The receiver of an audio message may be partially deaf, they may be in a noisy room or they may be distracted by colleagues or other phones.

NON-VERBAL COMMUNICATIONS

Most of what we have written so far seems implicitly to be about communicating with words, although we have referred to symbols that might be images or mathematical formulae.

One study of verbal communications has suggested that only 7% of the impact is carried by the verbal content, whereas 38% comes from the vocal inflection and the remaining 55% comes from the facial content (Mehrabian, 1971), and other studies have also indicated the importance of inflection and facial content, but we need to be wary of accepting *these* figures too literally, because they are a result of laboratory experiments and were about the vocalising of feelings and attitudes. What we can be sure of is that much affect is communicated by inflection and facial content, and affect is often an important part of what is being communicated within organisations. Verbal face-to-face communication is an example of rich communication, Fisher (1993). If we telephone, we lose the facial content of the communication and we have a less rich communication. If we email someone, then we lose the vocal inflexion *and* the facial content. The percentages vary between languages. English is a very rich language where words can be used to express very precise communications because of the huge English vocabulary, but Mandarin is a much more contextual language, where you need to know the context within which the words are being used if there is to be a comparably accurate communication, and thus facial content may be more important in Mandarin.

Non-verbal communications (NVCs) are those communications that are not word-based, and, as the above percentages suggest, they can be crucial to accurate communication.

NVCs have several aspects, including artefacts, body language and stereotyping, several of which are discussed below:

- *Artefacts*: what do our car, clothes and furniture say about us? Why do senior executives often have the biggest offices and desks and the most expensive cars? Are they trying to tell us something? – look how successful and powerful I am.

- *Body language*: what do our *facial expressions, gestures* or *body movements communicate?*

    □ *Facial expression*: the main facial expressions are happy, sad, neutral, angry, disgusted, fearful and surprise. These expressions seem to be universal, and until recently it was believed that we all learnt to decode these facial expressions accurately, but Jack et al, (2009), note "Central to all human interaction is the mutual understanding of emotions, achieved primarily by a set of biologically rooted social signals evolved for this purpose—facial expressions of emotion. Although facial expressions are widely considered to be the universal language of emotion … some negative facial expressions consistently elicit lower recognition levels among Eastern compared to Western groups…". It seems that East Asian groups find the emotions of "fear" and "disgust" particularly difficult to recognize (to decode). The research showed that East Asians tend to see "surprise" when the expression was fear, and "anger" when the expression was disgust. The facial expressions that indicate "fear" and "disgust" are universal, but not the ability to recognise them. The research of Jack et al. (2009) suggests that this is either because East Asians tend to concentrate on looking at the eyes when they decode facial expressions (as the research showed), and Western Caucasians look at the whole of the face (as the research showed), or that the emotions of fear and disgust are culturally less acceptable in East Asian countries. The eyes are ambiguous when fear and disgust are experienced.

☐ *Body language (movement and gesture)*: Morris (1994), Pease (1986) and Wainwright (1985) have all written good books on body language, and Morris in particular looks at how gestures differ from one country to another, hence saving the reader from getting into serious difficulties if their gesture is decoded in a way that differs from the coding of the gesture maker. We take just one hand gesture as an example – the "hand ring", where the thumb and the first finger touch at the tip to form a ring. In much of Europe and the US this gesture means good or OK, but in Germany, parts of Latin America, Russia, the Middle East and a small number of other countries it is a sexual insult; in Belgium, France and Tunisia it means zero or worthless; in Japan the gesture means money, or that something is of high cost; in South America it means perfection and in Italy it means "what are you talking about?". Clearly it pays to be fluent in hand gestures! Even a nod of the head can mean "agree/yes" or "disagree/no" dependent on which country you are in. Imagine asking "Do we have a deal?" and assuming that a nod meant "yes" when you are in a country where a nod means "no". How people stand and use their bodies also speaks volumes.

☐ *Stereotyping*: in order to decode, people often use stereotypes. The stereotype may be associated with gender, skin colour, religion, politics, oral accent or any number of other characteristics by which we assign someone to a group. We may use the fact that someone is a Muslim to decode what they have said, but they may be a Muslim who does not conform to our culturally determined stereotype, and thus our decoding will be incorrect and the communication may fail.

■ *Using all senses*: all the senses can be involved in communicating – sight, sound smell, touch and even taste. If I cook you a meal what might that communicate deliberately and inadvertently? As a young academic I was visited repeatedly by a female student with an endless stream of fascinating intellectual problems. After a number of weeks of visits, I noticed that whenever she came to my room she smelt of a delightful perfume, but when I met her by chance then she never smelt of perfume. My sense of smell had eventually enabled me to decode the unspoken communication as an invitation to dalliance and not intellectual endeavour!

Case Study 9.1: Decoding the meaning of a moustache

Some years ago in a multicultural MBA class with 25 different nationalities, the author rather foolishly tried to demonstrate international cultural differences by saying that in Britain the majority of men with a moustache were either policemen, in the armed services or homosexual, but that many men in Germany and Poland who had moustaches fell into none of the three categories. Shortly after, the author, who then had a moustache *and* a beard, received an email seeking a "date" from a homosexual MBA class student who was attracted to "older men"! Clearly, the communication that I thought that I had sent had been decoded incorrectly!

Case Study 9.2: The case of the police officer's turned up toes

A few years ago the author was teaching a class of police officers about the importance of body language as a form of communication. A female firearms officer was asked to think for 30 seconds about someone that she liked very much. Then she was asked to think for 30 seconds about someone that she did not like. The people in the class observed the officer for both 30-seconds. Then the observed officer was asked to think of the taller, blonder, older, etc., of the two people. As she thought of the taller, the rest of the class had to "guess" whether the person being thought about was the liked or disliked – the only clue being the officer's observed body language. Every time, everyone in the class was correct. We had all noticed that when she had thought of the person that she liked, her toes had turned up.

BARRIERS TO COMMUNICATION

Most of the barriers to communications, that are in the following list, are standard ideas, and a full discussion of them is to be found in a standard text like Fisher (1993), but we will briefly outline the standard barriers, plus some more recent barriers:

- *Differing frames of reference*: engineers make sense of the world in one way, and marketing people in a different way, as a result of their differing implicit and explicit theories and any possible personality differences between a typical engineer and a typical marketing person. This can be reduced to "differing sense making".

- *Selective listening*: we may only hear or decode what we want or expect to hear or experience. The author recently overheard a conversation that for one person was about the difference in weather between the UK and Australia, and for the other person was about how different Christmas celebrations are in Australia and the UK. The "Christmas" person responded, "Yes, Christmas must be very different" only to eventually realise, when the conversation grew confusing, that the other person had commented on the "crispness" of UK weather in December. The "Christmas" person decoded "crispness" as "Christmas", because of selective listening.

- *Value judgments*: the shop floor workforce may believe that the management always wants to cheat them, and thus are always looking for the "true exploitative message" in a communication.

- *Source credibility*: how credible is the source of the communication? "Can I trust this person to have anything sensible to communicate to me as they have never said anything sensible in the past and they don't share my knowledge, education and experience; so I won't bother to read their email."

- *Semantic problems*: where the sender and the recipient do not share the same first language and/or culture, then each may understand a single word to have different meanings. What possible meanings can be attached to the message "the business is sick." The head of a university may ask each department to submit a brief report on their research. What length is "brief"? - 500, or 5000 or 50,000 words?; what period is to be covered – the last academic year, the last 5 years, the last semester? The reports that the University Head receives will constitute feedback on the original communication (the request), and are likely, in some cases, to vary significantly from what the Head had actually wanted (*if* they were clear about that, in their own mind, at the time of the request).

The way a word or sequence of words is understood may vary because of differing colloquial uses of the words. The author recently replied to a German relative's enquiry as to whether he was cold and replied, "Ich bin warm", "I am warm". Technically the vocabulary and the grammar were correct, but the answer produced peals of laughter, because colloquially I had replied that I was gay/homosexual. The USA and Britain were said by Winston Churchill to be "two nations divided by a single language". The communication receiver may also not understand the diagrams and mathematics that form part of the communication – they do not understand the meaning of the symbols.

■ *Filtering*: as communication rises up through an organisation, it may be edited to make it briefer at each stage. This may be acceptable if the person editing understands the communication exactly as it was intended by the original communicator, but if they do not, they may omit elements that are important. An interesting occasional different problem is that a receiver decodes a communication and "realises" that something is missing, so they add that missing element before they pass it on. Thus elements of the communication are not only lost but also invented.

Even if there is no need to make a communication briefer as it passes up or down the organisation, it may get changed as each recipient makes it into a form suitable for the next person in the hierarchy.

A further manifestation of filtering is that, within organisations, no one wants to be the communicator of bad news, so it is edited out as the communication rises up through the organisation. The result is that the executives at the top of the organisation may only receive good news and information, and thus make inappropriate strategy. Reluctance to hear bad news or criticism, or the ignorance of it, was discussed in Chapter 7, where it was written about as being typical of narcissistic leaders.

■ *In-group language or jargon*: many of us have had the experience of asking an IT person about our PC or software, and we often cannot understand the answer because there is so much jargon in the reply. Within an organisation, the different functional specialists tend to have their own jargon/vocabulary/language, which prevents satisfactory communications with another function that does not share the jargon or specialist language.

■ *Status differences*: a university Vice-Chancellor may not expect that an email from a cleaner will have anything of importance, and not may bother to read the email.

■ *Proxemic behaviour*: when we are talking to another person, the distance we stand from them varies from one country to another, depending on the relationship between the two people and on what is being communicated. Hall (1966) first used the term proxemics to define the study of the distance between interacting people. He distinguished intimate, personal, social and public distances (each greater than the preceding distance) and noted that the distances were smaller in Latin countries and Japan, and greater in Nordic countries. If you stand too close to me, I may not pay attention to what you are actually saying because I am feeling uncomfortable with your closeness, or because I am wondering why you are standing so close – what are you communicating by your closeness?

■ *Time pressures*: if an emailed document arrives just before the meeting for which it is an input, then the receiver may not have time to read it carefully; thus there is a miscommunication. The receiver may also wonder why the document was sent so late, and whether this was deliberate. In effect, the receipt of the email has layers of communication to be decoded. A summary and/or a content list might help to partially overcome this problem of time pressure.

■ *Communications overload*: partially dependent on how an organisation is structured, certain people may be overwhelmed by the number of communications they receive. It is common to hear even relatively junior managers complaining of the high number of emails, telephone calls and faxes that they receive in a day. If a manager is in a flat organisation, with few levels of hierarchy, wide spans of control and a management style that requires each of the subordinates to "report in" each day, then that manager will receive very many communications per day. How will they know which communications are the most important? The problem is exacerbated by the ease with which large circulation lists can be attached to emails. Perhaps there needs to be a negotiation about *who* needs to receive *what* communication. Even as a junior academic, the author once returned from a 2-week holiday to find 200 emails awaiting attention.

■ *Poorly subject-labelled emails*: if the author receives an email with the subject given as "hello big boy" and an unknown sender, then I am likely to delete it unread. Email "subjects" need to indicate something of the content.

■ *Time differences*: if managers in China and the UK wish to communicate, the overlap in working hours is very limited as a result of the 8-hour time difference. In Chapter 8 we talked about relay advantages of virtual organisations, but an 8-hour time difference means that today's California communication emailed to London may not be able to produce a considered response until the next Californian working day.

■ *Punctuation*: incorrect punctuation can completely change the meaning of a piece of writing. Lynne Truss's book "Eats, Shoots and Leaves" beautifully explores the problems of ambiguity in writing, including those brought about by punctuation (Truss, 2009). "Eats, Shoots and Leaves" is very different than "Eats Shoots and Leaves" If this brief sentence is presented with a picture of a black and white panda, then we can all manage without punctuation, because we assume, rightly or wrongly, that the statement is about pandas and what they eat; hence, context can add to communication and aid decoding.

■ *Regional accents*: how we pronounce words can aid or hinder communication. Even different regional accents may cause confusion. In Germany, someone from Düsseldorf may find it difficult to understand someone from Bavaria who is also speaking German, but with a very different accent. In Germany all letters in a word are normally pronounced, but in English this is not so. A German will say "bom bing" and a Britain will say "boming", when they both mean "bombing" – confusion can reign (or rain)!

■ *Cultural differences*: in Chapter 3 we wrote of the meaning of time in different cultures. If an English person invites you to dinner at their home, and the invitation (communication) specifies 8.00 p.m., this message may be culturally decoded in different ways. An Indian guest may think the invitation means, "some time between 8.00 and 10.00 p.m."; and a German may think that the invitation means "arrive at 8.00 p.m. precisely". The English host is likely to have meant "arrive between 8.15 and 8.30 p.m.". Internationally, different cultures, as sense making, can lead to very different decoding.

In Japan the response to the question "do you understand?" is usually to say "yes", whether there is understanding or not, so that question is a poor way to elicit feedback. The author once asked a Japanese MBA student whether it was true that Japanese people would normally respond with "yes", and the answer was "yes", plus much laughter!

AN INSTRUCTIVE COMMUNICATIONS GAME

What follows is an amusing and instructive example of what can happen to a communication as it passes from person to person. The activity was developed by Bond (1986). The first member of a team is shown an illustration of an owl, which they can look at for 30 seconds or so. The illustration is then turned face down and the viewer has to reproduce all they can remember of the illustration. The second member of the team then looks at the first member's illustration for 30 seconds, it is then turned face down and the second team member has to reproduce all that they can remember of the illustration that they looked at. This sequence goes on through the entire team and then the sequence of drawings is examined to see how the visual communication has changed as it moved through the team. Reproduced below is a typical output of a team of engineering undergraduates. Bond (1986)

A number of conclusions are obvious when we examine the sequence of drawings:

■ The longer the chain of communication the greater is the distortion.

■ People leave out elements that they think are unimportant.

■ When people think they know what the message is, and that there is an element missing, then they will add it to the communication.

■ Retaining the original would prevent distortion.

■ Feedback at each stage would prevent distortion.

■ The chain of communication is only as strong as the weakest link – one person can ruin the communication for everyone who follows after them.

■ Someone who is visually poor can wreck this communication chain. Neuro-Linguistic Programming (O'Connor and Seymour, 1990) suggests that people

FIGURE 9.1

The owl and the pussy cat

have a favoured medium of data collection and processing – for some people it is about images, for others it is about the written word and for others it is about hearing the information, implying that communications should be about telling, writing and images, so that everyone can understand the communication in their preferred way.

■ People from countries that do not have owls are handicapped in this communication process. People from the Middle East are unlikely to be able to make sense of a communication that is about wintry snow and ice conditions – it is not in their experience or their working vocabulary.

FORMAL AND INFORMAL COMMUNICATIONS

In the village that the author used to live in, people say "what they don't know they make up." If there is a failure to formally communicate, then research suggests that there will be rumours circulating, or information will circulate informally on the "grapevine". Some research, Walton (1961), suggests that grapevine communications are more than 75% accurate. The 25% may well lead to unhelpful rumours, speculation and inappropriate actions. It seems important to prevent a communications "dark hole" to minimise the grapevine and rumours. A common observation about rumours is that they should not be believed until they are officially denied!

A ROGERIAN APPROACH TO PERFECT COMMUNICATIONS

Rogers (1951) developed a style of counselling that was called Client- or Person-Centred. This style of counselling offers a model of perfect communication that may have something to tell us about communicating successfully when truly accurate communication is essential; for example, when an important decision has to be made by a group of two or more people where all information, all thinking and all feelings have to be clearly understood by everyone in the decision-making group. We will illustrate with a communication between two people. The first person (the communicator) tells their "story", explaining what they want the listener (receiver) to understand. The listener listens intently to the words and the verbal emphasis, and watches the body language, and then feeds back to the communicator what the listener understood the communicator to have said and be feeling, in the listener's own words (they should not be a human voice recorder that simply parrots back the words that they heard). The communicator can now reflect "is that what I wanted to communicate, and has the listener understood how I feel about the communication?" After the reflection, the communicator can now feedback to the listener and say something like "These parts you understood, but there are other parts that you did not understand, and I am not sure that you really understand how strongly I feel about this matter". The listener now responds by inviting the communicator to have a second attempt at getting the listener to understand the full richness of the communication. Now the communicator is forced to think "Exactly what is it that I want to communicate, and how exactly do I feel." Asking this question of them-self forces the communicator to clear their own thinking. They have a second attempt at sending their "message". The whole circle of statement and feedback continues until both the sender and the receiver can agree that the listener does truly understand the message in all its richness and complexity. The end result is something approaching perfect communications. An unexpected result of the process is that it helps the sender to be clearer about what they want to communicate, and how they feel, than they were when they first sent their message. The key is the feedback and the determination of both the sender and the listener to fully understand.

VIRTUAL ORGANISATIONS AND COMMUNICATIONS

If the term "communications" is used as a literature search term, then very few papers come up, which seems to indicate that there is not a lot of research and theorising being done in the area of communications. When, however, "virtual organisations" is the search term, then there are very many hits, and an important part of that literature looks at the role of communications in virtual organisations. The literature looks at the impact of virtual organisations' communications systems on the formation of groups, the development of trust and cohesion in groups and the process of decision making in virtual groups. In this section, we will look at some of these topics and the issues that flow out of the virtual communications literature.

The essence of a virtual organisation, as discussed in Chapter 8, is that workers are not co-located, they are spatially separated. This definition does not draw a clear line between virtual and non-virtual organisation. If we reflect on a company HQ, with perhaps hundreds of workers, what we know is that many of them are never in physical contact with one another as they are in separate offices all over the HQ building. Someone on a course, 20 years ago, complained to the author that, since the introduction of email in his organisation, he actually met his colleagues much less often, and that most communication was through impersonal emails, where the personal touch was missing. Thus we argue that almost all organisations have some degree of virtuality about them, and not just organisations with no company building or buildings. If this point is accepted, then communications in virtual organisations are just a special case of communications in all but the very smallest organisations.

The literature shows quite clearly that where a physical space is not shared by workers this means that communications have to be via means other than speech to someone that you can't see, and this usually means electronic communications. In high-context cultures, like those in Asia and the Middle East, what is *not said* is often as important to communications as what *is said*, and this raises the possibility that virtual organisations will be ineffective in these countries, Cascio (1999). The consequence of electronic communications is that it may be harder to form relationships with the people who you work with because the non-verbal communications are missing and feedback is less likely in an electronically communicating team. Axtell et al. (2004), commenting on proximity of workers, observe that "A substantial body of research has demonstrated a positive link between the proximity of others and interpersonal liking… and…that relates to higher levels of communication." (p. 207). Rich information is better at reducing ambiguity and uncertainty and at facilitating shared meaning (Axtell et al., 2004). These ideas seem to support the idea that because virtual organisations have to use some non-rich communications, like emails and the telephone, it will be harder to build up teams that can successfully interact.

Other research, such as Technology Adaptation theories (see for example DeSanctis and Poole, 1994), suggests that these conclusions may not hold as people learn how to use electronic means of communication in a better way once they are used to them, and that there may actually be advantages to electronic communication. We may note the everyday experience of people using chat rooms and social networking sites, where one of the problems can actually be the high intensity of the relationships that are formed electronically. (Axtell et al., 2004) comment that "Impressions and interpersonal relationships via communications technology can also be more extreme and intense than face-to face relations." (p. 213). Certainly it seems that people feel much less inhibited when they are communicating electronically, for example, in a chat room. The author took part in an experiment organised by one of his colleagues, where a number of small group tutorials were run in an electronic chat room rather than in a classroom. The discussion was much more fast and furious than ever occurred in the classroom and there was very little deference to the status of the author as tutor. Most students felt more able to join in with the discussion even though they knew that the class would subsequently return to a conventional classroom. Social Context Cues Theory argues that "… lack of social cues increases anonymity which results in a state of deindividuation… This is argued to result in uninhibited, antinormative behaviour such as reduced politeness, intolerance, greater conflict and hostile behaviour." (Axtell et al., 2004, p. 211). Sigel et al. (1986) and Sproull and Kiesler (1986) have argued that this disinhibiting effect will lead to positive effects such as status equalisation and more equal participation.

The other result that comes out of the virtuality literature is that because virtual organisations have to make more use of communication media which lacks richness, there has to be some compensation, either by learning to use the media in a rich way (DeSanctis and Poole, 1994) or by having more communications so that quantity makes up for the reduced richness of the communications media. One solution is to arrange more opportunities for staff to physically meet on away days and similar events.

CONCLUSIONS

The literature on communications makes it clear that communications are fraught with difficulty and that poor communications will lead to slow and ineffective processes.

To improve communications, we simply need to avoid the problems that we have listed and examined. It will also help if we are empathic, in the sense of thinking about the person that we are communicating with, so that we anticipate any problems that they will have in decoding our communication; are they short of time, is the language of the communication their first language, do they share our culture and technical jargon, are they dyslexic and would it help to use more than one media (by using not only words, but also diagrams and illustrations)? If we get to know the person with whom we are communicating, then it is easier to code and pick a media that will help the communication; this is particularly the case when there is some degree of virtuality about the relationship between the two of you. Whilst formal feedback takes time, it does help the accuracy of the communication and ensures that the feedback is not of the kind where the communicator tries to make sense of the silence in the absence of any formal feedback.

If both parties to a communication (the sender and the receiver) know one another, then communicating can be more accurate and efficient. Communicating is a form of relating, and the better people relate, the better they can communicate, and the better they communicate, the better they relate – a virtuous circle.

REFERENCES

Axtell, C.M., Fleck, S.J., Turner, N., 2004. Virtual teams: collaborating across distance. In: Cooper, C.L., Robertson, I.T. (Eds.), International Review of Industrial and Organizational Psychology. John Wiley.

Bond, T., 1986. Games for Social and Life Skills. Nelson Thornes Ltd.

Cascio, W.F., 1999. Virtual workplaces: implications for organizational behaviour. In: Cooper, C.L., Rousseau (Eds.), Trends in Organizational Behaviour. John Wiley.

DeSanctis, G., Poole, M.S., 1994. Capturing the complexity in advanced technology use: adaptive structuration theory. Organizational Science 5 (2), 121–147.

Fisher, D. (Ed.). In: Communications in Organizations, second ed. West Publishing Company.

Hall, E.J., 1966. The Hidden Dimension. Anchor Books.

Jack, R.E., Blais, C., Scheepers, C., Schyns, P.G., Caldara, R., Cultural confusions show that facial expressions are not universal. Current Biology, available online, 13 August 2009.

Mehrabian, A., 1971. Silent Messages. Wadsworth, California.

Morris, D., 1994. Bodytalk: A World Guide to Gestures. Jonathan Cape.

O'Connor, J., Seymour, J., 1990. Introducing Neuro-Linguistic Programming: The New Psychology of Personal Excellence. Mandala.

Pease, A., 1981. Body Language: How to Read Others Thoughts by Their Gestures. Sheldon Press, London.

Schramm, W., 1953. How communication works. In: Schramm, W. (Ed.), The Process and Effects of Mass Communication. University of Illinois.

Siegel, J., Dubrovsky, V., Kiesler, S., McGuire, T.W., 1986. Group processes in computer-mediated communication. Organizational Behaviour and Human Decision Processes 37 (2), 157–187.

Spoull, L., Kiesler, S., 1986. Reducing social-context cues – electronic mail in organizational communication. Management Science 32 (11), 1492–1512.

Truss, L., 2009. Eats, Shoots and Leaves. Harper Collins.

Rogers, C., 1951. Client-Centred Therapy. Constable.

Wainwright, G.R., 1985. Body Language, Teach Yourself Books. Hodder & Stoughton.

Walton, E., March–April 1961. How Efficient is the Grapevine? Personnel.

Appendix: McGregor's Theories X and Y

In many organisations, managers hold implicit theories and make assumptions about behaviour. These are implicit in the sense that they are beliefs about organisations that are not made explicit, and flow from the experience and beliefs of the manager and not from academic theorizing. They encapsulate the way that the managers make sense of their experience.

In 1960, McGregor formulated some of these implicit theories or assumptions into what he called Theory X and Theory Y. These two theories were about the beliefs that managers held about the attitude of employees towards work. What McGregor did was make explicit the implicit assumptions and theories that he observed to be widely held by managers, see McGregor (1960) in Pugh (1990). McGregor set down two sets of beliefs that he observed managers to hold.

Both Theories X and Y are a set of assumptions or beliefs about workers or employees. The following definitions of Theories X and Y are quotations from McGregor (1960) in Pugh (1990).

THEORY X

- "The average human being has an inherent dislike of work and will avoid it if he can.

- Because of this human characteristic of dislike of work, most people must be coerced, controlled, directed and threatened with punishment to get them to put forth adequate effort toward the achievement of organizational objectives.

- The average human being prefers to be directed, wishes to avoid responsibility, has relatively little ambition and wants security above all else." (Pugh, 1990, pp. 358–359).

THEORY Y

- "The expenditure of physical and mental effort in work is as natural as play or rest.

- External control and the threat of punishment are not the only means for bringing about effort towards organizational objectives. Man will exercise self-direction and self-control in the service of objectives to which he is committed.

- Commitment to objectives is a function of the rewards associated with their achievement.

- The average human being learns, under proper conditions, not only to accept, but also to seek responsibility.

■ The capacity to exercise a relatively high degree of imagination, ingenuity and creativity in the solution of organizational problems is widely, not narrowly, distributed in the population.

■ Under the conditions of modern industrial life, the intellectual potentialities of the average human being are only partially utilized." (Pugh, 1990, pp. 367–368).

McGregor suggested that managers tended to believe either Theory X or Theory Y.

It is obvious that if the founders and senior managers of an organisation hold a set of beliefs that we recognise as Theory X or Theory Y, then the organisation will reflect those beliefs.

We can see that Theory X beliefs underlie Taylorism and Scientific Management (Taylor, 1947), Fordism and the assembly line approach to manufacturing and the classic organisational structures and management behaviours that are a reflection of much of Fayol's (1949) theory of organisations and the bureaucratic organisational form.

Taylorism and Scientific Management (Pugh, 1990) subdivided the work process into very small parts where each worker performed their narrowly defined job exactly as instructed. In these organisations there was no scope for individual creativity on the part of the workers, and they were paid on the basis of what they produced, that is, it was assumed that they would work if they were paid for each thing they did, and that if they were paid a salary, and were not closely supervised, then they would be lazy, as Theory X assumes.

Bureaucratic and classically structured organisations are also based on the assumptions of Theory X, where workers have narrowly defined jobs, the worker is rule bound and is closely monitored and supervised.

The motivation theories of the 1960s were very much based on a Theory Y set of beliefs, based upon the then fashionable ideas of self-actualisation. Even in the 1960s, the idea seemed to be that low-level jobs that only satisfied the basic needs of workers, as defined by Maslow (1943) (physiological, security and social needs), would be filled by people who needed strict supervision and for whom there could be no scope for creativity. Self-actualisation was seen as something for managers and more senior workers.

One of the mysteries of Theories X and Y beliefs is the way that managers who hold Theory X beliefs assume that they apply to lower workers, but not to managers. This is despite the fact that the managers who may well have been promoted up from low-level jobs where they presumably were Theory X-type people who could not find work rewarding, and were lazy. Do the managers think that when a worker is promoted into a managerial position they suddenly changes their beliefs and behaviours and become conscientious, diligent and creative? An alternative is that managers believe that all workers are lazy and uncreative because they know, or believe, that managers are also like that, but disguise the fact. Psychotherapeutic theory would suggest that managers project their own characteristics onto their workforce, that is, managers know that they are lazy and will do as little work as they can, and to make themselves feel better they assume that everyone is like they are.

One study of employees (MOW, 1987) asked what people would do if they suddenly became so rich that they did not have to work in order to generate an income. The general result, in a wide range of countries, was that the majority of people would continue to work, although not necessarily at the same job, or under the same conditions. In Britain 31% said that they would stop working, and in Germany the figure was 30%, but in the USA only 12% would stop working and in Japan it was only 7% who would stop. This study, and other similar studies, clearly indicate that the rewards of working are not limited to the material rewards of money income, pensions, etc.

One other possibility is that if people are treated as though they are lazy, uncreative and untrustworthy, then that is what they become. If you design jobs, payment schemes and management styles on the assumption that people are lazy and uncreative, then perhaps that is exactly how they will behave. Conversely, if you design jobs and organisations on the Theory Y assumptions, then you may find yourself with a workforce of motivated, involved and creative workers.

You might like to look at individual organisations, with which you are familiar, to see if they have been designed by people who believe in Theory X, or whether the designers' beliefs are Theory Y. Your familiarity may be because you are, or have been, an employee, or because the organisation is one where friends or parents work, or because parents or friends founded the organisation.

We end this appendix with two small case studies that illustrate some of the features of Theories X and Y, and that pose some questions for your consideration.

Case Study 1: The sales executives

I was doing some consultancy in a Sales Department in the UK headquarters of a large international organisation, and had negotiated a brief that I would comment on anything that I thought was worthy of comment.

One issue that came to my attention was the very rapid turnover of the sales executives (as they called their sales staff); on average staff stayed only 12 months. It took 6 months for staff to learn about the products that they were selling, and thus they were only likely to be effective for 6 months before they left their job.

When I interviewed the sales executives, they told me that they did not like being treated by the management as though they could not be trusted and creative. They all agreed that they were hired as adults and then treated as foolish and idle children. The whole management style was clearly Theory X based. This seemed worthy of comment.

The Head of Department agreed that the department was probably not getting all it could out of the sales executives by hiring them as adults and then treating them as idle children. It was agreed that an effort should be made to change the management style of the sales managers from Theory X to Theory Y.

The two sales managers protested that their staff were lazy and uncreative (that they conformed to Theory X) and that meant that they had no alternative but to supervise them very closely and do all the thinking for them. They both believed that was how all people were, not just their staff, and thus it was impossible to recruit Theory Y-type people, as they did not exist.

Continued

An interesting point here is to wonder whether the two managers were making a statement that they too were lazy and uncreative, or were they the only two exceptions when they were working as sales executives before being promoted to management? (I didn't ask the question.)

Under pressure, they agreed to start treating their staff differently, in a Theory Y-type manner. The experiment failed within a fortnight, not because there was clear evidence that their staff were Theory X, but because the managers could not stop themselves from treating their staff as though they were lazy and uncreative; their unchanged beliefs meant that they could not change their behaviours.

It should be mentioned that the experiment might have failed in the short run even if the managers had been able to change their beliefs and behaviours, as the staff were very suspicious of the declared change in management behaviour and may well have behaved in a Theory X way in order to test their managers.

A further complication was that I subsequently learnt that one of the managers had a very successful businesswoman as a wife, who was very much in control in their marriage. Perhaps his behaviour at work was about his need to find somewhere where he *was* in control.

Question

1. How easy is it for managers to change their beliefs and thus their behaviours?
2. Can people change their behaviours without changing their beliefs?
3. Do managers hold Theory X beliefs because they know/believe that they also are lazy and uncreative?
4. Do some people have reasons other than their beliefs for behaving in a Theory X manner?

Case Study 2: The chief executives

I was teaching on a course for the senior executives of a major European car manufacturer and we were looking at organisational culture and beliefs. On the course were two Chief Executives, one from the company's Belgium business and the other from the company's French business. I asked each of them if they required their assembly line staff to clock on and off at the start and end of each shift, that is, to electronically register the time when they entered and left the assembly plant. One Chief Executive said, "Of course they have to clock on and off; I can't trust them to start and end on time unless I make them "clock"." The other said "No, I don't make them clock; why would I do that?"

Each man could not understand the belief and behaviour of the other, but it is hard to believe that French and Belgium car assembly workers are really so different just across a common national boundary.

REFERENCES

Fayol, H., 1949. General and industrial management. In: Pugh, D.S. (Ed.), Organization Theory: Selected Readings, third ed. Penguin.

Maslow, A.H., 1943. A theory of human motivation. Psychology Review 50 (4), 370-396.

McGregor, D., 1960. The Human Side of Enterprise. In Pugh, D.S., (Ed.), Organization Theory: Selected Readings, third ed. Penguin.

MOW International Research Team, 1987. The Meaning of Work. Academic.

Pugh, D.S. (Ed.), 1990. Organisational Theory: Selected Readings, third ed. Penguin.

Taylor, F.W., 1947. Scientific management. In: Pugh, D.S. (Ed.), Organisation Theory: Selected Readings, third ed. Penguin, pp. 203-222.

Index